NO TIME
FOR TEARS

COPING WITH GRIEF
IN A BUSY WORLD

 REVISED AND UPDATED SECOND EDITION

JUDY HEATH
PSYCHOTHERAPIST (LISW-CP)

FOREWORD BY BERNIE SIEGEL, MD

CHICAGO
REVIEW
PRESS

Copyright © 2015 by Judy Heath
Foreword copyright © 2015 by Bernie Siegel
All rights reserved
Published by Chicago Review Press Incorporated
814 North Franklin Street
Chicago, Illinois 60610
ISBN 978-1-61373-164-2

Library of Congress Cataloging-in-Publication Data
Heath, Judy.
  No time for tears : coping with grief in a busy world / Judy Heath ; foreword by
Bernie Siegel. — Revised and updated second edition.
      pages cm
  Summary: "NO TIME FOR TEARS is a guide to help not only people struggling
through grief due to the loss of a loved one but also those who counsel them.
Psychotherapist Judy Heath offers practical and useful ways to traverse the pitfalls
that may lead to unresolved and lasting grief and to find comfort and peace. Those
who counsel the bereaved will find new ways to inspire their practices and many
tools to assist those in need. This second edition includes updated information about
medication and grief, children and grief, coping after a loved one is murdered, and
lessons learned in treating survivors and victims' loved ones after 9/11"— Provided by
publisher.
  Includes bibliographical references and index.
  ISBN 978-1-61373-164-2 (paperback)
  1. Grief therapy. 2. Grief. I. Title.

  RC455.4.L67H43 2015
  155.9'37—dc23

                              2015002289

Cover design: Marc Whitaker / MTWdesign.net
Cover photos: Shutterstock.com
Interior design: Sarah Olson

Printed in the United States of America
5 4 3 2 1

DEDICATED TO
THOMAS
CARLL, ABBY, AND BRITTANY

CONTENTS

FOREWORD

"And we ourselves shall be loved for a while and forgotten. But the love will have been enough; all those impulses of love return to the love that made them. Even memory is not necessary for love. There is a land of the living and a land of the dead and the bridge is love, the only survival, the only meaning." —Thornton Wilder

"Try to remember that a good man can never die. . . . You will feel him in all things that are here out of love, and for love. . . . The best part of a good man stays. It stays forever. Love is immortal and makes all things immortal. But hate dies every minute." —William Saroyan

———

I couldn't agree with Judy Heath more about our society leaving no time for tears. When we see people crying we are more apt to hand them a tissue and tell them everything will be all right than to deal with their grief and allow them to experience it. I see the difference in our cancer support groups, where grief and tears are not something terrible but are viewed rather as a natural act related to life's difficulties.

I also know that endless grief serves no purpose, so our society needs to learn how to accept and experience grief but not let it take over our lives. This is something I think many people fear and, therefore, deny their grief. In a book I have written, *Buddy's Candle*, I deal with this issue. Let me summarize it by saying if we never stop crying we extinguish our beloved's celestial candle. Would our departed loved one want us to enjoy the day or grieve endlessly? So therapists, doctors, families, and those who realize and accept their mortality need to feel free to express feelings and shed tears. Just as moisture softens a hard, dry sponge, so tears help to heal our wounds. When the grieving is done we can then resume our lives with a new understanding that loss is our teacher and not something to be denied.

The reason many people feel abandoned by doctors when their loved ones die is because doctors are often not taught how to care for people and deal with loss. Doctors tend to think rather than feel. In a study at Yale in which surgeons were asked how it felt to be a surgeon, they answered, "I think" (it is like such and such), rather than "I feel . . ." Famous paintings depict dying adults and children with the doctor sitting by the bedside with chin in hand, thinking.

Because of the pain I experienced as a physician and had no chance to express in a medical environment, I have written to the dean of my medical school several times saying the instructors taught me to be an excellent surgeon, but they did not teach me how to deal with my feelings and care for my patients. No one answered my letters. The American College of Surgeons' Pledge says, "I will deal with my patients as I would wish to be dealt with." I cannot get them to change the words "deal with" to "care for."

Doctors see death as a failure and rarely even use the term when a patient dies. Families see death as their loved one losing a battle, and so they empower the disease by focusing on the enemy and make their family member feel guilty for being a loser. Most patients die in the hospital at night when the doctors are not there to interfere with the process and their family is absent so they do not feel guilty for leaving.

Remember we have a great deal to say about *when* we die. So do not feel guilty if your beloved dies when you are not present. I have seen this with my parents, patients, and even family pets. My father had no problem sharing his last minutes with our family, while I knew my mother and some others would not die when their loved ones were in the room with them.

What we need to be taught is how to help people to live between office visits and die when they are ready to leave their bodies. I have found when people have support and love, dying is not as hard to do. My father died laughing with his family by his side listening to stories about his life. We left his hospital room with no fear of death and free to express our sadness but with no guilt about feeling joyful.

We also forget that if we attend funerals and are present when someone dies we can be healed by the family who appreciates our care and love. I know from experience. When we focus on avoiding death our lives become doomed to failure. I always recommend the movie *Harold and Maude* as therapy. In it, Ruth Gordon plays an eighty-year-old who is into life and meets a young man who is into death. At one point the young actor says, "I decided I enjoyed being dead." His mother gives him a car as a gift and he turns it into a hearse. The last scene shows the young man's hearse going over a cliff after the character played by Ruth Gordon dies. You assume he has committed suicide, but then the camera shows him walking away playing his banjo. I realized what he did was eliminate death as the focus of his life. He could grieve over his loss, but now he was truly alive and not denying his mortality.

Woody Allen writes about two guys talking, one of whom is in great despair about life. His friend asks him, "What are you doing Saturday night?"

"Committing suicide."

"What about Friday night?"

It may seem strange to talk about how to handle loss and the death of loved ones by saying that death, for me, is not the worst outcome. There is a point in everyone's life, no matter one's species, when one's body no longer will function and is not a comfortable place to be in. I see this in the actions of people and pets I have loved and cared for.

Symbolically, when people draw purple balloons, butterflies, and kites going up into the sky they are telling me, often unconsciously, that they are ready for the healing that comes when they make the spiritual transition and leave their bodies. Death is about beginnings and not endings. We do not call graduations *terminations*. We call them *commencements*, and so it is with death. Every caterpillar and butterfly understands what the transformation means better than most people.

Saroyan shares these words at the end of a story in which a young man dies; he becomes "dreamless, unalive, perfect." And I know that he is right. As a four-year-old I had a near-death experience, choking on a toy I aspirated, and I can tell you when you leave your body you will most likely not want to come back. Even blind people see when they have a "NDE" and are upset when resuscitated and find themselves back in their body and blind again.

Harry Chapin's song "Circle" shares these words:

It seems like I've been here before, I can't remember when;
But I have this funny feeling, that we'll all be together again. . . .
Our love is like a circle; let's go 'round one more time.

Yes, when the circle ends, be it expected or due to a tragic accident, we should be free to grieve the loss of our loved ones and take the time to shed tears. To live in the darkness while denying our feelings and hiding our tears is not what we are here for. Crying is not a waste of time. It is a time for healing to take place.

I can remember building a cairn over the grave of one of our dogs who died and bringing a rock to the site every morning as I walked by his grave. Then one morning I thought what I wanted to bring him was beauty, and I picked a flower to place there. From that morning on I looked for beauty because of my loss and not a cold stone. I have the candle that represents every one of our dead loved ones, and I do not want to put out their candles with my excessive grieving and tears.

I have learned to forgive myself as I know they would forgive me and to use my pain to nourish myself and others and make our lives meaningful. When one is hungry one does not get angry at one's body; one seeks nourishment. So do not deny your feelings; use them to help you nourish yourself and your life by finding what you need. "What is evil is not the disease but to not respond with compassion to the person with the disease." We must use our loss and express our compassion, and when we do the curse becomes a blessing and helps us to become complete too.

The key to life is enjoying the day as children and animals do. When I thought one of our sons, at age seven, had bone cancer and a year to live, I was not doing well. He came to me and said, "Dad, can I talk to you for a minute? You're handling this poorly." His tumor turned out to be a rare benign tumor, but he taught me a great deal. I learned from him to enjoy the day and the time we were experiencing and not grieve over what I thought would be. Think about this: if right now you had fifteen minutes to live, what would you do? If your answer isn't "I'd buy a quart of chocolate ice cream and eat it," you have some work to do. What I mean is that we all need to define what our chocolate ice cream is and live it.

The way to die laughing and give those around you the freedom to feel and express their grief is to accomplish what you are here to accomplish, and animals do that much better than we do. To quote a veterinarian who let her patients help her through surgery, "I can amputate a leg or jaw and they wake up and lick their owners' faces. They are here to love and be loved and teach us a few things." A Hindu myth shares the words of a seven-year-old who is about to give up his life to save another: "Consider this, sooner or later my body will perish at any rate, but if it perishes without love, which the wise declare is the only thing of permanence, of what use will it have been?" and "Let me be born again and again on the wheel of rebirth so again and again I may offer this body for the benefit of others." When the boy is about to die he bursts into joyful laughter, and all the people stop and clasp their hands together in an attitude of prayer.

Since consciousness is not local, a part of all our departed loved ones is still here for us to experience and share with. I could tell endless stories about the experiences of loved ones who have lost family members and had them return spiritually or symbolically after their death. After my mother, Rose, died we kept finding roses and pennies everywhere. Finding pennies is my way of knowing I am on the right path, and my mom's great-grandchildren started spontaneously calling them pennies from heaven. This consciousness will eventually become a part of the consciousness of those who come after us. So, remember, life is a school, and the more you learn the more you can pass on to future generations. A perfect world free of afflictions and death is a magic trick and not creation, so share your love and allow yourself to express your grief and receive love and healing, thus making life meaningful and creative.

Death is the greatest teacher there is about life, so live and learn and let the tears that are inevitable soften your journey.

—Bernie Siegel, MD

―――

Bernie Siegel, MD, is an internationally recognized expert in the field of cancer treatment and complementary, holistic medicine. He is the bestselling author of over a dozen books, including The Art of Healing; Love, Medicine & Miracles; *and* Peace, Love & Healing.

PREFACE

——

GUIDANCE AND HOPE

A griever stands bewildered in a room full of chatter. "Well, he had a good long life," her neighbor consoles while taking her hand. She knows she should be thankful for her friend's words, but instead she feels annoyed and confused. In another room in the same funeral home, a pale man and his weeping wife stand by a tiny closed coffin. "God doesn't give us any more than we can handle," a well-wisher offers. In response the young father feels the growing knot in his stomach tighten.

After twenty years in the field of bereavement, I am amazed at the misconceptions about grief that still persist. On September 11, 2001, only forty miles outside of New York City, my hometown of Huntington, Long Island, was struck with tragedy when the World Trade Center was attacked. In the wake, my colleagues and I were inundated with difficult bereavement and posttraumatic stress disorder cases. Being a specialist in the field of grief, my phone rang off the hook. The calls were not just from people in need of help but also from other therapists and counselors who were suddenly besieged with these cases. I found myself teaching crash courses to my peers.

It was then I realized the misinformation about the treatment of grief that persists. What I took for common sense in my practice was not common at all. Having written articles, a children's book, and courses on bereavement for professionals, I had always intended to write a guidebook to help people struggling with grief and those who counsel them.

Grief is underrated. No wonder people often feel they are going crazy after a loved one dies. We are ill prepared for the roller coaster of emotions, our lack of focus, or the sometimes absurd comments that spring from the lips of those around us.

When my five-and-a-half-month-old son, Jesse, died of sudden infant death syndrome (SIDS), it was the end of my life as I knew it. That was my entrance into the long, dark forest from which I thought I might never emerge. What I didn't know was that Jesse had sent me on an incredible journey down a road I might have passed by if my life had gone another way. On that path I met others like me whose losses had transformed their lives. Jesse taught me to cherish my family, live each day to its fullest, and have passion and conviction about my beliefs. Today, nearly twenty-five years later, I try to provide a lantern to others traveling through that seemingly endless forest.

If you have lost a loved one, my wish is that this book might gently guide you through the process of grief, answer your questions, and provide you with some hope going forward. The stories of many souls have been woven into its pages, to help illustrate terms and ideas. You will meet John, a captain in the New York City Fire Department who lost over thirty friends on September 11; Judy, a woman who lost both her mother and her sister to cancer; Harold, who discovered a new way to celebrate holidays after the death of his wife; little Melissa, a girl who thought she carried her deceased grandmother around "on her shoulders"—as well as many others.

For those of you who counsel the bereaved, it is my hope that *No Time for Tears* might inspire your practice and help you to bring more healing tools to those in need.

Family and friends who read this book will discover ways in which to console and aid one another through the process of grief. There is also a helpful frequently asked questions section at the back of the book, compiled from many years of questions I have received about death and dying. National resources, groups, organizations, and Internet links also appear at the end of the book. In some of the case examples used in this book, names and identifying information have been changed. Where they were not, the person generously agreed to make his or her story public. Regarding gender pronouns, rather than writing "he or she" or "him or her" every time I refer to an individual, I alternate between feminine and masculine pronouns throughout the book.

Although there is no more powerful force than death to shatter our world, leaving us crushed and abandoned, there is no other event in our lives that carries with it the ability to realign our priorities and grant us perspective in such a monumental way. "Grief changes us," a wise man once told me, "but how we change is up to us." Death of a loved one is life-altering and it can be transforming. Please join me on this journey for a while as I attempt to share with you the wisdom, tears, and hope that I have gathered along the way.

1

THE THINGS THEY DON'T TELL YOU ABOUT GRIEF

What is grief? Is it the tidied-up snapshots we hold in our minds? One person may instantly visualize the composed figure of Jackie Kennedy and her children at the funeral of her husband, while another might imagine scenes of nameless dead soldiers. The media presents us with countless images that hardly do justice to the experience of grief. What we don't see in this collective composite is the true devastation behind these representations, yet we all know it's there, lurking behind Jackie's sad eyes. Look closer and you'll see the sleepless nights, the residue of never-ending tears, and much later, the emotional detachment. Dive beneath the surface of the war footage and you will hear the anguished cries of mothers and fathers whose young men no longer rummage through snack cabinets or track mud onto their carpets, whose lifeless bodies will not bring along the grandchildren for whom they longed. This, my friends, is true grief.

It's easier isn't it? The two-dimensional representation of grief, preferably in black and white so as not to see any blood. In contrast, I for one dislike it when the news media gets too "up close and personal" with grief, as seems to be the trend these days. Let's interview this poor mother whose child lies before her, a bullet hole through his chest. As sobs that seem to emanate from her very soul escape her lips, she is pushed to answer some inane question. I *feel* the violation of her privacy as the microphone is thrust into her face. She deserves to do this privately. Doesn't she?

Bereavement is my life's work, and it will take me a lifetime to truly understand all of its facets. Each of us faces loss at one time or another. We know that it is a process, and most people understand that there are stages of grief. Fortunately, more complete information has begun to emerge in literature and in studies due to the extensive research that has been done in the past thirty years since Elisabeth Kubler-Ross swung open that door.

Imagine a bad actor attempting to portray a drunk; he may get the slurred speech and the swagger, but without an underlying knowledge about alcoholism there would be no subtext and his performance would be superficial at best. Our understanding of grief as a society is like that—superficial, but improving.

Most of us are familiar with the dominant characteristics of grief, things like shock, denial, and sorrow, but there are many more lesser-known characteristics that surprise most grievers. Traveling through this process with so many souls through the years has made me aware of its far-reaching effects as well as the small ways in which loss invades our lives.

"I think I am going crazy!"

A statement uttered by nearly every griever, young and old, male and female alike. I myself have known this feeling. I have walked the dark and lonely path of loss. To me it is a chilling wooded pathway where craggy-branched trees block the sun. Be aware of the dips in the wet leaves of its dirt floor and small stumps to catch your feet along the way. Throw your collar up and close your jacket against the pounding winds and rain. I will walk this path along with you, for I remember. There is a place where the branches part and you can feel the sunlight against your skin once more, I promise.

THE LONELINESS

"When my brother died I felt so alone," Sandra explained. "He had been my best friend since childhood. Our parents were great, but they were so into each other that they really didn't pay much attention to us. So Paul and I became a team. We built forts together, watched TV, and always confided in one another. We remained close throughout our lives. After we were married we talked on the phone every couple of days. We shared the same humor and knew each other's whole history. My husband never really understood our closeness. He grew up as an only child. When Paul died I lost a part of myself, of my history. My husband didn't totally get it. My children loved their uncle, but they didn't miss him the way I did. That first year was the loneliest time of my life."

Sandra's story touches upon the intense loneliness experienced by the bereaved. Consolation with clear attention paid to the *loneliness* of the griever seems to be most easily given to widows and widowers (for a time, anyway). Less attention is given to the loneliness factor after other kinds of losses. In Sandra's case, her brother Paul held an exceptional place in her world. Both her parents had passed away, and Paul was her only link to her past. It is a misconception that because Sandra was surrounded by loved ones after the death of her brother that she would be spared the loneliness. Almost everyone I have ever seen in my practice talks about being intensely lonely after the death of a close friend or family member—no matter whom they've lost.

There is a hole in the world that only one person can fill. Although talking about the person might temporarily bridge the gap, the void reappears, sometimes swallowing the griever. Some people run from activity to activity to avoid that hole; some cling to their loneliness like a lifeline that meets their deceased one on the other end. Perhaps to other mourners the loneliness is a deserved penance acquired through guilt over their loved one's death.

Whatever the circumstance, be aware that loneliness is one of the major manifestations of grief. As friends, family members, or counselors, we should acknowledge and attend to this significant aspect.

HOW TO HELP YOURSELF WITH THE LONELINESS

If you have lost a loved one and are dealing with intense loneliness, you might want to talk to another human being about your loss. It is not mandatory that you join a bereavement group or see a therapist, although this would be ideal; you can talk to a friend, a clergy member, or even a stranger. It is healing to verbalize your feelings. Now, all you macho types, don't shut this book! Remember, I counseled many New York City firefighters, and you don't get much more macho than that! And guess what? They told me that talking helped. And they kept coming back. If you just can't bring yourself to verbalize or would like a few other suggestions, here are some ways that my wise patients have taught me over the years to help deal with the loneliness.

1. Pets are helpful. With pets you don't have to talk. Take walks with your dog through the woods or to the water. If you're in a city, go to the nearest park. Think about the person you lost and share your feelings with your pet through a hug or a run. Caring for another living being helps with intense loneliness, and animals don't ask for too much in return.

2. Gather all the photos you have of the person who died and make a special photo album. There is healing in remembering times that you spent together. In some instances this may be too painful right after a loss. If you find you become too overwhelmed by this project, stop.

3. Some people feel less lonely in a place of worship. I have had many people tell me that they prefer to go when there is no service in session and that lighting a candle or saying a prayer in a quiet church or temple soothes them.

4. Of course some people feel less lonely at the graveside of their buried loved one. Dominic, an old Italian patient of mine, used to bring lunch and a lawn chair to his beloved wife's grave every week. "I had lunch with my Millie," he would say, "and filled her in on everything that happened

with the family this week." Smiling through tears, he added, "I feel I've had a visit."

HOW TO HELP THE GRIEVER WITH LONELINESS

None of these things takes away our loneliness, but anything that helps, even temporarily, is good. As friends and family members, what can you do to help with the griever's solitude?

1. Be open to talking about the person who died when the griever is ready to do so. Do not feel that it is your job to bring it up in every conversation—that is not helpful. Wait for a window of opportunity. Be a good listener to your loved one, and don't be afraid to mention the deceased person's name or tell a story or two about him or her. That person will let you know whether or not it is a good time to talk about it.

2. Patience is required. People have the need to repeat and examine the circumstances of death. There is a healing power in this repetition.

3. If you are a spouse or partner, you should be aware that touch is an important antidote to loneliness. A hug, a caress, or hand-holding goes a long way at these times. Sex is a little trickier. For some people, bereavement is a time when they lose all interest in sex for a variety of reasons. Loneliness is just one of those reasons. The intensity of the sex act can feel "too close" to another person in time of grief. In other cases people have reported using sex as a kind of antidote to the loneliness. "I forget about my son's death during sex. I feel close to my wife and for a little while I don't think about everything else," one man told me.

4. Sometimes people in grief are quiet but really do want company. Perhaps just being there for comfort is enough. Conversation isn't always necessary.

After her mother died, Debra did not wish to have sex with her husband for several months. Debra's husband asked to come along to one of our sessions, during which he complained profusely about their lack of intimacy since Debra's mother's death three months earlier. In frustration, he cried out, "Don't you love me anymore?" To which Debra replied, "Of course I do, I just miss my mother." He looked puzzled. "What does missing your mother have to do with sex?" Without any forethought Debra blurted out, "I'm too lonely for sex!"

This response fascinated me, and in her next private session, Debra explained, "Frank and I have always had very intimate, connected sex, but I'm just too sad and alone to be that close to another human being right now. It's not that I don't love Frank. I know that when I'm not so lonely for my mother, I'll be normal again. I'm just not there yet."

Try to be patient with the griever if he or she happens also to be your sexual partner. Don't punish him or her by withholding affection. Believe me when I tell you that in most cases, he or she will come back to you.

OUT OF SYNC

This is a strange by-product of grief, seldom mentioned in literature but often spoken about by the grief-stricken. Melanie came to me after the death of her two-year-old son, Michael, from a congenital heart defect. "I feel like the whole world has sped up and left me behind." She was a stay-at-home mom whose world consisted of soccer games for her eight-year-old daughter, being class mom, and all the daily hustle and bustle of a young mother. "I'm around all the same people I was before, but I'm just not able to keep up. They all seem to be moving so fast, and I'm just thinking and moving slower."

I'm an old *Star Trek* buff, so this characteristic of the griever reminds me of the episode when the crew of the *Enterprise* encountered an alien race that moved around so much more rapidly than humans that, to Kirk and his gang, they sounded like buzzing insects. To this grieving mother, other people's chatter sounded like meaningless buzzing. Cars sped by at alarming speeds. The whole world buzzed around her and she felt *out of synchronization* with it. If you've never had a great loss, you might imagine how this feels by remembering the last time you were really exhausted and had to attempt to act normally.

"It's like I'm in a fog," an NYC firefighter explained. "I just don't feel safe in a fire anymore. My reactions aren't the same."

HOW TO HELP YOURSELF WITH FEELING OUT OF SYNC

1. Take fewer commitments for a while. Quieter, more peaceful surroundings and activities seem to help. Limit your time around large groups of people. This might include avoiding some social gatherings for a time.

2. The more you try to force yourself to be "in sync" with the world, the more anxious you will become when that is just not possible. Don't worry; you will return to the world as the grieving process moves forward.

3. If your job requires being around noise, people, and general chaos, take quiet breaks away from everyone. A book or soothing music on earphones might help.

4. You may find yourself more comfortable around senior citizens than your own peers at this time. No, you are not prematurely aging; you've just slowed down for a time. Take advantage of not being as driven as the rest of your generation for a while. This is a time to take long walks in nature, watch old movies, and visit your grandparents (you'll appreciate them in a whole new way). Play cards or a board game. Take a yoga class. . . . Get the idea?

HOW TO HELP THE GRIEVER TO FEEL LESS OUT OF SYNC

Wouldn't any of us like an excuse to slow down for a time? Our lives are so hectic in today's society. If you want to communicate with a friend or family member who has just had a life-altering loss, observe how this loss has affected him or her. As a therapist, I have honed my observational skills to better interpret the unspoken language of my patients. We live in a verbal society where unsolicited opinions abound. It is often forgotten that data is needed to formulate intelligent conclusions. How do we know how a person is truly feeling if we don't observe her unspoken cues?

You *know* how to do this; let's face it, our observational skills are practiced when we deal with children prior to their verbal development. Little Justin is upset, and his mother automatically watches for nonverbal cues to help determine the source of his discomfort. Is his diaper wet? Does his tummy hurt? Is he tugging on his ear to indicate another ear infection? She looks for these cues in an attempt to remedy the situation, but how often do we extend this same courtesy to other adults? We expect adults to tell us when something is wrong, but what if they don't exactly know what is wrong?

Observe people in grief and you will see quiet people walking slowly, often with their head down. When they do look up, their eyes are filled with weariness and sorrow.

Much of what takes place for the survivor after the death of a loved one happens on an unconscious level. If we are aware that people feel out of sync in grief, maybe we can help them by listening and then by validating their reality. There are other ways too. Friends and family members may be encouraged to:

1. Slow down with the griever. Suggest quiet activities like going for a stroll, sitting by a fire, walking on the beach, or watching television.

2. Limit social activities to only a few people.

3. Be understanding about complaints that the griever can't keep up or needs to rest. Suggest naps and giving in to the need for sleep when it is practical. Most people in grief do not sleep well for long periods at a time.

4. If this person was formerly a bundle of energy, willing to do anything or go anywhere, make allowances for the temporary change in personality and find other people to fulfill those needs for you at this time. This will alleviate unnecessary pressure for this individual. Don't neglect spending time with the griever, merely tailor your time to the person's energy level.

PHYSICAL CHANGES

"I don't understand it," Natalie protested, "I was always able to do so much in a day. Now I'm falling asleep at my desk. What the hell's the matter with me?" I was so happy to be able to reassure this woman that she was not terminally ill and going to die as her sister recently had. Grief is exhausting! It drains one's energy. When my husband was mourning the loss of his father, he slept constantly. "It's so strange; I go to bed early and wake up tired again." And he looked tired too. Many of my patients are exhausted all the time. Pale-skinned and with dark circles under their eyes, they complain that they can't sleep or that they can't stop sleeping.

Grief may also affect one's eating habits. One of the first questions a therapist asks a patient when trying to determine if he is depressed is "Have your sleeping and eating habits changed?" Doesn't it stand to reason that a person in mourning *would* be depressed? Of course this patient is depressed! Sadness is a natural by-product of grief, along with sorrow and even despair. However, this depression is expected and even a necessary part of healing.

One young lady whose father died in the Twin Towers gained forty pounds within six months of her father's death. Eating for Terry was a *comforting behavior*. She found solace in the food. Other individuals cannot eat and grow gaunt and sallow. The physical manifestations of grief are too numerous to outlay here, but the powerful relationship of body to mind has been the study of much research in my field over the past two decades.

Weeks after my infant son Jesse's death, I experienced a most frightening, yet amazing, physical manifestation. As I lay in bed one morning, I was overcome by searing pains traveling up and down my arms; I was certain it was nerve damage of some kind. The family physician found nothing wrong, but still the pains continued and were soon accompanied by a paralyzing heaviness that had settled into my arms. I felt certain I had lost my mind along with my son. It was then someone told me about the "aching arm syndrome," which often occurs in mothers who have lost infant children. This is a psychosomatic manifestation attributed to a mother who longs to hold the child now absent from her arms. Had I not experienced this myself, I might not have thought it possible. It was the most profound lesson I have ever personally learned about the power of the mind over the body.

As a psychotherapist I have since witnessed many physical manifestations in grief. Many patients complain about being cold all the time. One woman told me, "I put on sweaters and blankets and I am still cold. It's like I'm chilled from within." Another less common occurrence is a form of "sympathy pains" with the deceased. Dominic's wife died of a heart attack, and he would often experience pains in his chest. He drove his poor daughters crazy with trips to the ER. But after six months these phantom pains subsided and he and his girls were able to laugh about it in my office.

Some research has indicated that extreme mourning can disrupt menstruation. Young women who have begun menstruating might find that their periods have become erratic or have ceased altogether. At the other end of the spectrum, one of my clients experienced the sudden onset of menopause during grief. Stress affects women's cycles and is inherent in grief. If there is a disruption to your cycle, do not hesitate to contact your gynecologist.

Common physical symptoms of grief include:

- Difficulty sleeping
- Sleeping more often

- Weight loss or gain
- Low energy or fatigue
- Menstrual irregularities
- Headaches
- Digestive difficulties
- Hair loss
- Dizziness
- Chest pain
- Sexual impotency
- Racing heart (palpitations)
- Shakiness or tremors

PANIC ATTACKS

"I thought I was dying!" Amanda exclaimed. "I was just sitting in math class and my heart started beating really fast. I was shaking and I couldn't breathe. My friend Brianna asked me if I was all right. I shook my head, but I couldn't feel it move. It was the weirdest thing and it just wouldn't go away."

Imagine a world where you wake in the morning to your mother's voice urging you to hurry and get ready for school, a quick breakfast and a hug, "Love you, Amanda," and you're out the door. Same girl, weeks later: a loud alarm rings several times before she acknowledges it. Dad has already left for his early commute to the city. Alone, she decides to skip breakfast. No hug. No mother's voice expressing love. This is Amanda's life since her mother died a month earlier in a car accident. Her reaction? Anxiety that leads to her first panic attack.

"So why do people have panic attacks?" she asked, and I filled her in on the "fight or flight" theory. Our body's primitive, automatic reaction to perceived danger is to kick into high gear. Everything in us prepares to either fight or flee. Our respiratory rate increases, as does our heart rate, while blood is pumped to the muscles and limbs to ready us for either situation.

"Have you ever been really scared?" I ask Amanda.

"Sure." Her eyes grow big as she remembers. "Once I thought there was a burglar in my house."

"Remember how you became aware of every noise or movement? How you scanned the room with sharper eyes?" She nodded. "That was your body on high alert."

Panic attacks are like that, and in this state everything may be seen as a threat. It is also known as an acute stress response. Our bodies get into patterns and cycles. People can get stuck in high alert, and it is a draining place to be.

Here are some signs of panic attacks (if you experience three or more, seek professional help):

- Increased heart rate
- Sweating
- Trembling or shaking
- Chest pain
- Shortness of breath
- Dizziness or light-headedness
- Nausea
- Fear of losing control or dying
- Derealization (feelings of unreality)
- Depersonalization (being detached from self)
- Paresthesia (numbing or tingling)

So how do we help people to stop having panic attacks? Some people have anxiety disorders that require them to take medication to stop the cycle of anxiety. Antidepressants, SRIs (serotonin reuptake inhibitors), and benzodiazepines are all drugs used in treatment of anxiety disorders. Grief is not an anxiety disorder. So, when I see people in grief who are experiencing panic attacks, we first try to use other means to stop the cycle.

COGNITIVE/BEHAVIORAL TREATMENT FOR PANIC ATTACKS

A good psychotherapist applies different treatment methods for diverse problems and people. If you are old enough to remember Felix the Cat and his magic bag of tricks, think of a good therapist as having a comprehensive "bag of tricks." Although medication might be necessary for a griever experiencing panic attacks, I like to be conservative in my approach. Amanda was being assaulted on all fronts. Anybody who has truly known grief understands what I'm talking about. The world she had come to trust was a lie. The ever-present parent who formerly guided her daily life had been viciously torn from her, leaving holes and broken pieces all over. Her thoughts about her life and the world in general had become distorted and untrustworthy. Amanda saw threats everywhere.

The cognitive part of cognitive/behavioral therapy has to do with a person's thoughts, or *cognitions*. We needed to help Amanda change some of her thoughts. This was accomplished through first identifying misinterpreted thoughts and feelings. Since her mom's death, Amanda was afraid to ride in a car at all. This made life difficult, since she lived in the suburbs, where cars are essential. There was no late bus at her school, so she dropped all her after-school activities—things she dearly loved, like writing for the school newspaper and choral arts. Amanda's fifteen-year-old world had been closed off, making her even more anxious. We involved Amanda's father in her treatment by having him slowly drive her around a quiet parking lot for her first foray back into a car. They did this three times that week until Amanda felt less anxious. For the subsequent two weeks Amanda accompanied her father driving around their neighborhood daily. Where originally she would break down crying hysterically and beg her father to stop the car, her outbursts now came only when another car passed by. Soon they graduated to running small errands together, and within months Amanda was able to resume her after-school activities. This kind of cognitive/behavioral treatment is known as exposure therapy, and it really works with anxiety.

Imperative to changing a person's thoughts is educating that person about what is happening to him or her during a panic attack. Knowing that the panic attack is an instinctive "fight or flight" response that cannot kill you can take some of the sting out of it. Fear of the unknown is mighty powerful! Amanda was eventually able to talk herself through an attack. *OK, now my heart is racing, my hands are tingling, but I'm not going to die or even pass out. This will end. I rate it as a number four.* I taught her to rate her attacks on a 1–10 scale, a technique that allows the person to take control over the attack.

The behavioral part of therapy for panic attacks has to do with relaxation and breathing exercises employed before or during an attack to calm down. These changes in Amanda's thoughts and behaviors allowed her to take control over her body again and end the attacks without the use of medication. She still had to deal with her monumental loss, but at least now she could do so without the added fear that her own body was acting against her. This also gave Amanda a sense of control in her life again, rather than beginning a dependency on medication.

HOW TO HELP YOURSELF WITH PHYSICAL CHANGES

Mostly you live through them and don't panic. So much about understanding the grieving process is acceptance—acceptance that in most cases there is a beginning, middle, and an end to the ordeal of grief. That is not to say that you ever truly get over the loss of a loved one, but hopefully you will learn to incorporate the reality of that loss into your life and move forward. Sometimes that does not happen, as when grief is unresolved or "complicated," but in most cases there is finally acceptance.

You may lose or gain weight. This is normal. If you lose or gain a large amount in a short time, please see a doctor. This may be an indication that some therapeutic intervention is needed. If you have trouble sleeping, there are some effective low-dosage, over-the-counter sleep aids. I do not suggest you take these daily. Try taking them every three of four days. The human body can make it through sleep deprivation for a few days. Most times patients get really tired by the third or fourth day and finally sleep. This pattern usually disappears, becoming more normal through the natural process of grief.

Get yourself a physical. Grief is physically and emotionally wearing. Knowing where you stand physically will put your mind at ease and help sort out what are psychosomatic and what are physical symptoms. I know most of you really don't care about your health at this moment, but your loved ones do, so do it anyway!

1. Do not rule out talking to a therapist or joining a bereavement group. It helps.

2. Expect a change in eating and sleeping patterns. Acknowledge that you might be eating as a comforting behavior and try to substitute other behaviors that might be less destructive.

3. Bring a sweater along in the car and throw an extra blanket on the bed to attend to that chill.

4. Psychosomatic symptoms, particularly panic attacks, come from the anxiety you feel. Please do not ignore this anxiety, as it can be destructive to you, mentally and physically.

5. Some people journal through grief. Writing down daily feelings and thoughts may give them less power to build into a physical symptom.

The old saying goes, "What doesn't kill you makes you stronger." I believe this can be true, although it doesn't seem possible. When we start on this path we are beaten and weak. As with every journey, we learn a lot about ourselves along the way.

HOW TO HELP THE GRIEVER WITH PHYSICAL CHANGES

1. Do not tell her it's all in her head. This is a maddening old phrase that reeks of ignorance. We live in our heads! Just accept that the griever's reality is different from yours right now and listen without judgment.

2. Perhaps the gift of a massage, or running a hot bath to help the griever relieve his anxiety and relax, might be appropriate.

3. If you see she's not eating, present her with a food she rarely turns down (this is encouraging without nagging).

4. Rent a movie that he loves, even if it's not your favorite. Be compassionate; you may need that person to help you through a rough time someday. Try to imagine what might help him to be less depressed or anxious.

LACK OF FOCUS

"I think I am going crazy," said a member of my bereavement group. (There's that phrase again.) "I have always been so organized, and now I can't even get my grocery shopping done."

"My memory is shot," another chimed in.

It really helped these people to realize they were not alone in their "insanity." What I call *lack of focus* shows up in many ways for the griever. In the task of readjusting to a new reality, the mind becomes preoccupied and not fully present to the bereaved individual.

People speak of "walking around in circles" and forgetting why they went into a particular room. Previously organized individuals suddenly find it hard to locate things. You are not going crazy; you are a normal person in an extraordinarily difficult time. Yes, we all know that death is a "normal" part of life; so is pregnancy, and although there is much good literature out there on both, grief is generally underrated. It constantly amazes me when a patient is made to feel guilty for displaying the normal characteristics of bereavement. "Shouldn't I be better by now?" We may unwittingly contribute to the pressure placed on the grief-stricken by trying to push them along in their healing. Our motive may be as simple as wanting to see someone we love "be happy" again, but this push can make the griever feel inadequate.

When pregnant women complain of mood swings or cravings, we as a society tend to smile and nod, accepting of the biological and emotional trappings that accompany pregnancy. Yet too often we tell the grief-stricken to "just get on with it." And although in the end, I do believe that it is important to *get on with it*, we often fail to realize that grief is a process that must run its course in order for us to move on.

HOW TO HELP YOURSELF WITH LACK OF FOCUS

Many of the suggestions that have been made for dealing with lack of focus are the same techniques used for people who are getting older. Makes you feel great, huh? But these techniques really work. Think of these suggestions as something you would do for a beloved friend and treat yourself gently. At this time, you must be your own best friend.

1. Make lists. I don't care if you never made a list before in your life. You will need them now! Grocery lists, lists at work, lists of chores you must accomplish. Make them and mark them up. Remember, the effects of grief are temporary, and you won't have to do these things for the rest of your life.

2. Sticky notes. Don't be embarrassed—stick them everywhere! On the phone to remember to call the piano teacher or on your computer screen to remember to file that report. Help yourself out. If so inclined, set reminders and alarms on your cell phone to help remind yourself of deadlines, appointments, and even errands.

3. Ask friends and loved ones to help—even if it is against your nature. When we ask others for help we invite them into

our grieving process, which, in my opinion, is an honor. We also demonstrate to others, particularly our children, that grief is an acceptable process. This teaches children to be more accepting of their own grief and to have compassion for others.

4. Talk out loud to yourself. We've all done this, haven't we? Charlie, a towering New York City cop and the sole male member of a Loss of Spouse group said it best: "I go from room to room and can't even remember why I'm there. So now I have a running dialogue with myself. I say 'Charlie, feed the cat,' so I feed the cat, and then I say, 'Now you have to make some phone calls and do the bills' . . . and like that." He unleashed his wonderful grin on us, and we were all thrilled at his success.

5. The workplace is often the biggest challenge to those in the process of grief. Many companies still allow only three days of leave for the death of a loved one. After which the griever is expected to get right back to normal. Some lucky people report that they are able to forget about their grief at work and function quite well. In many cases, though, people find that this disrupting lack of focus follows them into the workplace. If you have an understanding boss, coworkers, or staff, you might mention that you are not fully operating on all cylinders yet and ask for patience. I have seen some miraculous results come from taking this tact.

A Wall Streeter who was in treatment with me had a no-nonsense boss with a "type A" personality. Bill found it challenging to concentrate around all the noise and usual hustle and bustle of his firm after the death of his father. Wary to mention it to his boss, he tried his best to work around it for several days. Finally, when he was unable to take his clients out to dinner later that week, he went to see his boss. When he explained his circumstances, his tough boss shared the loss of his *own* father with Bill, and they both reached for the tissues. For the next few weeks, coworkers fulfilled Bill's nighttime obligations and he and his boss became friends.

I wonder who taught us to be so embarrassed by typical feelings of loss. How many times have you seen someone apologize for tears that came naturally when speaking of someone who died? We have loved these individuals—isn't it normal that we miss them?

HOW TO HELP THE GRIEVER WITH LACK OF FOCUS

1. Lower your expectations that this person can do all the things he did prior to the death. You can help by not having unrealistic expectations of a person in grief.

2. Traditionally neighbors have brought food to the grieving family. This is a wonderful help, until the refrigerator becomes overstocked. People need other kinds of assistance. Volunteer to pick up groceries or dry cleaning. Take a grieving friend's children for a while. Be creative. Ask the person what she needs and don't let her off the hook with "nothing, I'm fine." Perhaps you can make some phone calls for her. I am not advocating becoming a nuisance. If you never had a close relationship with this person to begin with, it is not likely that she will want you hovering around now. But, if you are a close family member or friend, you *can* be of assistance in some small way.

2

IN THE BEGINNING: THE ROLLER COASTER OF EMOTION

"How do you *feel* about that?" the comic-strip therapist asks his patient. Most of us expect a one-word answer: "Angry," or perhaps "Excited." The truth is that we often experience more than one emotion within a short span of time, even about the same subject. This is particularly true during the grieving process. Sometimes the emotions conflict with one another.

"What is wrong with me?" a well-groomed forty-year-old woman asked me. "How can I be so sad and yet relieved at the same time?" She spoke here of the death of her elderly father, who suffered from Alzheimer's. During the year before his death, Mary juggled family and career with constant visits to the adult care facility where her father resided. How could she *not* be conflicted?

Many bereaved people feel confused about the rapid-fire emotions inherent in grief. It's like being readmitted to puberty with the constant assortment of sensations that barrage the griever. You feel *out of control* and sometimes crazy! The mood swings and array of these emotions, while challenging for most, are absolutely brutal for those of us who like things *in control*. When overwhelmed by the myriad of sentiments flooding him, the in-control individual can medicate with or without a doctor's assistance through drugs and alcohol or may choose to escape the feelings through compulsive behaviors like eating to excess or working around the clock. Some folks simply shut down or in the worst-case scenario may even commit suicide. Not very appealing choices!

Here's the good news: there is no real control over the emotions of grief. Once you know this and realize that you have not lost your mind, it helps a little. You need to remember that feelings are just *feelings* and that even though they may create anxiety, you *do* have some choice about how to deal with them. Overwhelming negative emotions cause people to do almost anything to escape them. It can seem impossible to just let them run their course.

The widow's loneliness is a dreadful daily barrage, and so she seeks to alleviate it by finding somebody to fill the loneliness. This can lead to a really bad judgment call in a new partner. If she can wait out the loneliness, a day at a time, the urgency will lessen and she will have more control over her choices. But try convincing someone in *that* kind of pain to wait awhile. It's not easy.

However, we all do better when we know what to expect. For many years I was fearful of roller coasters. My husband and children would hop right on these frightening contraptions wearing broad grins, and when my youngest was tall enough to gain admittance, she hopped on right along with the rest of them, squealing with delight. Oh, I'd force myself to tag along sometimes, white-knuckling my way through, eyes shut, sporting a contorted grimace. "Are we having fun yet?" Then one magical day, in Disney of course, my husband offered to help me enjoy the Big Thunder Mountain Railroad roller coaster. "Open your eyes," he encouraged. "It's not as scary if you know what's coming up ahead." Well I'm here to tell you, it took everything I had to pry open my eyes, but when I did I understood what he was saying. The fear of the unknown added to my anxiety. He talked me through it. "OK, now we're going to take a bend to the right . . . there! Now to the left."

And so on. I was able to let go of control if I knew what to expect. We human beings are like that.

In this chapter we touch on the many emotions of early grief in an effort to help you "keep your eyes open" about what to expect. However, the answers about ways to deal with some of these reactions are not simple how-tos. Hopefully, understanding that these reactions are somewhat universal will normalize them for you.

It's kind of like that roller coaster I mentioned; if you let these feelings pass, your mind and body will naturally flow through them and come out the other side. Shock, denial, sorrow, despair, and even anger usually pass in time. However, guilt, shame, and deep-rooted anger may require counseling to move through completely. So let's identify some of these emotions together.

SHOCK

The shock you experience after your loved one dies is like what happens when you've been out in the cold for too long. Remember that feeling when your feet and hands began to grow numb? As a child, I recall going ice-skating one morning and having so much fun that I lost track of how long I'd been outside. Upon returning home and removing my skates, I found cold, colorless feet with no feeling. When your loved one dies, the mind and body provide a buffer much like the numbness that shielded me from what next ensued on that cold winter's day so many years ago.

"Daddy, Daddy, I can't feel my feet! What's wrong with them, help me, help me!" Daddy came to the rescue by peeling off my socks and rubbing my feet. As they began to turn pink, it felt like pins and needles and the tears came. After a while he had me place my ailing tootsies on a warm radiator. Slowly but surely my feet returned to normal. Gratefully I hugged my father.

To all those who minister to the bereaved, remember that shock is there for many reasons. Among them, shock gives the griever time to adjust to what follows. All too soon the painful "pins and needles" of reality invade the fuzzy buffer of shock. I like to think that we as friends, family, and counselors may provide the loving foot rub or the warm radiator that eases the griever back into reality. Although she may get there on her own, we can help make a grueling transition more comfortable.

Shock is a strange phenomenon; most of the time when you are in shock, you don't know it. If you ask a person who has just experienced traumatic loss how he is doing, quite often the reply will be "fine," and at the time he believes this to be true. A year later that same person will speak of memory lapses and being "really out of it" during those first few weeks or months. But there are physical cues that give people away immediately. Few people exhibit all these signs, but most exhibit some:

- Lack of focused eye contact
- Fixed, vacant stare
- Dilated pupils
- Stiff muscles
- Remaining in same posture for long periods
- Nervousness, tremors
- Cold, clammy hands
- Shallow breathing
- Slow speech patterns
- Tight jaw
- Being easily startled
- Chronic tiredness
- Dizziness
- Body numbness
- Inability to remember blocks of time

It is incredible how well people can function while in the state of shock; this is due to the fact that they are temporarily buffered from the reality of their circumstances.

"I was perfectly fine right after my wife died," Mitch explained. "I did what I had to do about the funeral and getting help with my daughters. I went back to work." He shook his head. "Everyone kept telling me how strong I was. I just had no idea what the hell was going on." It was four years later, after much alcohol abuse and nearly losing his job, that Mitch found his way into therapy. A proud man, he didn't want to disappoint his family and friends. "When the shock wore off and I realized Karen wasn't coming back, I just couldn't face it. So, I started numbing myself every night. Then I got my friend to give me a prescription for Xanax so that I could stay numb all day, too."

Mitch's judgment became increasingly impaired, and he began having a blatant affair with a married woman at his office. "I nearly broke up her marriage, and I wasn't even in love with her," he confided.

I have seen far worse results occur as people attempt to run from the pain of their loss. To those of you who are experiencing this pain right now—you are in the thick of that darkened forest I mentioned earlier. You may be tempted to run to escape the pain, but do not forget about the rocks and stumps beneath you. If you move too fast, you will not see them in time to avoid them. Grief is a process. Just hang on and move forward, a step at a time.

Denial

Most of us are familiar with the book *Sybil*, in which the main character is so horrendously tortured by her mother that she develops the condition known as dissociative identity disorder. In an effort to escape her abuse, she actually developed alternate personalities. This is a most vivid example of the power of the human mind when trapped. Perhaps it can help us to understand something about the element of denial in the grieving process. Contrary to Kubler-Ross's original findings, the stages of grief do not necessarily follow in order. Although shock *does* come first, denial is a thread woven throughout the very fabric of grief and may appear at any time throughout the process.

Anthropologist Margaret Mead is widely quoted as saying, "When a person is born, we rejoice, and when they're married, we jubilate, but when they die we try to pretend nothing happened."

We have all become familiar with the defense mechanism that Sigmund Freud labeled *denial* and have experienced it in everyday life. Your son stares at you with a straight face and tells you he really hasn't watched *that much* TV today—and he believes it! Denial. The wife who finds the receipt from Victoria's Secret in her husband's pants pocket and yet never received any lingerie tells you he would never cheat on her—denial. Need I go on?

Most therapists believe that it is not appropriate to shatter a patient's denial all at once. Denial serves a purpose for the mind. Even if you wanted to drag someone out of her denial, she would employ strong mental strategies to cling to her beliefs. Many patients leave therapy because their denial is threatened. Just try convincing an alcoholic that he has a problem.

Just as shock numbs the mind, denial gently cushions it. "I can't believe that after all these months since she died, I still expect to hear her voice when I pick up the phone," Fran shared with the group.

"I know, I know," Sondra chimed in. "I still have my father's false teeth—like he's going to use them."

Denial is sneaky. It wakes up with you in the morning, when you find yourself reliving the whole reality that your loved one is actually dead for the umpteenth day in a row. And the pain floods right back in. I once treated a brilliant middle-aged woman who confessed to me that she stalked a man all through the mall. "He looked so much like my Joey; I just had to follow him. Intellectually, I knew it couldn't be Joey, but I just had to see." She wasn't crazy; she allowed herself to play out her denial. Of course she knew Joey was dead and that this stranger could not be him. When she saw it wasn't her son, she went back to her car and had a good cry. She was healing, and her denial was bridging the gap between fantasy and reality.

As acceptance grows, denial falls away. Eventually Janet was even able to laugh about this episode. "All I needed was a trench coat. I was hiding behind mannequins and everything, just to get a glimpse of this poor guy." Laughing at herself made the whole thing feel less ominous. People should be able to laugh at the insanity of life and death. Don't worry about a little denial. A little denial is healthy.

So, when is denial not so healthy? I was appalled when less than nine months after September 11, an article appeared in our local paper applauding one of the widows for moving on with her life. The article glorified this woman's wedding to the new man in her life with a quote from her clergyman about how wonderful it was that she could pick up the pieces so quickly. This, my friends, is unhealthy denial. When I saw the look of shock and dismay on her children's faces, I nearly cried for them. When society and even your minister are telling you "how strong you are" and "how wonderful for you that you can move on so quickly," then denial is being reinforced on a societal level. Instead of being encouraged to move naturally through the grieving process, people are being asked to deny their feelings. Now, mind you, there are some widows who secretly celebrate their husband's passing and can't wait to *move on*, but even so, shouldn't a proper grieving time be allowed for the children who have lost their father? To deny the grieving process can lead to *unresolved grief,* putting the griever at greater risk for many consequences.

Normal denial is commonplace after the death of a loved one. If the griever refuses to believe that the person has died, he should seek professional help. Most therapists who specialize in bereavement can quote stories of patients whose denial was so profound that it impaired or *complicated* their grief. True unhealthy denial shows up in a variety of ways. The griever who cannot change or move anything that was touched by the deceased loved one, years after the death, may be stuck in denial. Those who refer to the deceased in the present tense years after that person's death display denial. Sometimes the mere inability to talk about the deceased can be an indication of denial. Unhealthy denial indicates a need for therapeutic intervention.

Many parents create a shrine to their child who has died. I know this grief—I have experienced it firsthand and helped many through it. The loss of a child damages many people permanently. Trapped in her own denial, an individual can inadvertently harm herself or others. How is it for the surviving siblings who can never fulfill that parent's need to have the lost child back? Perhaps remembering our deceased children through a favorite blanket or an article of clothing or through photographs might help the griever without disrupting the forward motion of our families.

One of the most beautiful stories I know centers on this subject. My patient Elisabeth lost her fourteen-year-old son, Justin, tragically. Understandably, she was unable to change his room after his death. She and her husband and surviving daughter tried to move on from their loss. Years later, Elisabeth had a subsequent child, Sammy. And this boy was extraordinary. Sammy opened each family member's heart in the way only babies can. Elisabeth was healing, finally. At the appropriate time, she was able to move her deceased son Justin's bed into Sammy's room. She smiled at her three-year-old, "Now you have a big-boy bed!" Sammy proceeded to climb up on the bed and lift the window shade to look out at the sky. "Justin is here with us," he told her.

GUILT

> *For of all sad words of tongue or pen,*
> *The saddest are these: "It might have been!"*
> —*John Greenleaf Whittier*

This part of the journey is painful—but please walk a bit with me through the snakes and thorns. It is important to face guilt as an aspect of grief so that you might emerge healed from its haunting hold. In my tenure I have learned that guilt almost always accompanies grief. Whether it be the mother who wasn't home when her child died, the child whose last words to his dead brother were spoken in anger, or the wife who forgot to tell her husband she loved him the day he died, in all these cases guilt was present.

"I should have hidden the keys to his truck," the weeping mother cried. Logically she knew that she could not hide the keys to Josh's truck every evening. Josh was twenty-four years old, and sometimes he had a few beers after work. On the night he died in a car accident, he had too much to drink and decided to take his truck out well after his parents had gone to bed. This was probably *not* the first time he drank and drove, but usually he was more responsible or his parents just didn't know about it. So, when is it not his parents' fault anymore?

We have all heard the phrase "Stop beating yourself up about it," and this is indeed apropos in many cases. Grievers beat themselves up over the death of their loved ones. They keep themselves up at night wondering what they could have done differently. Preoccupied with what they did wrong, they bash their shins on chairs, barrel through stoplights, and bite holes in their lips.

Many of us harbor our guilt like a festering secret we dare not admit. To put words to your guilt might make it more real. Guilt is like a fist, waiting to punch you in the gut every time your mind wanders in its direction. Of all of the reasons to enter into counseling after a loss, to dispose of guilt is the most compelling. Yet it is the fear of the admission of this guilt that keeps many grievers away from counseling.

Guilt is an imposter that usually withers under scrutiny. It whispers doubts into the griever's ear, like, "I should have forced him to go to the doctor" or "We never should have gone out that night." As if one small decision could eliminate the tenuous nature of our mortality. People die, and nothing we could have said or done can change that eventuality. Grown adults refuse to go to doctors, and people *do* go out. These behaviors are really quite normal and often do not end in death.

Unfortunately, we are not that powerful. Maybe when a person grasps for ways he could have changed the outcome, if only he had done *this* or said *that*, he is really trying to exercise control over the uncontrollable. The loss of a loved one (particularly an unexpected loss) is just not acceptable to the mind. It is that simple. So we look for reasons for the unreasonable, even if the explanation includes a self-indictment. *If I can logically explain this away, maybe it never really happened at all.*

Ridiculous? Perhaps, but who ever said the human mind always makes sense? Obviously none of this kind of thinking takes place on a conscious level, but desperation can be a great motivator. Again and again, I have been amazed at the transforming effect admitting the secret of hidden guilt can have on the griever.

I wish I had a magic wand that could instantly alleviate guilt, because it is a tricky devil. If I simply try to convince the griever who sits before me that he didn't cause his loved one's death, he may smile and nod, but he'll probably call me a "quack" behind my back. I actually had one patient, Catherine, tell me that it was because I was the first person *not* to tell her that she didn't kill her mother that she returned to therapy the following week. In no way did I believe that Catherine caused her mother's death, but had I told her so, I would have been just another voice arguing with the truth the way she saw it.

Trudy came into my adult Loss of Parent group with all the signs of shock. For weeks she sat relatively silent, letting others share about their losses. Her lovely face was tight, her jaw locked. Sometimes I noticed her hands shaking, and they were cold to the touch. After years of witnessing people keeping secrets, I knew the look. I was guessing that when and if it ever came out, it would be a doozy. It took time and trust for Trudy to unload her secret. But, magic happens in bereavement groups. Somebody reveals his guilt, which in turn triggers sharing by another member, and finally Trudy felt safe enough to unburden herself.

Trudy's elderly mother lived in her home. Trudy described her mother as "full of life," and though she did suffer from the early stages of dementia, she was still quite vital. One night the house alarm was inadvertently left off. To this point, Trudy's mother had never ventured outside at night, but *this* night she did just that. The family had gone to bed, and Trudy's mother opened the sliding glass doors, wandering outside into the freezing night. In the morning her body was found in the snow.

The verbal admission that this had occurred provided some relief for this woman immediately, as her body shook, her shoulders sank, and she sobbed. Another woman placed her hand on Trudy's back. "It's OK," she chanted quietly. "It's not your fault." She said this over and over again, as Trudy cried. Someone got her tissues. Everyone waited until she was able to lift her head. The outpouring of compassion from the group members was heartwarming. It was the beginning of healing for Trudy, who transformed before our eyes in the months to come. It turned out that even her own sister, from whom she was estranged, blamed her for their mother's death.

Trudy also entered into one-on-one therapy. Attached to her guilt, as it is to all guilt, was the feeling of shame. The dictionary defines shame as "a negative emotion that combines feelings of dishonor, unworthiness, and embarrassment." What a fitting companion to guilt. Trudy did not run from her guilt and shame after her mother's death. She faced these emotional bullies and fought back. It takes *emotional courage* and support from others to work past the crippling effects of guilt and shame.

Medication can mask the anxiety or depression that exist as symptoms to inform the griever that his underlying feelings have not yet been dealt with completely. That would be fine if the meds could permanently alleviate the source of the pain. But medication is a poor substitute for necessary therapeutic work, and though negative thoughts may be temporarily hidden, they often reemerge in self-destructive behavior. Negative thoughts and feelings will have to be dealt with anyway, eventually. The process of grief has already been interrupted and must now be resumed.

Guilt and shame color grief for individuals of every age, including children. In the section on survivor's guilt in chapter 4, we further determine how guilt in death affects people.

YEARNING

Much has been written about the yearning or pining after a deceased loved one. What exactly is *yearning*? It is a need so overwhelming that you ache with it. The presence of your loved one is so desired that you play games with yourself to feel him close again. Maybe you spray her perfume, wear his sweater, watch her favorite movie, set an extra place at the table, or carry his favorite toy around in your pocket. This is not denial. Unlike denial you are all too aware of the person's absence; this is yearning.

Every day, Cynthia went into her son's room, which she had not altered since his death a year before. She sat on his bed, closed her eyes, and imagined him there. She visualized his back as he sat at his desk and imagined she could hear his voice on the phone. She held his old teddy bear close and pretended that it was *him* in her arms. To some this may seem strange, but in the early stages of grief, this is actually a healthy coping behavior, allowing the griever to adjust to the loss.

A recent study, published in the *Journal of the American Medical Association*, researched the common belief that people go through stages when they grieve. Husband and wife researchers Holly Prigerson and Paul Maciejewski followed 233 grieving people for two years. The emotion most often experienced by these individuals was not anger or sadness but yearning. Prigerson called it "a sense of heartache" and "pangs of grief." This study consisted primarily of people who had lost spouses. Many died of natural causes and were expected to die of illness. These findings should not be generalized to other kinds of deaths, and certainly not to people who are dealing with sudden, unexpected death. Yet it is clear that yearning is at the core of grief.

Don't judge yourself too harshly in the first six months after a loss. Although some of these behaviors may seem strange to those around you, they are not warning signs that you are grieving in an unhealthy manner. These judgments about "the proper" way to grieve are most likely made by people who either deny their own feelings or who have never experienced great loss.

Anger

When something of value is taken from a child, he knows enough to get angry. As adults, we find a way to camouflage our emotions and complicate things beyond measure. "Of course I'm not angry," she tells me while wildly tapping her crossed leg against my poor wooden coffee table. "How can I be angry? It's nobody's fault." Many patients seem reluctant to speak about their angry feelings after a death. But sublimation of such feelings may lead to self-destructive behaviors later on.

People have all sorts of misconceptions about displaying anger; some think that anger flies in the face of God, so they feel guilty for their own deserved angry feelings. Others believe that they have no right to be angry because terrible things have happened to many people and not just to them—again, guilt. Who taught us we don't have a right to our anger?

Anger is a natural reaction to loss. In our sessions, I encourage individuals to allow their angry feelings to surface. It is better to release such emotions in the confines of therapy than to transfer these bubbling toxins onto your living loved ones.

Exercise is a natural antidote to strong negative emotion. One client I saw used to chop wood to release his anger. Anyone who has felt true anger comprehends the energy locked within it. Anger has fueled people to sue doctors who they believed indirectly or directly caused their loved ones' deaths. It can motivate people to fight for worthy causes, or it can rip a family apart at the seams. Channeled and directed, anger can be useful, but unchecked or unacknowledged, its energy may run roughshod over a person's life.

We are all acquainted with bitter, unhappy people who dwell in the clutches of anger; theirs is a dark, unwelcoming world. Grievers must make a conscious choice to avoid taking up residence in that world.

SORROW AND DESPAIR

Two ubiquitous partners to grief. Throughout this book, the sorrow of grief is explored at great depth, so here I will just mention its ever-present existence.

THE RITUALS OF GRIEF

"Who the hell came up with these bloody rituals?" Spensor spat. "I'm sick to death of them, and if I get one more damned casserole . . . !"

Although we all seem to receive some casserole dishes from well-wishers, this handsome fortysomething Brit got a few extra from his unattached female neighbors after the death of his wife. "You wouldn't think they'd wish to advertise the fact that they really can't cook," he chuckled.

Many bereavement books are available to explain the derivation of each religious group's rituals, and they are quite interesting. What they all have in common is the need for group healing and comforting. Emotionally battered survivors are forced to choose coffins, final resting attire, and even hymns to be played at these rituals. Most speak of floating through these early days "in a fog." This of course is the shock I mentioned earlier. Understand that these rituals are *for* the mourners and should not make matters worse. In the best-case scenario, many of these details were decided upon before the person died; however, this is seldom the case.

In grief, you should be as involved as you wish to be with all of the "details after death." This is where a good friend or relative might be helpful. But this is only if you want it that way. Others should not condescendingly assume that the griever just can't handle it. Some survivors actually take comfort in making these decisions themselves.

In my years of grief counseling, I have developed some pet peeves when it comes to rituals. Some people make the ritual more important than the people. Certainly tradition is important, but there are some folks who see themselves as the self-appointed guardians of these traditions. What they fail to realize is that the ritual was originally conceived of as a comfort to the mourning family. When rituals fail to achieve their purpose, they become meaningless. If you are being bullied by someone to do things a certain way that is not comfortable for you, it is your privilege and your right to tell the person "No, thank you." Do not worry about protocol. This is the one time in your life when you can let go of guilt. There is enough guilt that accompanies death anyway. This is useless guilt.

Well-meaning people do outrageous things in the early days after a death. Beth, an only child, came home to live with her mother after her father died. Four years later Beth's mother died of breast cancer. Upon returning from the funeral, Beth found that her mother's neighbor had come into her home and removed all of Beth's mother's clothes from the closet. Beth fell weeping to the floor when she opened her mother's closet looking for an old bathrobe she might hold against her face. "I was trying to help," the neighbor told Beth. She had dropped all of her mother's things off at Goodwill, in an effort to shield Beth from distress. The neighbor was projecting her own feelings onto Beth. Just because one person reacts a certain way about death, that does not necessarily mean another person will. What comforts one person may upset another. Never assume.

You know those "guardians of the traditions" I spoke about earlier? Here is another of my pet peeves. These people may show up anywhere on the path of grief; I call them "the judgers." Where there are vulnerable people, the judgers are there. And who is more vulnerable than the bereaved? Judgers say things like, "Well, maybe if he didn't work so hard, he might not have had that heart attack." Now, just imagine you are the wife of the man who died—can you feel that guilt start to crawl along your skin?

Or how about "I think you should sell this house right away—it would be the best thing for you." Excuse me, but nobody knows what is best for you but *you*. And now is *not* the time to make any major decisions.

The judgers can be anybody, even family members. I am not saying they are malicious; they're sometimes just misguided. It is understandable when another grieving family member has an ill-formed opinion—after all, he too is experiencing grief and may not be thinking clearly. What I am suggesting is that you are most vulnerable. If possible, all major decisions should be postponed for six months to a year. If you find another family member is pushing hard for her own agenda, remember that she may be experiencing great anxiety that she seeks to alleviate, and this may be the motivation behind unwarranted suggestions. This is not your problem! Grief is a time to be self-caring without apology, and it is perfectly acceptable for you to say, "Thank you for your opinion, but I'm not ready to make that decision just yet." If that person pursues the matter regardless of your sentiment, simply indicate that you no longer wish to discuss the topic.

Funerals, wakes, and various other death rituals came about for a variety of reasons in different cultures and religions, but almost all have three things in common: the body of the deceased is being prepared for its final resting place, the soul is being readied for its transition, and the living are joining together to mourn.

3

GRIEF INTERRUPTED

We are a nation of people who want quick fixes. In fact, we are becoming addicted to speed in all things. Healing takes time, and in our hearts we know this is true. There is no quick fix for grief. A busy mother whose own mother had died told me she didn't have *time* to grieve. I sympathized with her words. I, too, was a young mother when my son, Jesse, died. If I hadn't taken the time to heal, I might never have been able to move on and be a compassionate mother to my other children and a good therapist to my patients.

I'm not sure when it started happening, maybe ten years ago or so, that grieving patients began coming to me already taking antidepressants or antianxiety medications for which they had gotten prescriptions from family doctors, gynecologists, and neighbors. Pills were everywhere—and it's only gotten worse. The magic pill will fix everything, even death.

An article titled "For Some Bereaved, Pain Pills Without End" appeared in the *New York Times* Health and Science section about five years ago, citing a Columbia University–based study that showed a "surprising trend." More than half of the doctors in the study prescribed Xanax and other potentially addictive drugs specifically for bereavement. I do not mention this to indict the medical profession but merely to illuminate a development that worries me.

The human mind and body compose a most extraordinary machine with natural instruments of healing that we can enlist or impede, depending on our level of arrogance. To regularly prescribe medication for those in grief is irresponsible and often counterproductive to the healing process. Of course there are exceptions to this policy, as when a patient is experiencing prolonged or *complicated grief,* already medicated for a preexisting condition, or thought to be suicidal. If you have just lost a loved one and are placed on medication, be cautious. It may be necessary, but it could also impede your process.

In my work with the victims of the World Trade Center tragedy in New York, I was appalled to discover how many of the grieving survivors were immediately prescribed drugs. In a society that medicates for everything from feeling uncomfortable in social situations to tingly legs, is it any wonder that pills are seen as the simple solution for the sorrow of loss? Why not? It keeps us quiet and believing we are doing better. Why am I suddenly picturing Jack Nicholson in *One Flew over the Cuckoo's Nest*? Only now the cuckoo's nest has moved out of the asylum and into our homes. "Just take two of these and call me in the morning." It makes life so much easier for others, including the therapist, when the griever stops making such a big deal about everything.

Grief is not a disorder to be medicated away; it is not pathology or a disease. Our ancestors were given the dignity to travel through this process more naturally. Although painful, it is the necessary path to healing. Being depressed after your loved one's death is more than natural—it's normal. Features common to grief are crying, feeling empty, and an overwhelming sense of loss. This is not a disorder requiring medical intervention. Now the overconfidence of our own intellectual superiority combined with the "big business" of the pharmaceutical industry has determined that we don't need to grieve anymore.

When my sisters were placed on hormone therapy years ago, deemed the new savior for menopausal women at the time, my wise mother warned us all to be careful about disrupting the natural process of our bodies. Years later, one sister faces the only case of ovarian cancer in the history of our family and the other sister stopped taking hormones when they were found to be dangerous. As a consequence, she is reexperiencing all the symptoms of menopause—twelve years later! So, did the hormones stop the symptoms or just delay them?

The point is that we do not know the consequences of disrupting the body's innate path. Have you ever listened to the laundry list of side effects for the drugs advertised on television? It's enough to make your hair curl. (That's probably a side effect right there!)

There are reasons to prescribe conservative medication during grief. So how do you know if medication is right for you? An onslaught of psychosomatic symptoms like ongoing panic attacks or physical ailments may indicate a medical intervention is necessary. If you just cannot function in your job and your livelihood is threatened, medication may be a temporary solution. Certainly if you fear taking your own life, you may need to be evaluated. A person may have a preexisting diagnosis that would render him or her less able to cope or function, which should also be taken into consideration. It should not be construed as a "lack" or a "failure" on the griever's part if medication *is* found necessary, but neither should it be automatically accepted as a matter of course for those suffering a loss. Most people who are prescribed meds might also benefit from attending bereavement counseling to help them regain functionality and eventual movement toward weaning off medication entirely. Unfortunately, it has been my experience that the exact opposite often occurs—that once a person starts on medication, a vicious cycle of growing tolerance, higher dosage, and new and better pharmaceutical cocktails often ensues.

Too many nights without sleep for some patients may call for a mild sleep aid; however, *that* intervention doesn't always have to be chemical. Many people have reported help from melatonin, which is a natural substance produced by our bodies to help regulate sleep and wake cycles and can be purchased at a health food store. In cases when an individual has developed chronic anxiety or depression over time due to complicated grief or in some cases of posttraumatic stress disorder (PTSD), medication may be needed.

I realize that if you are overwhelmed by the agony of your loss at the moment, it is tempting to medicate. When my son Jesse died, I was immediately handed valium by a doctor. I was tempted to take not just one but the whole vial! I took the pills for about four days, yet something inside of me cried out. I didn't want to push away my sorrow—wasn't I entitled to it and every other emotion that went along with a good-bye that never should have been said? In some way, those feelings were all I had left of my son.

Don't let anyone rob you of your sadness, your anger, or whatever other emotions you are entitled to. You have already been robbed. And if you need to talk about these feelings, you owe it to yourself to find a safe place in which to do so. There are some amazing, healing listeners out there who will not ask you to repress your thoughts and feelings. There are also wonderful bereavement groups available. It takes emotional courage to proceed down this path. The real experts will tell you that it is the only way back out into the sunlight again.

Societal pressures

In the early 1900s, most Americans died at home, and consequently death was seen more as a part of life. It was expected for people to live and die surrounded by their loved ones. When a family member grew sick, he or she might receive treatment in a hospital but probably came home to die. By the 1950s, more people were hospitalized, but over 50 percent of deaths still occurred at home. Today, over 80 percent of people die in hospitals or long-term care facilities.

Early-twentieth-century doctors cared for the chronically ill and the elderly at home, and the family members helped in that care. This also allowed relatives, particularly children, to watch the natural progression of life to death, including the gradual fading away of their loved ones. If that sounds barbaric, I pose this question to you: is it any more humane to see a loved one perish in the sterile environment of a hospital, surrounded by strangers and hooked up to cold machinery?

As a society, we have grown frightened of the inevitable end of life and thus have made it a stranger to ourselves. In removing death from our lives, we may have gone backward in our understanding of it. Always a mystery, death now becomes a distorted intruder we turn away from as a culture. So, when it hits, it feels abnormal, impossible. Consequently, the attempt to baffle death has become an entire industry of "antiaging" products and plastic surgery. We don't even want to see people getting older anymore, let alone dying.

So how do we individually accept what our society denies? Think back to childhood, when you first explored the world. Nature was the best teacher for understanding the life cycle. I remember being fascinated by the smallest creatures, the turning autumn leaves, the tiny egg found in an abandoned bird's nest. Our very hearts beat to the rhythm of life and death. As a culture, however, we do our best to avoid it. We construct skyscrapers, obsess about the garments we wear, and spend a tragic amount of time consumed with the pursuit of money, growing ever more distant from the natural rhythm of ourselves as creatures of the Earth.

In grief, many patients report a rekindled interest in the simple things. The irrelevant is somehow stripped away, leaving only the bare bones of life. How do I get out of bed today? Did I remember to eat lunch? This is a time to stay focused on all those minute details of life that we left behind in childhood. Thrust back into the rhythm of nature, there is no $200 handbag or shiny new car that can hold us in the artificial. Everything becomes just *too real*. A loved one has died, which means that someday *I* will die too. Society with its youth orientation and many distractions has helped us to avoid this eventuality rather than helping us to accept the unavoidable truth. Haven't we learned that we are better able to accept that for which we have prepared?

I do not advocate sitting around thinking about death all day— quite the contrary. I believe if we are conscious of ourselves as *beings* that possess the miracle of life upon this Earth, we will derive more meaning and joy from each moment and stop busying ourselves in empty pursuits. This brings a certain peace to the soul. Think of those rare individuals who smile broadly and seem to find pleasure in the simple things of life. We all know them; perhaps we have even *been* them at particular times in our lives. These special people have somehow managed to derive pleasure from just being human.

For the bereaved there is no choice but to crash into humanity, for to be human is to be mortal. Life becomes a series of daunting tasks, where even a trip to the grocery store can be fraught with uncertainty. When you are in deep grief, the unnecessary falls away. You can do only that which is within your temporarily impaired capabilities. As the shroud of sorrow lifts, you will add cautiously on to your diminished world.

There will be some surprises as your priorities automatically realign. You may decide that your job has become inexplicably meaningless or that you've lived for years in a way you can no longer tolerate. But the deafening throng of loss needs to be quieted before you make any impulsive life-altering decisions.

Reconstruct your life with the insight that mortality has granted you. This is heady, philosophical stuff for those of you who despair so deeply at this moment. But the time will come when you emerge from the fog and reenter the "real" world. Isn't the reality of life and death more credible than the age-defying, artificial culture we inhabit? So, when you walk back out of the shadows, do not discard the torch you used to find your way out—the knowledge of what is truly significant in this world.

THE CONSEQUENCES OF UNRESOLVED GRIEF

Psychology produces words that seep into popular culture. When I was a young girl, the buzzword was *neurotic*—everyone was "neurotic." If you were a fan of the game show *Password*, you could almost see the host Allen Ludden whispering, "The password is . . . *neurotic*." For a while the word in vogue was *denial*. Jokes sprang up like "De Nile is not just a river in Egypt, you know!" Then, just as suddenly, it seemed like every boy had attention deficit hyperactivity disorder (ADHD). Lately, the buzzword is *bipolar*.

I remember a case of twins, years ago, in which one of the two little girls was diagnosed with ADHD, when both had just lost their mother. One child became quiet and withdrawn, while the other was acting out by displaying many of the same characteristics of ADHD. She could no longer sit still in school and had trouble focusing. A counselor mistakenly placed her on Ritalin until she was properly diagnosed. Along the same lines, more recently, an article in the *Journal of Psychiatry and Neuroscience* cited a "disturbing" trend in overdiagnosis of bipolar disorder. Unfortunately, the therapeutic community is not above being influenced by the diagnosis du jour. Also, diagnosis is not an exact science, and symptoms of different disorders do overlap. Although grief is not a disorder, it often mimics some of these characteristics and so goes misdiagnosed. Many times I have seen this in patients who come in to my office.

It's fascinating to watch knowledge spread through popular culture. Recently the term *unresolved grief* has been popping up in the media. So, what exactly does it mean? Does anyone ever completely resolve grief? Is there a formula for mourning properly?

Lynn walked into my parental loss bereavement group one night. She was twentysomething, short-haired, pretty, and overweight. What struck me immediately about Lynn was the look of shock on her face. She appeared dazed, with an almost vacant stare. Judging from her face, I was sure her loss had been very recent.

"Is this the group for people who have lost parents?" she asked.

"Yes. Please join us. We were just making introductions for the new people who have joined us tonight."

A man shared with us that he had lost his mother to cancer two weeks earlier and that his minister suggested he get some help. Now it was Lynn's turn.

"My mother died when I was eleven and my dad died when I was sixteen. I can't live like this anymore. Every day I dread getting up in the morning. I always wanted to be married and have children. Now that I finally achieved my dream, I thought I would finally stop feeling so horrible. My husband asks me, 'Isn't this what you wanted?' I love him and my daughters more than anything, but I am still depressed. What is wrong with me?"

Stunned by Lynn's words, the members of the group weren't sure how to relate to this woman who had lost her parents over a decade ago. Looking at her vacant face, I recognized the destruction of unresolved grief. I took her aside after the group and she entered into private therapy with me the next day. In working with Lynn, I learned of the harrowing circumstances of her teenage years.

"After my mother died, my father sent me to a neighbor's. I was not allowed to go to her funeral or anything. When I returned home every trace of my mother had been removed from the house—all her clothes, her jewelry, even pictures of her. It was like she never existed."

She delivered these words with a distant look in her eyes. "My brothers and sisters were older and they had all left home, so I was stuck alone with my father."

It turned out that Lynn's father was an emotionally abusive alcoholic who slipped further into his cups after his wife's death. He neglected poor Lynn, who cooked and cleaned for them both. "I had very little time to do schoolwork and no clothes that fit me. I had to work to buy my own clothes."

By the time she turned sixteen, Lynn's father drank himself to death. This child had suffered the loss of both parents, neither of which was ever acknowledged. "I guess I was pretty smart, but no one seemed to care about me at school."

No one at the school ever offered this girl help. She just slipped through the cracks. Amazingly, she was able to graduate and go on to become a dental hygienist. She found a wonderful man to marry and had two beautiful children. Despite her depression, Lynn was an accomplished individual. When she wandered shell-shocked into our bereavement group, she was nearly suicidal.

Some of the elements of Lynn's story are all too familiar. There was a time, not too many years ago, when adults thought they were protecting children by leaving them out of the mourning rituals. Articles of the deceased were quickly scooped away by well-meaning friends, so as not to "remind" family members of their loss. We have learned a lot since then. The old saying goes, "A joy shared is doubled, while a sorrow shared is halved." A griever needs to mourn. This may be done in many different ways, but left undone it catches up with you. Studies show that unresolved grief can lead to substance abuse, high-risk behavior, chronic depression, insanity, and even suicide.

What is unresolved grief? According to Webster's, one of the definitions of *resolved* is "to find an answer." *Grief* is defined as "emotional suffering." So, when a person is unable to find a satisfactory answer for his emotional suffering, he continues to grieve. For some, that answer may be spiritual, while for others resolution may come as an acceptance of life and death as a natural order. Others may feel that their loved one's death served a purpose, such as ending long-term suffering or serving his country in the military. We may never make sense of the death itself, but we can come to terms with the loss of our loved one. So why is one person able to "make peace" with her loss and another never able to get past it? If it is never gotten through, it is always there, coloring everything.

Janice was six months pregnant with three small children at home when she came into my bereavement group. She worked hard to keep a "brave face" for her family after her mother died. Grandma had been a constant part of her children's lives, helping with all household chores, including babysitting. After Grandma's death, Janice was intent on keeping everything the same. She and her husband worked twice as hard to take up the slack.

"I want my kids to be happy. I don't want to bring grief into my home," she resolutely stated to us one night.

"Janice . . . it's already there," I gently responded.

She was working so hard not to upset her children that she couldn't see how angry she had become. The children were confused because no one was talking about Grandma. Mom's anger implied that the children had done something wrong, while the unexpressed grief was interpreted to mean that it was inappropriate to express feelings about loss. In turn, each child suffered greatly. The two oldest boys began physically fighting with one another and breaking things. One of them began drawing very disturbing pictures. The youngest child cried constantly. Dad began drinking more heavily to escape his emotionally unavailable wife and insane household. All this because no one wanted to acknowledge the great loss that they had all experienced together.

So how do we work to resolve grief? There are several ways. First we acknowledge the loss. Janice learned that it was OK for her to talk about her grief without overwhelming her children with it. This in turn gave her children permission to talk about their own losses.

Janice accomplished this by joining a bereavement group for parental loss. It is my experience that groups are most effective when they deal with a particular kind of loss. There is enough diversity in members of most groups to begin with; add to that different kinds of losses and a member can become alienated from other members and the group as a whole. Although all bereavement encompasses a whole host of emotions, parental loss has its own specific issues that are different from the loss of a child or spouse. If a specific type of bereavement group is not available, it is still far better to seek out help than to suffer in silence. Even bereavement groups with different types of losses can be extremely helpful, as all loss is similar in some way. Talking about the loss of her mother was essential for Janice. She was truly comforted by the other members who dealt with many of the same issues.

"My mother was my best friend," she told us one night. "I just don't know how I'm going to raise these kids without her!" Other women in the group had similar circumstances. We brainstormed to help one another, not only with the sorrow of losing one's parent but with the practical concerns of how to manage a household without Grandma. Part of grief resolution in this case included practical solutions for child care. If in unresolved grief you are looking to find answers to your emotional suffering and you are constantly reminded of your loss, it becomes complex to move on. If Janice was unable to face the very real concern of finding help for her children, she would reexperience the loss of her mother every time she needed that extra pair of absent hands. She could sit in a therapist's office for the rest of her life talking about her loss, but unless she attended to the realities of her life, she might never move on.

There is often a great deal of practicality involved in grief resolution. For example, how can an elderly member of society be expected to come to terms with the loss of a spouse with whom he has shared the better part of his life without finding something else constructive to help fill his lonely hours? In this instance a good counselor doesn't just listen but might help guide him to a card game at the senior center or a bereavement group for widows and widowers. I have seen many a happy senior find companionship through one of these groups.

Clinical psychologist Therese Rando talks about the six "R" processes of mourning necessary for healthy accommodation of loss:

1. Recognize the loss. Acknowledge the death. Understand the death.

2. React to the separation. Experience the pain. Feel, identify, accept, and give some form of expression to all the psychological reactions to the loss. Identify and mourn secondary losses.

3. Recollect and re-experience the deceased and the relationship. Review and remember realistically. Revive and re-experience the feelings.

4. Relinquish the old attachments to the deceased and the old assumptive world.

5. Readjust to move adaptively into the new world without forgetting the old. Revise the assumptive world. Develop a new relationship with the deceased. Adopt new ways of being in the world. Form a new identity.

6. Reinvest.

The lyrics to an old song go, "Why do the birds go on singing? Why do the stars shine above? Don't they know it's the end of the world? It ended when I lost your love." Isn't that what we're talking about here? Lost love. The love within each of us meant only for the person who has traveled to a place so distant that no amount of crying or postage or calling of a name can elicit the response you so desperately need? One word, one touch . . . You would do anything, go anywhere, for a mere whisper, but you are denied even that.

So, who cares what the so-called experts say, you might ask? What the hell's the difference if grief is resolved or not—it still feels horrible! We've talked about grief being a natural process, but so much conspires to divert us from what is natural. To go forward, you must go *through*. Your mind and body cannot help but mourn, if you let them. This process requires nothing more than allowing the process to advance. You are important to this world, to those around you.

When someone dies, those left behind inhabit a kind of limbo nestled on the periphery of the real world. We "half" live through gray days and sleepless nights. Like zombies, many of us walk unconsciously through meaningless jobs carrying on vacuous conversations. But one day the sky looks blue again and little things start to matter again. There is a place for us among the living, and it does not require that we abandon our dead to find it. Trust me and keep reading.

WHAT IS COMPLICATED GRIEF?

Complicated grief is also referred to as pathologic, chronic, morbid, or abnormal grief. All these terms indicate grief that is extended and presents with various symptoms. Complicated grief for some individuals shows up as the inability to experience normal grief reactions. A person might avoid any reminders of his deceased loved one. Other complicated grief looks almost exactly the opposite, where the individual cannot stop thinking about the person who died. Long after a normal mourning period has passed, she is still preoccupied with the deceased. She may dream constantly about this person and speak of little else. She is unable to integrate the death into her reality and begin to live again.

So why do some people get stuck in the grieving process? Studies show that there may be circumstances of the death itself that predispose the griever to complicated grief. Sudden, unanticipated death, especially when traumatic or violent, can be one of those factors. Sometimes death from an overly long illness can leave a person open to complicated grief as well. Loss of a child carries with it the seeds of complication. A person might sincerely believe that he could have done something more to prevent a death. An overly dependent relationship with the individual who died, or an angry, ambivalent relationship, can cause complications. If someone has suffered more than one loss in a short period of time, is unusually stressed, or has a mental illness, he is more likely to get stuck in grief.

I was seeing a young girl who was having great difficulty adjusting to her mother's death when I noticed that the girl's father often referred to his wife as though she were still alive. Amy kept asking me to come to her house. Something told me that I should honor her request, so I scheduled a home visit with Amy when she was out of school with the mumps. During my visit, her father, Glenn, took me on a tour of their home, and I was surprised to find that after two years, he had not removed any of his deceased wife's articles from the master bedroom or bath (OK, so I'm nosy). Everything had remained the same since the night she died. There were half-used toiletries on the bathroom sink and even a pink toothbrush alongside his in the holder. Her shoes lay scattered about the closet floor, along with her clothes, which still hung in the closet. It was as though she still lived in the house. I knew for a fact there was no other woman living there, but it was rather eerie. No wonder Amy was having such problems. Amazingly, even at six years of age, she knew something was wrong in her house. What she didn't completely understand was that her father's mourning process had stalled. The next week I began seeing Amy's father.

Glenn's wife's death had many of the characteristics that predispose a person to complicated grief. His wife was hit by a car while walking the dog at night while Glenn was supposed to be away on a business trip. In actuality, Glenn was having an affair with a coworker and they were spending the night in a hotel. Normally it was Glenn's job to walk the dog at night. Glenn's wife was struck violently and died instantly. On top of this, Glenn's grief was further complicated by the fact that he was still mourning his younger sister who had died recently of cancer. Talk about complicated grief!

Glenn had so many issues to work through, including the trauma of his wife's death. It was necessary to deal with the trauma of the circumstances before attempting to touch upon Glenn's grief. His posttraumatic symptoms included intense nightmares and intrusive memories that sometimes made it difficult for him to work. Glenn experienced panic attacks almost daily when he drove past the area where his wife had been killed. Medication was necessary to even attempt therapeutic intervention. But suffice it to say that it was more than a year before we had worked through Glenn's trauma to even touch upon his grief.

4

THE LANGUAGE OF LOSS

THE STORY OF THE DEATH

Every time someone dies, the *story of the death* is created. Most of us have a need to repeat our story of the death over and over again. The story of the death is composed of the words a person chooses when he or she describes the death of a loved one. That story could be completely accurate and true, but it is always colored by the perceptions of the person telling the story. The story is like a recipe where the basic meal remains the same yet is altered by those ingredients added by each particular chef. The story of the death for one family member may include an abundance of denial, while another family member may sprinkle guilt liberally into the mix. So, why is the story of the death important? Allow me to illustrate with one woman's story.

"It was my fault that my sister died," Donna said very matter-of-factly. There was no change in her affect as she related this information to me, as though it was just another fact of her childhood. She actually seemed surprised when I asked her for further explanation. Her expression seemed to wonder, *Doesn't everybody know I killed my sister?* She paused for several seconds before answering. Her next words came from an expressionless face, as though memorized from a script: "We were playing outside. I was supposed to be watching Jenny, but I saw a really cool butterfly and started following it. Jenny ran out in the street and got hit by a car and she died."

That was it, thirty-seven words to sum up the most traumatic event of this patient's childhood. Donna seemed eager to move on to another topic, becoming visibly uncomfortable when I chose to linger on the current subject.

"Have you ever done any therapy around this issue?" I asked.

"No, don't you remember? I've only done marriage counseling and it didn't work."

I remembered. It was the marriage counselor who sent Donna to me for individual counseling.

"Tell me about Jenny," I said.

"She never made it to the hospital—internal injuries," she quickly replied.

I knew this level of denial could only be defending a deeply *internalized* guilt over the death of her sister. This was going to take time. If I pressed her too much further, she would surely not return for her next session. Over a period of several months Donna broke through her denial. She began by remembering things about her sister and she even brought in a picture of them together.

A short time each week was devoted to this subject, cushioned between other things we were working on. This kind of exploration made Donna extremely vulnerable and required patience. As her denial lifted, Donna was undefended against the guilt and possible self-hatred she was harboring. I worried about her hurting herself. With Donna's permission, I share some excerpts from a breakthrough session:

"How old were you when your sister died?" I asked.

"I told you already, I was five years old."

"And Jenny?"

"I told you, two!" She grew impatient.

"Right, sorry," I smiled slightly. "Donna, tell me again the ages of your own children?"

She looked puzzled but answered, "Kyle's seven and Dean's one and a half."

"So how often do you let Kyle babysit for Dean?"

"Of course I never let Kyle watch Dean for more than a few minutes at a time. And I know where you're going with this—but it's not the same." She shook her head.

"Isn't it?" I asked. Those words just hung in the air as she truly considered this concept, maybe for the first time.

"No, because boys are different; they never sit still. You *expect* them to go running after things. And besides, my mom only left me there with Jenny for a few minutes to answer the phone because Dad was calling all the way from England."

"So she left you to watch an active two-year-old on a busy street?" This was said without an incriminating tone. I watched Donna's face as she allowed the reality of these words to penetrate the denial she had been working so hard to preserve for all these years. And I added, "You did say it was a busy street, right?"

"Yes."

"How long was your mother gone?"

"I don't know, maybe ten or fifteen minutes."

"And then she came outside?"

"No," she replied, "then I ran in to get her because the car hit Jenny." Finally the blank affect was shattered and the long-awaited tears began to flow.

"So, she didn't even hear the accident? You had to go and get her?"

Her next words were spoken emphatically through her tears. "I wouldn't do that! I wouldn't leave my sons outside like that. Not in Queens on a street like that!"

The last she screamed with a rage that shook her whole body.

Yes, now Donna would have to deal with the reality of the situation and all that went with it. But I felt sure she could handle *that* better than the story she'd been living with for most of her life.

The story of the death is powerful. What we tell ourselves and others about our loved one's death is crucial to the grieving process. One widow repeats the story of the death, day after day, as if in the retelling, her story becomes more acceptable to her. A father claims he feels closer to his son by these constant recitations, maybe his last way to hold on to his son.

Some families make up the story of the death together and use exactly the same words. I've seen this in suicide. Perhaps this helps with the enormous weight of guilt felt by such families. Sometimes these stories can harm us, like in the example of Donna and the story that had unknowingly been agreed upon by mother and daughter. Words designed to alleviate her mother of the guilt she could not bear had kept Donna imprisoned for thirty years. We owe it to ourselves to each look at the words of our own story of the death.

What do your words tell you about how you view what happened? Some stories seem way too short. "Yeah, he smoked." A lot is conveyed in a story like this. The subtext goes something like this: *I blame him for the death and I don't want to talk about it.* Men often have shorter stories of the death, but those few words might just be the tip of the iceberg.

Does your story convey large portions of guilt or blame? This is probably an indication of work you might want to do with a bereavement counselor or group. You might need to view the circumstances of your loved one's death more objectively or completely, in order to *let go* of the negative consequences it may have on you emotionally and even physically. Remember what we learned about unresolved grief?

SECONDARY LOSS

When a loved one dies, you don't just suffer the loss of that individual. Many other losses accompany the death. I refer to these losses as *secondary losses*. Secondary losses can be numerous and crippling. When I work with people, I break secondary losses into two categories: *practical* and *self.*

PRACTICAL SECONDARY LOSSES

These are those types of tangible changes that accompany death. For instance, if your spouse died, along with that loss, you may have also lost part of your household income or the person who kept the outside of your house in order. A parental loss might produce the need for trustworthy child care. Almost every loss includes practical secondary losses.

Loss of status can also accompany a death. Sometimes the major breadwinner dies and a whole family can find themselves struggling financially, in addition to experiencing grief. Children may have to adjust to living in a different school district and moving to a smaller home in addition to a loss of friends. Mom or Dad may go from being part of a couple to single parenthood and working overtime.

At first we grieve the person, but practical secondary losses often keep happening months and even years after the death, causing us to reopen the healing wound again and again.

"SELF" SECONDARY LOSSES

Those losses to "self" when your loved one dies are less tangible and yet may be even more distressing than practical secondary losses. The self loses the relationship with that other person, which can produce lowered self-esteem, lack of confidence, loss of a person to confide in, loss of future hopes and dreams, and extreme loneliness, to mention just a few.

Another less tangible secondary loss is the loss of the future with the individual who died. Parents may be mourning the loss of a child's future, while an older couple may lament the retirement dream they shared when one prematurely dies.

Loss of a first child imposes the loss of one's role as parent, while loss of a spouse causes an immediate change in role from married to single. Roles also change when another family member dies. This adjustment can prove to be a key part of finding one's place in the world again. *Who am I without that other person there?* Depression may set in as you realize that the way you have defined yourself no longer exists. Many grievers talk about feeling like *they* died along with their loved ones. Self secondary loses are often at the center of these feelings.

HOW TO HELP YOURSELF WITH SECONDARY LOSSES

In the early stages of grief (the first few months), you may not even be sure what secondary losses you've suffered. As time passes, these losses become more apparent. A boy loses his father and immediately that loss is felt, but over time when there is no dad cheering him on the soccer field and he and his family have to move to a smaller house in a different town, the secondary losses mount and take their toll. It may be important to consider what secondary losses this child has suffered to better understand the true breadth of his loss.

For you, whatever type of loss you have suffered, it includes many secondary losses—practical and self. When you can think again, making a list of these losses might help in working through them. Why would you want to make such a list? If you inform yourself about what this loss will do to change your life, you will be more prepared to assist yourself through these underrated secondary losses. If it is too painful to approach this alone, elicit aid from your counselor, friend, or family member.

Several years after her mom's death, Meagan's dad brought her in for counseling. Bewildered, his main complaint was "Just when I think she's doing better, she becomes withdrawn and depressed all over again." Dad couldn't understand why Meagan's grief never seemed to lessen. Part of the reason was that as Meagan entered different developmental stages she was forced to miss her mother in new ways and to *re-grieve* again and again. Together, Meagan and I made an extensive list of her secondary losses. It was mind-boggling and taught me once again to respect the power of grief. On the top of the next page are just a few of the secondary losses she mentioned.

The list went on, but I'm sure you get the idea.

A true understanding about the scope of this girl's grief allowed me to better help her heal. It was at this point that Meagan's dad hired a nanny to lessen a good many of Meagan's secondary loss issues. The woman was a youthful mom herself, who had already raised a family. She helped with household chores, but more important, she provided

"Self" Secondary Losses	Practical Secondary Losses
Feels different from other girls	Doesn't have anyone to shop or to pick out clothes with
Low self-esteem	Too many household chores that a mom usually does
Embarrassed by her period	No woman's touches around the house

a female role model and became a friend to Meagan. The chemistry was evident, and I saw true affection between the two. They even went clothes shopping together. In no way did this solution serve to alleviate the greatest loss of this young person's life, but in a very practical way it helped. In what ways has your loss changed your world? Think about the many roles that the person who died fulfilled in your world.

SURVIVOR'S GUILT

Not so long ago I was undergoing a lovely massage at the expert hands of a talented massage therapist. Mostly I spend this time quietly as a treat to my mind and body, but on this day, Laura and I struck up a conversation. She asked what I did for a living, and when I answered, she felt compelled to share with me her incredible story. After this massage we became instant friends. This is a by-product of loss—members of *this* lonely hearts club have a deep connection that can happen even in a dark, quiet room without eye contact. Her story is one of the most amazing accounts of *survivor's guilt* I had ever heard.

Laura grew up on the same street as Jenn in a town called Bexley, Ohio. Both girls shared an interest in marine biology, which they discovered during an educational high school program to Andros Island in the Bahamas. Later they attended the College of Wooster back in Ohio, but returned to the Bahamas for an independent study project. After graduation, Laura and Jenn once again returned to the field station on Andros Island as teachers of marine biology. Their days were filled with turquoise blue water, white sand, and sunshine as they lived in small huts and became friendly with the people of Andros.

During this time they befriended Mark, a handsome native Bahamian who became a diving instructor for the field station. The three grew inseparable, bonded by their easy wit and love of the water; they made a dynamic team engaging the "too cool" high school and college students with their humor and playful repartee while teaching them the mysteries of the sea. And they dove. Laura and Jenn increased their diving certifications. At some point, Laura began to have some trouble with ear infections, which kept her from diving deeper. But Jenn and Mark loved to push the envelope. They dove deeper than Jenn's certification justified, and they began exploring the underwater caves around Andros. Some of these "blue holes" or "sinkholes" required special certification and equipment that neither Jenn nor Mark possessed.

It was on New Year's Day 2002 when Laura woke up and proceeded to gather up her equipment for a very special dive. It was to be her sixtieth, the last dive necessary to receive her master diver's certificate. This dive was to be special for another reason as well. It was the day that Jenn and Mark would take Laura to "King Kong." She had heard of the amazing beauty of this enormous blue hole that descended more than five hundred feet into the ocean and spread out in intricate cave designs in all directions. Because of its unique structure, it was safe for Laura to dive down about one hundred feet or so and swim around the perimeter.

The divers were warned never to drink alcohol the night before a dive, but because it was New Year's Eve, Laura *did* have a beer. She didn't feel entirely comfortable about it. As she began to gather her equipment, she realized that her ear was bothering her. Disappointed, she told her friends that she would not be joining them on the dive that morning.

"I remember how it felt when I hugged Jenn, before she left," Laura told me. "I remember what she was wearing."

Jenn and Mark never returned from that dive. Their bodies were never found, though divers looked for days.

Now in my living room, this lovely twenty-five-year-old woman recounted her story of the death. "We were like the same person, Jenn and I."

In this short story I heard words to suggest that Laura felt part of *her* was lost beneath the ocean that tragic morning.

"Did you ever do any counseling for this?" I asked.

"Not really."

"Do you believe that you *did not* cause this to happen?" I asked. Her sweet face contorted with the pain from within that I've witnessed so many times before.

"I don't know if I believe it deep down in my core." She hesitated before deciding to go *there*, one more agonizing time. "I should have 'sat surface.' I should have gone with them." She explained that "sitting surface" was a diving term for staying up above and basically watching out for the other divers.

"People tell me that it wasn't my fault. I even tell myself. But I would give anything to be on that boat." She stared vacantly into the space where I guessed she imagined herself on that boat.

"Why? Because you think you could have changed something?" I asked.

"Yes," she paused, "I should have told them it was stupid to take the chances they were taking. I should have stopped them!"

"Would they have listened to you?"

Long pause. "No."

"Could you have stopped them?"

"No," she shook her head and sadly smiled.

This is the guilt of the survivor, the one who made it out while her friends perished. It is the same guilt that plagues so many.

Laura shared with me some insightful things about her personal journey toward healing.

"It was the community on Andros that saved me from falling apart."

"How?"

"It was their loving kindness and their faith." Laura proceeded to explain that she had grown up with religion in her life, but she had never truly understood faith until she lived among these Bahamians. She spoke of their gratitude for even the smallest things. They told her that she would never understand what happens here in this world but that she can still believe. They made it that simple.

When Laura went home to Ohio, she faced everyone asking, "Why?" It was the simple faith of the Andros natives that sustained her. She realized that she had stopped asking why. But the greatest gift she had been given were the simple words from a Bahamian woman who told her, "God kept you here for a reason."

Another piece of this story has also brought Laura some solace. Survivors often speak of doing something in memory of those who died. It helps with the resolution of grief. Jenn's family was obviously devastated by their loss. It is a custom of the marine biology field station to give out gifts to the natives at Christmas each year. Many of the natives of Andros are quite poor, and they appreciate these gifts tremendously. Since her daughter's death, Jenn's mother has spent each year collecting gifts and clothing for the people of Andros, distributing them at the Christmas ceremony in honor of her daughter. Also, Jenn's mother and her former high school collect books each year and have started a library for the people of Andros.

This was the only such conversation I was to have with Laura on this subject, as she was headed back down to Andros Island. After working in Charleston, South Carolina, as a massage therapist for some time, she decided to return to work at the marine biology field station. She said she felt guilty about not finishing the work she and Jenn had started together. I was concerned that she might be headed back for a different reason.

Unchecked, survivor's guilt can lead a person to self-destructive behavior. At times, the subconscious is a powerful adversary. The desire to join a loved one who has died can be a motivator to shed these mortal coils. So, I made this apprehension known to my friend Laura, even though I did not believe she intended herself harm. Her motivation for returning to her beloved island probably involved her own personal closure and to begin the journey of discovering the purpose for which she believed she had been spared. Laura has since returned home, married, and moved on with her life. Each of us is here for a purpose. Do not allow the toxic tendrils of guilt to keep you from living the life you have been given. Seek help and constructive release from this inner turmoil.

One the best films ever made on the subject of survivor's guilt remains *Ordinary People*. Although slightly dated, the story, acting, and directing of this movie make it a marvelous tool in the understanding of survivor's guilt.

HOW TO HELP YOURSELF WITH SURVIVOR'S GUILT

If you suffer from survivor's guilt, you know it. Guilt of any kind makes it difficult to sleep without the wheels of anxiety constantly churning. I cannot advocate strongly enough for those who suffer or who are watching a loved one suffer from this all-encompassing negative type of guilt to get help, *now!* An individual counselor is most appropriate in this case. You might be reluctant to voice these kinds of feelings in a group. If you cannot bear to disclose these negative feelings to a mental health professional, at least tell a trusted friend or confidante.

Be aware that substance abuse, depression, high-risk behavior, and even suicide can be the consequences of survivor's guilt. If you spend an inordinate amount of time justifying your actions before or *at* the time of a loved one's death, you might be trying to overcompensate for guilt.

Some survivors make statements like "It should have been me" or "I am so lucky" after this kind of loss. The survivor might become preoccupied with thoughts of the "other's" death and obsessed with the circumstances surrounding it. You might be looking for someone else to blame and adamantly pursue an irrational line of reasoning in an effort to shed the toxic heaviness of guilt.

Be aware that depression often accompanies survivor's guilt. If you dig, you may find that you don't really feel entitled to enjoy your life anymore.

HOW TO HELP THE GRIEVER WITH SURVIVOR'S GUILT

So how can others help those who suffer with survivor's guilt? By quietly listening to the story of the death a few times before starting to point out small inconsistencies in the griever's perspective of the death. If you just say, "Of course it wasn't your fault—you didn't cause his cancer!" this just doesn't cut it. The griever will merely dismiss your opinion as false and remain in his destructive form of denial (of the truth). Encourage this person to seek professional help.

I have found it useful to look into a person's *motives* for making the decisions he made around a loved one's death. New York City firefighter John Newell lost his partner Bobby on September 11. They had switched shifts that day. Here is an excerpt from one of John's sessions:

> Therapist: So you changed shifts to help each other out?
> John: Yeah, we do it all the time.
> Therapist: So if you'd known that a terrorist was going to fly a plane into the Twin Towers and cause your partner's death, you wouldn't have switched shifts that day?
> *(John gives me his best "Are you nuts?" look before answering.)*
> John: Yeah . . . so? It doesn't make me feel any better! I know I didn't do it on purpose, but it should have been *me*, not him.

Believe it or not, this was an improvement from prior sessions. This time, John had used the words "I know I didn't do it on purpose." This was the first time he could ever say words to that effect, and it had taken us three months to get there! I use this example just to show the power of survivor's guilt over a person.

Something else that helps people with survivor's guilt is constructive action, as in Laura's story earlier. She gave back to the people of Andros Island, and this helped to ease the pangs of guilt.

ANNIVERSARY GRIEF

The old wives used to call it getting through "the firsts" (those old wives get smarter as I get older). The reason that *one* year of grief is perceived as such a marker is because in one calendar year you pass through each milestone at least once. You travel through the birthday of your loved one, the holidays, perhaps the day he graduated from law school, or her first day of kindergarten. Sorrowfully the year flows by and you are swept downstream by the current of time, taken further and further from that last touch, that last glance, or the final words of that special soul. On each such occasion you experience the piercing pain of *anniversary grief*.

On these days, you sometimes cry as though no time has gone by at all, as though no healing has taken place. And oddly, even if you have lost track of the days, it's as if your body remembers without you. This happens even years later.

"The strangest thing happened," one teen reported. "I'd forgotten that it was my mom's birthday coming up. I mean, I was so busy with school and band—I was happy, you know? Anyway, it was six years ago she died. I was in school and I kept on feeling tired and sad. I called my dad to pick me up early. He asked if I was having a hard time with Mom's birthday. It wasn't until he asked me that I even remembered."

It's as if the very blood that courses through our veins misses that person. Again we are reminded that we are truly creatures of this Earth for all our technical advances.

A holiday approaches and you recall the dress your mother wore that day. The leaves change color and a memory of picking pumpkins suddenly takes shape. Anniversary grief is everywhere that first year. With time the intensity of this fades, but there are occasions even years later when anniversary grief can throw you back in time.

In my work, I find this grief to become quite intense during the period leading up to the actual day the person died. Weeks and even months before the date, people begin to feel as though they are backsliding, when in fact this anniversary grief is just a part of the process. As stated previously, death often carries with it the characteristics of trauma. Unconsciously, our minds gather information as we go through our lives. We collect data through our senses that we don't always process consciously.

The spring was approaching and my lovely client had slipped into a depression. She couldn't understand why her favorite time of the year, with flowers blooming, made her want to stay inside with the blinds drawn. On further investigation we determined that it was this very time of year when her husband was diagnosed with an inoperable brain tumor. She remembered watering the flowers on her porch when he approached with this news. It doesn't take a psychology degree to figure this one out, yet we don't always see these obvious parallels when it comes to ourselves.

Anniversary grief sneaks up on you. Little things throw you into a time warp from the past. Soon the calendar shows you that next Wednesday is the anniversary of the day your loved one died. Each day leading up to it casts you further into the depths of hell. Along with this tumble comes the fear that you will never again emerge from your despair. Remember what I told you? This is a part of grief. You have crawled out of this black hole before and you will do it again.

Much literature mistakenly reinforces the idea that everything will be better after the first year. While a year is certainly a mile marker demonstrating that you made it through all your "firsts," there are no steadfast rules here. Each individual grieves at his or her own pace. The expectation that you will magically be done after one year can be disappointing and frustrating. Grief rarely ends completely, but you do become functional again. You may still miss your loved one but will learn to incorporate that loss into your life and go on. Does that mean you will never be happy again? Absolutely not!

Along with anniversary grief, you may encounter a revisitation of guilt. This is common. All of the "shoulda, coulda, wouldas" bombard you like never before and you are sure you will crumble beneath them. If you have left therapy, this might be a good time for a few refresher sessions just to carry you through this difficult time. Talk it out with someone you trust: a friend, family member, or whoever can help you gain some objectivity. Your mind may be a dangerous neighborhood right now. Time will grant you perspective.

Every time you grieve a loss, it loses a little of its power over you. Give yourself time for this anniversary grief—it will pass and lessen. As time passes, you might feel you are drifting further away from your loved one. Again guilt may rear its useless head: *Hey, how can I be starting to enjoy life again when he lies in his grave? Let me just sabotage this happiness, because I don't deserve it.* These are dangerous thoughts that can take on a life of their own. Weed them out. Talking to other grievers can be helpful. People often join bereavement groups after a year of mourning. The groups are there whenever you are ready to live again.

RE-GRIEVING

Re-grieving has been tossed into much bereavement literature under the heading of secondary loss, but I believe they are different. Although it is most predictable and prevalent with children climbing the developmental ladder, I have seen re-grieving by many people and have learned to look for a trigger that often precedes the re-grieving episode.

Occasionally a patient returns to therapy—sometimes even years later. Let me explain why by way of example. Jake was a forty-four-year-old man whom I saw after his wife died of cancer. His grieving process was difficult, and his secondary losses included losing a mother for his children and a partner in life. He no longer felt comfortable around friends who were couples. Jake worked through all of these issues and finally rejoined the land of the living. He gained back the weight he had lost after his wife's death and he looked healthy again. He ended therapy and I did not see him for five years. So, what triggered this man's re-grieving episode?

When Jake came back into therapy, he looked awful. He had started losing weight again and couldn't sleep. He began having panic attacks and his irritable bowel syndrome had returned. These were all of the original symptoms that he had come into therapy with five years earlier.

JAKE: I've got to do something; I'm going to lose my job! I can't be running to the bathroom every five minutes!
THERAPIST: Have there been any significant changes lately?
JAKE: No, not really. I just can't stop thinking about Julie [deceased wife], and I feel like I'm back to square one.

Jake was obviously frustrated and broke down in the office. I asked about his children, who were all doing well. His job at the post office was fine, except for his recent sick days. Nothing had changed—except:

JAKE: Oh, and you remember Helen?
THERAPIST: How is that going?
JAKE: Well, it's going great. In fact, we're getting married in April.

Bingo! This was the triggering event for Jake's re-grief. Falling in love was permissible, but getting married was unacceptable and disloyal to his deceased wife. I never said grief was logical. Several months of therapy and a few sessions with his wife-to-be, and the symptoms were gone. A beautiful spring wedding ensued.

In posttraumatic stress disorder, stimuli associated with the original trauma can trigger symptoms. I do believe that all loss is traumatic and stimuli associated with the deceased loved one can trigger symptoms of grief. Many people speak of hearing a certain song or smelling a perfume that triggers tears before the stimuli is even consciously processed. True re-grieving is more profound than these painful reminders. There are anniversary pains that can even send a person hiding back under those covers for a day or two on the calendar date of an important event. However, true re-grieving is something else; it feels more like a setback to the griever. It places her back into a physically and emotionally vulnerable state for a longer period of time and may require additional therapy. Rest assured that "this too shall pass" and it is not truly a setback in the sense that much of the grief work has already taken place. With a little bit of work, life will resume. You will not feel like this forever.

5

COMFORT

Watching what people do to themselves to escape emotional pain is mind-boggling. The self-created complications that obstruct our path to happiness, or even just contentment, are unimaginable. Many of these behaviors begin as the shock wears off and the real pain begins. So how do we guard against this very vulnerable time for the griever?

COMFORTING BEHAVIORS

In my practice we talk about *comforting behaviors*. These are things a person does to help himself through a painful time. Most of us are familiar with destructive behaviors—things like drinking too much alcohol, overeating, or participating in high-risk activities like motorcycle racing. Unfortunately for the human animal, our destructive behaviors often double as coping mechanisms. This is fine until the destructive behaviors begin to cause more problems than they solve. At this point these destructive behaviors may have even become compulsive. Why not address this very real possibility before getting to that point?

So, how do *you* generally deal with difficulties? Do you crawl into bed with a bag of chips, go on a shopping spree, take long walks, or talk to a friend? How you deal with stress is key to helping you deal with loss. Self-examination reveals constructive ways in which you comfort yourself, even if the destructive ways are more tempting. Think about the things that made you feel better when you were a child. Watching a favorite television show, reading comic books, or just kicking a ball around might have served to comfort us before some of us grew up and discovered wine, fast cars, and meaningless sex. My patients share their memories with me in an effort to explore their comforting behaviors.

"Well, let's see. I seem to remember climbing up a tree to get away from my family," one patient told me. "I'd just sit up there and look out at the world. No one knew where I was, and I would just stay quiet up there for a long time. Sometimes I even brought a book with me." Much to her relief, I did not advocate that this grandmother of three start climbing trees again. Instead, we used this information to come up with a brand-new comforting behavior for Michelle. Imagine her elation upon transforming a long-vacant upstairs bedroom into a "tree house." Her new hideout featured a cushy red chair and mahogany shelves filled with her favorite books. Sun dappled in through lace curtains as Michelle would sit, reading, knitting, or just enjoying the splendor of her lovely garden below. "No one bothers me up there. Sometimes I just close the door and have a good cry for myself."

Comforting behaviors need not be as elaborate or expensive as creating a room for yourself. In our fast-paced, stressful environment, easy answers to anxiety relief are tempting for all of us. If you can take away those bad feelings with chocolate, why not? If you go home to an empty house after work and have to face the anguish of your loss, why shouldn't you smoke a pack of cigarettes? The numbing effect is quick and easy. But none of these represents a lasting solution.

Imagine yourself as a New York City firefighter after September 11. You spend day after day sifting through rubble, looking for the remains of your friends and colleagues. On your time off, you attend dozens of funerals for these colleagues as a sign of respect to their families. What would you or I do to escape such insanity? Does having a drink or two or six really sound so bad?

I'm sure that some of the guys I counseled probably wanted to throw something at me when I started talking to them about comforting behaviors, yet they listened and, more important, they talked. One fire-fighter asked if he could bring his wife to therapy to help support him. Together, the three of us came up with an idea for a comforting behavior that really worked for Eddie. Firefighters have fluctuating schedules, which *did* present some problems, but we worked around them. It seemed that outdoor exercise was the only thing that took Eddie's mind off the nightmare he was living through. Luckily, his wife Tracey was looking to lose weight. They began to find time to walk, run, or bicycle the three-mile trail at the nearest state park together. Eddie was thrilled that Tracey consented to this schedule, as she had never before shown any interest in exercising with him. Soon it became a part of their life together. I am not going to say that this was the end of Eddie's problems, but it was more likely the beginning of a solution.

In Eddie's case, nature provided a sense of comfort. I sometimes wonder if we realize how far away from nature we have drifted. Technology has taken us prisoner even as it has freed us. Between windowless offices, e-mail, Facebook, text messages, cell phones, computers, and televisions, some of us can go days before feeling the actual sunlight upon our faces. However, we remain biological creatures with natural cravings. We have all heard about seasonal affective disorder (SAD), in which people experience depression due to lack of sunlight. As children, many of us spent hours playing outside investigating plants and animals. For the newly bereaved, the world hurries by. Nature often acts as a counterbalance to this chaos. The list of comforting behaviors that include nature is vast, but here are some that I have seen work firsthand:

1. Exercising outside: this includes walking, running, outdoor sports like tennis or golf, boating, and fishing
2. Planting or tending a garden
3. Just sitting outdoors with a friend
4. Barbecuing, picnicking, or eating at an outdoor café
5. Spending time at the beach
6. Backpacking and camping

Comforting behaviors are often a form of escape for the griever: a temporary, much-needed respite from mourning. Television or a good book can also provide a diversion. Many grievers have difficulty concentrating on books during early grief, and television becomes more accessible to them; even magazines may be easier to digest. As mentioned earlier, touching, affection, and even sex may be comforting to some individuals, while a hot bath works for others. Whatever helps without injuring yourself or others is good. Your body needs a release from the constant stress of grief; children intrinsically understand this. As you will see in chapter 7, children grieve differently than adults—one minute they may be crying and missing their departed grandparent, and five minutes later they are laughing and playing. They often get through the process of grief with less wear and tear on the body and mind.

In the hilarious classic movie *Airplane!*, Lloyd Bridges exclaims, "Looks like I picked the wrong week to quit smoking!" Yes, grief is a ridiculous time to suggest that you tackle addiction. There is not much meaning in anything for the newly bereaved, and you may even harbor a secret wish to join the person who died. Would you believe that those feelings might lift? And there may even come a time when you feel it is your duty to live life to the fullest *for* your loved one who no longer can?

Some people's comforting behaviors include spirituality. A church, temple, mosque, or ashram may provide you with a level of peace. I speak here not just about organized religion, although this provides comfort for many, but also about individual spirituality wherever a person might find it. Some find spirituality in twelve-step groups, some in nature, some in prayer, some in meditation. I have heard it said that the difference between prayer and meditation is that prayer is talking to God, while meditation is listening for his voice. This may be a time for you to explore your spiritual side. By the same token, many people become angry with God, and this should be explored as well.

The most important point about comforting behaviors is the following: if it makes you feel better, it doesn't matter what other people think! No one has the right to judge these comforting behaviors in the early stages of grief. At times, people do things to make themselves feel closer to their missing loved ones. A mother whose child has died may spend hours in that child's room, touching his things and even smelling the sheets and his articles of clothing. This woman is connecting with her child in the only way she has left. If this same woman constantly engages in this very same behavior a year from now, there may be cause for concern, but in the beginning, it's just fine.

Fran was a funny, endearing woman who attended a Loss of Parent bereavement group at a community center where I interned. I learned a lot about comforting behaviors in that group.

"So, I'm sure everybody in that cemetery thinks I'm nuts—but I don't care!" Fran exclaimed. "I go there with pictures of my mother and father and I put them down by their graves and I talk to them. Is this crazy?" she asked the group. We laughed without judgment.

"No, Fran, because if you're nuts, so am I," Stanley chimed in. "I talk to my dead father all the time. I ask him for advice about work or whatever. This makes me feel better, so why should I care what people think?"

"Well, I can't go to the grave at all. I get no comfort there," another woman offered. "My parents aren't there. It's just their bones. Me, I get comfort when I'm with my aunt, because she is so like my mother."

Listen carefully when the griever talks about what makes him feel better. We have so much to learn from each other.

BEREAVEMENT GROUPS

"But I'm not a joiner!" Katie was adamant about the many reasons why a group would not be a good idea for her. "I do better one-on-one." She had not convinced me, so I countered: "Just give it a try one time," I suggested. "If you still don't want to go, I won't bring it up again." She attended the one that night and ended up returning for all nine subsequent meetings. Months afterward, she admitted that the group had been a rewarding and therapeutic experience. When asked what had changed her mind, she explained:

> I thought it would be depressing and it turned out to be really very uplifting. I no longer felt alone and I actually made a friend from the group that I could relate to better than to some of my other friends who had not had any losses.
>
> Also, it felt good when I could say something that helped another person in the group who wasn't as far along in their grief process. I was worried about breaking down in front of them, but then I realized that this was the *one* place I could totally be myself. It's strange, but these people understood how I felt better than anyone else, and I could say anything I wanted without feeling like they would judge me. Even though we were from different walks of life, I truly love each and every one of the group members. Even grouchy Rita! The whole thing just made me feel more normal.

Katie does a great job summing up the benefits of a grief group after a loss. The leader should bring up pertinent topics and provide some helpful literature, as well as keep things moving along so everyone who wishes to share gets a chance. An experienced leader will alter the agenda to accommodate the group when necessary and will ideally possess a broad base of knowledge on the subject. Someone who has not personally experienced her own loss will have a more difficult time with credibility. Textbooks just don't cut it when you're facing an assembly of individuals who have recently suffered loss.

Joining a group is not in lieu of individual grief therapy for most major losses buts works well in conjunction with, before, or after one-on-one sessions. This does not always apply for "senior" loss of spouse. Many churches and Jewish community centers have excellent group programs for this population and individual therapy may be unnecessary.

COMFORT IN THE WORKPLACE:
HOW TO HELP YOURSELF AFTER A LOSS

If you are headed back to work after a loss, Helen Fitzgerald, training director for the American Hospice Foundation, has excellent advice for you. Before returning to work she suggests that you make sure the "powers that be" know what happened to you and give them as much information as you feel comfortable sharing. If people want information from you that you are not yet comfortable sharing and may never be, just tell them so.

While you are out, you might ask to be kept up to date with what's going on at work via e-mail. Sometimes a person can be flooded with what Fitzgerald calls the "I'm so sorry comments" when first coming back to work. This can bring back the emotions of the loss and make it hard to work at all. A mere "thank you" is sufficient as an answer to these people. Fitzgerald also makes the suggestion that you might want to meet with coworkers for lunch before returning to work and get all the "I'm so sorry's" over with at once, instead of dealing with them piecemeal throughout the workday. She also suggests easing back into the workday, perhaps starting with half days.

You may wish to send out a group e-mail conveying that you'd rather not discuss your loss in the workplace, as it tends to upset you and might interfere with your concentration. Try not to be embarrassed or ashamed of feelings that are natural or for trying to protect yourself from the onslaught of well-wishers that may make things more difficult for you. You might ask your boss to convey this message to coworkers for you, or you can phone some folks before entering the workplace again.

When you do return, caution others that you may get emotional and need to leave a meeting or take some time to yourself for a while. Double-check your work, as your focus may not be up to your usual standards. You might even ask a coworker you trust to look things over for you. Post your deadlines where you'll see them easily. Tell others what you need right now. Remember, they might feel awkward and welcome any instructions you can give them. If you don't want to talk about it, tell them.

HOW TO HELP A COWORKER WHO IS GRIEVING

Don't be afraid to mention the loss and simply say how sorry you are. Take your cue from the griever. If your coworker wishes to talk about it, then be a good ear. If not—don't push it. Many people prefer to keep their private lives out of the workplace for a variety of reasons. Every time he is reminded of his loss, emotions may be triggered, and most people don't want to break down at work. A lot depends on the type of work environment you inhabit.

Communication is the key to helping your coworker or employee after her loved one has died. Keep questions to a minimum—the key is to ask the right questions. "Is there anything I can do?" is not specific enough; almost everyone answers no to this. If you really want to be of assistance to this person, tell the person so and then make a suggestion or two.

A sympathy card sent to your coworker's home is very appropriate, and in some cases attendance at wakes, funeral services, or whatever rituals are involved may also be helpful. Flowers or donations to a charity or organization requested by the family can also be a form or support. This may be done on an individual basis or as a group with other coworkers.

In my interviewing process for this book, I found that thoughtful things like bringing someone a cup of coffee during the day may be more appreciated than anything else. Depending upon the type of work you share together, pitching in to lighten your grieving coworker's load for a while may be a good idea.

Do not treat him as if he has the plague; just interact with him as always, but perhaps a bit more gently. Remember, he feels isolated in his grief. Don't add to this alienation by leaving him out of things because it's less awkward for you. Death is a part of life, and we owe it to one another to be there in whatever small capacity we can be.

WHAT EMPLOYERS, MANAGERS, OR
HUMAN RESOURCES PERSONNEL CAN DO

Determine the bereavement leave policy (more on this to come) for the employee and explain it to her. If it is only the standard three days, you might ask how much time the person thinks she might need for funeral arrangements and personal time. Investigate the policy to determine if the employee can tap into her family sick leave policy to extend the allotted time. Also establish if there is any counseling available for this person through your company's policy. All of this can be done in writing if you sense that the employee does not wish to discuss these things with you. It is the most practical, helpful information you can give to the griever at this time. Also, you might let her know that she can start back to work on half days at first, if this is an option.

Obviously, showing true concern and caring is of the utmost importance at this time. You don't need to launch into a diatribe about your own losses; just a hug or a pat on the back with a heartfelt "I am so sorry for your loss" will do fine. Don't just commence with the details of how things will be handled in your employee's absence, as she probably cannot concentrate on this right now. Just make the transition as simple as possible and keep her informed via e-mail or phone calls after the funeral.

BEREAVEMENT LEAVE

The pipeline for knowledge goes like this: A discovery is made or important information on a particular subject is accumulated until the knowledge base becomes concrete; this knowledge is then shared with a small group of people immediately associated with the subject matter. Findings are published, and other people who are affected by this new knowledge now become aware of it. Word spreads. The media becomes informed, and articles are written. Segments of television shows or the news start to cover the subject, and soon word spreads to the larger population. Inevitably there is a lag time between the accumulation of new information and the use of it. So it has been with bereavement leave.

A bereavement leave policy is a company's practice for employees' time off after a family member has died. This time is to be used for making funeral arrangements, attending wakes and funerals, sharing needed time with other family members, and dealing with loose ends left behind by the deceased, like possessions or wills. After all of the years of accumulated knowledge in the field of bereavement, most companies are still granting only three days off. This is a travesty.

According to the American Hospice Foundation, nearly eight million people will be directly affected by death this year, and half of them will be in the workplace during the grieving period. As our generation of baby boomers ages, the numbers keep growing. Isn't it time to look more seriously at bereavement leave? As my own little experiment, I started asking company owners and managers their opinion about the number of days granted for bereavement leave. I was amazed at their responses. Some had no idea *what* their own company policy was, while others felt that three days was adequate. A few owners thought it wasn't enough but weren't sure what to do. My overall observation was that these folks avoided the subject of death in much the same way our society does. This undeniable eventuality is skirted around until some poor employee faces a personal loss and finds out he has only three days of paid leave to fly halfway across the country and bury his mother! Come on.

I am happy to report that some companies and institutions *are* leading the way in this regard and have at least increased paid bereavement leave from three to five days. Other companies are allowing employees to tap into their family sick leave policy to extend their allotted time. This is a good start. Five days makes more sense but still may not be enough time. The idea of tapping into sick leave and vacation time after the five days are up makes a great deal of sense. The situation should be evaluated on an individual basis.

In recent years the concept of "family" has also broadened in bereavement leave policy. Leave is granted for death of a parent, parent-in-law, brother, sister, spouse, child, grandparent, grandchildren, brother-in-law, sister-in-law, son-in-law, and daughter-in-law. More comprehensive policies add "any other person who is a member of the established household." Domestic partners are also being recognized in some cases, but not in many, yet.

In a wonderful article by Kathryn Tyler, she explains how HR (human resources) departments might further help promote humane and appropriate bereavement leave policy within a company or an institution. She suggests that someone research the corporate and community resources available to grieving employees and place this information in a brochure for them.

It pays—literally—for companies to take grief seriously. Some large corporations have instituted policies to directly assist their grieving employees, because in the long run it benefits the company. In an article titled "Unresolved Grief Can Be Costly," reported in *Employee Benefit News*, Susanna Duff writes, "If not addressed by an employer, grief can rattle a workplace with an unhappy employee and uncomfortable coworkers."

Hallmark designed a program entitled "Compassionate Connections" that includes four free private counseling sessions for grieving employees. Follow-up visits are covered under the company medical plan. Besides being good, humane policy, the program helps with loss of productivity and distracted employees.

The Mobil Corporation started its grief program in 1990 and saw a decrease in medical, mental health, and substance abuse claims. Aside from offering support for grieving employees, this program also debriefs coworkers on how to deal with situations like when an employee's seventeen-year-old-son was shot and killed. American Express offers counseling and has held seminars to help managers learn how to help with employees' grief.

If you have recently suffered a loss and are not sure about your company's bereavement leave policy, you may wish to find out what the employee assistance program offers in terms of grief counseling, including therapists whose fees are covered by that company's particular health insurance plan.

The mental health care extended to our New York City firefighters following September 11 was so impressive that I simply must mention it here. Because it was a national disaster, a federally funded program called Project Liberty was set up to assist those stricken. Many of my patients were able to stay in counseling until their posttrauma issues subsided because Project Liberty filled in when their regular benefits ran out. The paperwork was challenging, but when I called the NYC Fire Department counseling unit with a question, I always got a caring human being on the phone, which is more than I can say for some insurance companies.

Counselors were sent in to talk to groups of firefighters to help with their overall issues and to suggest individual counseling for them. A hand was extended, although naturally not all chose to avail themselves of these services.

Having started my own practice, I understand the other side of things. Companies and institutions can go broke constantly extending helping hands to their employees. But look at it this way: if an individual is given the time and consideration to begin his grief process properly, he will be that much closer to a healthy resolution. I am happy to report that despite the large number of firefighters who sought early retirement after September 11, many who chose counseling returned to the fire department. Counseling allowed them to continue in the work they loved. Unfortunately, there were many men and women whose respiratory systems were compromised and so were forced to give up their careers.

The point is this: what are a couple of days of extra pay and a little guidance toward proper resources, in the larger scheme of keeping your employees mentally healthy? The goodwill a company can foster by lending support to its employee in a time of true need will result in a more productive person with a sense of commitment and loyalty.

There isn't much chance for fraud here. In some cases, employees have to present a death certificate or a program from the funeral of the person who died; however, most employers take the person's word for it. Let's face it, someone can get away with being sick a lot more often than she can pretend a family member has died.

It is important to mention that some people find comfort in their work. The maintenance of their usual schedule helps them to cope in a healthy manner. At the very least, one's work can sometimes serve as a distraction or even a needed temporary relief. If you find work helpful in this regard, this is a good thing. A pediatrician I was seeing mentioned that the only time she could concentrate on anything was at work. "It helps me to get out of my own head for a time," she explained. For her, this was not running away from the pain but rather giving her mind a rest from it. Contrary to some grievers, this doctor found herself alive and connected back in the world.

COMFORT THROUGH THE HOLIDAYS

Harold arrived, looking disheveled in a worn, drab raincoat. He was usually an impeccable dresser, but this evening's garments were wrinkled and chosen without his usual flair for style and color. A dignified Jamaican man in his late sixties, Harold came into therapy after the loss of his beloved wife, Tanya, who had been found stabbed to death in a parking lot on Thanksgiving eve. Tonight, nearly a year later, he looked as he had on that first night of counseling.

> HAROLD: I don't get it. I was doing so well for a while. Now I
> can barely get myself to work. What is the matter with me,
> Judy? *(His soft brown eyes implored.)* Suddenly I am back to
> sleeping on the couch again, and the other night I poured
> a glass of wine for my wife. I haven't done that in many
> moons.
> THERAPIST: So, what were you doing last year at this time?
> *(He stared at me as if to question what* that *had to do with
> anything.)*
> HAROLD: Well, let's see . . . Cecily [his daughter] would have been
> arriving with her husband and the baby. She was going to
> stay with us for a month. Her husband would have to go
> back after a week or so, because of his work. Tanya was so
> excited! *(He smiled slightly.)* I remember she was getting the
> guest room ready and bought lots of little goodies for the

baby. *(His head lowered and he shook it slowly.)* It seems like a lifetime ago. And sometimes it feels like yesterday.

THERAPIST: Did you decide to have Cecily visit this year? I know you were undecided about it.

We had discussed this when Harold was trying to determine how he would spend the Thanksgiving holiday this year.

HAROLD: It's so ridiculous anyway. *(He half-laughed.)* Thanksgiving isn't even *our* holiday!

I waited in silence for Harold to collect his thoughts. A great deal had transpired in a year. First Harold had taken a leave of absence from his job, and his daughter, Cecily, had stayed on to help him after her mom had been killed. A year later, although Harold was still grieving, he had returned to work and gotten his life back into a semblance of order. Cecily had returned to the Dominican Republic, where she lived. Now, Harold was undecided about how to deal with the whole holiday season. He couldn't bear to celebrate in his home without Tanya. He explained how she was the center of every event, how she decorated and cooked so incredibly.

HAROLD: I am just getting used to not having her around. It would just make the house empty all over again if she was missing at the holidays. It is too damned lonely, you know?

THERAPIST: Have you reconsidered spending some time at Cecily's?

HAROLD: It's too late to buy a plane ticket now. It would be highway robbery.

THERAPIST: Don't you get time off at Christmas? How about booking it ahead and spending your Christmas holiday differently this year?

(Harold seemed to warm to the idea.)

HAROLD: I guess I could just go to my friend Robert's for Thanksgiving. I wouldn't mind getting away from this place over Christmas. *(He threw me a sideways glance.)* But what happens if I break down at Robert's? They think I'm doing better.

THERAPIST: Harold, this is not like a cold you get over. You have the double whammy of experiencing the anniversary of your wife's death concurrently with a holiday. I'm sure Robert has seen you cry since Tanya's death.

HAROLD: Oh, yes, that is for sure. But I do not want to ruin Robert's holiday with his family.

THERAPIST: So why not explain to Robert that this is your first Thanksgiving since your wife's death and you may have to leave his home early if it is too uncomfortable for you? Do you think he'd understand that?

HAROLD: Of course he would. Robert and his wife are very good people. I guess I could try.

HOW TO HELP YOURSELF AT HOLIDAY TIME

If you are grieving, there is no better time to put self-caring into practice than during the holidays. This is going to be challenging, because it requires that you think ahead and try to anticipate your feelings at the holidays. Bereavement is not a time when "looking ahead" comes naturally. If you are in counseling or in a bereavement group, I suggest you tackle the topic of holidays long before they occur.

It is my experience that many clients think they will proceed with the holidays as usual after the loss of a loved one, and for some, this is fine. If the festivities of the holidays do not bother you, then feel free to disregard this section. It does not mean there is anything wrong with you—not every griever is bothered by the same triggers. However, for the many who do have difficulty with holidays, I implore you to listen to your heart. How do you do this?

We have already discussed the griever's lack of energy and decreased tolerance for chaos. I don't know about your family, but holiday time in my neck of the woods calls for a storehouse of energy and a lot of noise.

Holiday time for Harold brought back the memories of what was going on in his life prior to his wife's death. You may find that the holidays seem meaningless to you after a death and that you have no wish to decorate or send out "silly" cards. Guess what—you are entitled! If you don't want to do these things, for God's sake, don't! People in grief are redefining their whole worlds. Just because you don't wish to celebrate the same way this year doesn't mean you never will again. Things are different—*you* are different—right now.

One family who lost their dad on September 11 decided to travel to a tropical island over the holidays. This is something they never would have considered prior to Dad's death. Now they wouldn't spend the holidays any other way.

If I could log all of the hours spent discussing holidays with patients, I am sure the number would be staggering. This is not true of just the bereft but of all patients in general. More anxious thoughts are produced by the navigation of family during the holidays than beaches have sand. Whose house should we go to? What should I buy this one? Aunt Mabel isn't talking to Aunt June. Where will we sleep? What if the kids act up? . . . and on and on. The pressure for some is unbearable. Now is your chance to end all of that and create a new tradition. Here are some of the new traditions I have seen people start:

1. Only immediate family in attendance
2. Celebrate at a restaurant
3. Volunteer at a soup kitchen
4. Take a trip
5. Someone else cook this year
6. Friends instead of family

7. No exchange of presents among extended family

8. Lighting a candle in memory of the loved one

There are many grievers who make small changes to the traditions. In my Loss of Parent groups, there is always a great deal of pain around the holidays. This is often because Mom and Dad have been the keepers of the family traditions, and in their absence, things fall apart. This is a good time for a family discussion about how to redefine the holidays so that you might continue to meet as a family. Some families opt to have the celebration rotate from one sibling's home to another so that no one household is doing all the work. Sometimes families have grown and wish to celebrate in their own individual homes. There is no right or wrong here. The John Lennon lyric goes, "Whatever gets you through the night, is all right . . . is all right." How about "Whatever gets you through the holidays, is all right . . . is all right."

HOW TO HELP GRIEVERS AT HOLIDAY TIME

Numero uno: relieve their guilt. If your friend or family member is grieving the loss of a loved one and wants to celebrate a holiday differently because of it, tell that person it's OK. It's hard enough for people to share this need for change. Don't squash it. One can always return to former traditions later, if desired.

Hanukah and Christmas carry with them the burden of gifts for which the griever may not be willing or able to shop. A good friend or caring family member might volunteer to help with this task. Concentration may be faltering at this time, so a shopping buddy might be useful. If family is gathering and will be missing the person who died, the others might spend some time telling stories about their missing family member. Tears and laughter are medicine for the soul.

A young woman who lost her mother related the story of her family holiday gathering after her mom died. "We created a book of our mother's outlandish sayings. She had a 'saying' for everything, and none of us could remember them all, but together we were able to compile over fifty of Mom's unique phrases. I made a book out of them, and at the next family gathering I gave a copy to each family member as a gift. Before long we were doubled over in laughter reading them out loud together." How creative and memorable.

Help the griever to realize that all people mourn differently. It will take away some of the sting caused when those around her behave oddly. If we can love one another through a mutual loss at holiday time, the relationships may sustain the loss. If the "judgers" take over, we are doomed.

As an aside, Harold was not able to go to his friend's house for Thanksgiving dinner and instead ended up eating a Hungry-Man turkey TV dinner alone before crying himself to sleep. However, by Christmas, he was able to travel to the Dominican Republic and spend his vacation with his daughter and her family. In his words, "My granddaughter is the spitting image of her grandmama. When she puts her little arms around my neck, I feel like everything is going to be all right. I will go back next year."

BLUE CHRISTMAS SERVICES

A very unusual type of worship service has begun appearing on church schedules around holiday time; some call it the "Blue Christmas" or "Longest Night" service. In an effort to help comfort the bereft during the holiday season, some churches are holding quiet, somber services. Holiday cheer can get pretty obnoxious to those who are silently suffering. It becomes difficult to listen to those glorious Christmas carols when the heart is heavy.

The Blue Christmas service offers an alternative for the griever. Some churches decorate for the occasion with dried flowers and bare branches, while a more hymn-like music fills the air. The words presented by a minister, chaplain, or priest are meant to comfort and reassure those listening, allowing them their sorrow even in the midst of the holiday madness around them. One might hear others crying or comforting one another.

A healthy display of respect for the grieving process has developed this unique way for people to bring their pain to God. Removed and isolated, one may feel even more alone surrounded by joyous, singing families in a regular Christmas celebration. At the Blue Christmas service, the griever is not alone; now he stands amid those who know his sorrow, and there is a true reverence in that.

6

———

How Did Your
Loved One Die?

~~~~~~~~~~~~~~~~~~~~~~~~~~~~~~~~~~~~~~

Most people have very spotty memories of the first days after the death of a loved one, like a distorted collage of unreal scenes often within a shifting time frame. In the wake of death, most of us suffer from some posttraumatic stress characteristics.

"My father's face constantly flashes before me—the way he looked just before he died," Jenna said tearfully. "His face was distorted from the drugs and his lips looked blue. It was horrible! Now I'm afraid I'll never see him any other way."

"You will," I assured her, "and after a while that picture will fade and take its place among all the other memories you have of your father—good and bad. Right now you have been traumatized by the events leading up to your father's death and the loss itself. Give your mind time to do its work and put this whole ordeal into perspective."

People, by nature, seem to want to compare their grief, as if some fabulous trophy awaits the person in the most pain. Believe me, this is one trophy you do not want.

ANTICIPATORY GRIEF

The National Cancer Institute defines *anticipatory grief* as "a grief reaction that occurs in anticipation of an impending loss." In other words, this is the type of grief people experience when they watch someone they love leave this Earth "bit by bit" (as one family member described it).

A colleague and dear friend of mine, Helen Gibney Dubinsky, is a psychiatric nurse and professor of nursing at Molloy College in New York. Helen was part of the hospice movement when it finally made its way to the United States in the late seventies. Part of her life's work has been helping families with their grief.

"In anticipatory grief," Helen explains, "the timetable changes, but the grief process must still run its course." It seems that family members who go through the course of an illness with their loved ones begin part of the grieving process before the actual death. Helen notes that often the dying person accepts the reality of her death before her family is able to do so.

Helen and many experts have discovered that family members, often in an effort to protect their loved ones or because of their own denial issues, refuse to acknowledge the fact that the person is dying. If you face imminent death with a close friend or family member, take your cue from her. If she wishes to talk about her death, it takes great emotional fortitude to listen. In the long run it may help you both. You might wonder how the choice of speaking openly about the reality of the situation could benefit anyone. Many guilt-ridden caretakers have sat in my office bemoaning the fact that they were too afraid to broach the subject of death with their loved ones and that *Now it is too late.*

One woman tortured herself with guilt. "I should have talked to my father about his dying. He seemed to want to talk about it and tie up some loose ends, but I refused to acknowledge the fact that he might die because I didn't want him to think about it. Of course he was already thinking about it!" This wonderfully caring individual kept herself up at night with regrets about what she should have said to her father.

In some cases there is a chance that the dying person may pull through and family members are trying to stay positive. This is commendable, but if the person in that bed wants to talk about his wishes after death—we should listen. Reading this does not give you license to start beating yourself up if you chose not to discuss death with your dying loved one. Many times it is the person in the bed who wishes to protect his closest friends and family members by choosing not to discuss death at all. You may be surprised to find out after the fact that he talked extensively about death to a hospice worker or distant acquaintance.

Helen recommends allowing the dying person to write letters to his loved ones in the eventuation of his death. Sometimes dying people would like to leave a letter to be opened at a certain time. Perhaps it is a mother who will not live to see her daughter marry, yet she would like to leave some words of wisdom for her daughter to read before her marriage. Whatever the dying person might require—it will make the grieving family member feel better in the long run to carry out his loved one's wishes. Perhaps the person who is dying has some practical items to which she must attend. You might offer to do those things for her. Sometimes, all the person wants to do is talk about his experience of dying, and this might be the hardest thing of all for you or me to hear. Believe me, later you will be thankful to have had those words together. Try to think of death as a natural part of life. It happens to each of us, but it is not contagious. We traveled into this world and we will travel out of it. Let's help each other on this journey.

My patient Judy spoke to me of the death of her younger sister, Nancy, from breast cancer. "It's a learn-as-you-go process," she said aptly. It was six years between Nancy's diagnosis at thirty-four to her eventual death at forty. Nancy left behind two lovely daughters, ages five and eight, and her husband. "I was so focused on what needed to be done at each juncture that I lost sight of the most important thing—staying in the moment with my sister. Looking back, I wish I had talked with Nancy about her death, but I was always in the mind-set of 'She's going to get better!' So, I wouldn't dare say anything otherwise."

When I asked Judy what stopped her from talking about death with her sister, she responded, "It made it all too real."

This is such an honest response, and I thank Judy—and all who help us to learn about this difficult subject—for their candor. Talking about death makes it too real. *Too real* for the griever and *too real* for the person facing death. "My sister's dying of breast cancer was also frightening because it meant that I was at risk and so were the other six female children in our family."

Some years later, Judy's mother was diagnosed with malignant skin cancer that was too far gone for treatment. An amazingly courageous woman, Judy was determined to use the lessons her sister's death had taught her. This time around, she was in reality.

"I now knew how this kind of thing progresses," Judy said. "I could see my mother's declining interest in food and other indicators that she was on the same road as Nancy. This time I paid better attention to my mother. I talked to her about our relationship, her friends, my father. I had never had good communication with my mother, so I purposely took a step toward opening up with her. And she responded! I was left knowing that my mother felt she had lived a good life and had a very good husband in my father. My mother told me that she knew she was at the end of her life but that she believed she would be reunited with my sister Nancy."

Judy leaves us with these words about anticipatory grief: "Don't think about what's next—you must concentrate on *now*, because that person will be gone. That is the lesson my sister Nancy taught me."

If you harbor any guilt over words unsaid, understand that it is natural for us to want to protect the dying in any way we can. We don't get a chance to practice "doing death" before it is foisted upon us. Forgive yourself for those things you will handle differently next time. Know that there are wonderful groups available for those whose loved ones die of cancer and other diseases.

HOSPICE

Even though most people would prefer to die at home, this is not often the case. Sadly, people in our country mostly die in institutions. Things are changing, though, however slowly. More of us have become familiar with hospice, which is the interdisciplinary care for people in the terminal stage of an illness. Unlike the sterile hospital setting, individuals may be at home or in a setting devised for their comfort. They may be surrounded by the emotional support of their loved ones.

After watching her father die in excruciating anguish of bone cancer, my best friend, Jeannie, wrote a paper questioning the practice of our medical institutions to deny the use of heroin by suffering patients. In another article, I read a quote by the medical director of St. Luke's Hospice in Sheffield, England, who said:

> It's mediocre, pathetic medicine, this worshipping technology but not paying attention to the true needs of dying patients. I have often been disgusted seeing people who are going to be dead within a few hours, hooked up to all this blasphemous plumbing when all they really need is a friendly word, a nice cup of coffee, and some heroin.

Unfortunately, one of the by-products of our denial of death as a culture is the inability to properly accommodate the dying. In hospitals, people who die are seen as the failures when curing or saving that patient is seen as the solitary goal. Hospitals are constructed for the living, not the dying. Ideally, hospice helps to bridge this gap by being helpful to the dying. Fortunately, I have heard many more good stories about hospice care than I have horror stories. We must as a society continue this necessary forward movement to support the dying and their families. To do this, we have to accept that dying is something we will all face.

A leading figure in the development of Hospice Inc., the Reverend Edward Dobihal Jr., states, "They enable us to surmount the denial of death we have been taught. . . . The extent to which we can humanize the process of dying—by consecrating death as a part of life—is a measure of our ability to humanize the process of living."

My friend and colleague Alan Poe has served as the chaplain for the Hospice of Charleston. He has learned much about how families deal with death and had this to say about anticipatory grief:

> Often people are surprised to learn that the process of grief has started before the actual death of their friend or family member. In reality, grief may begin as early as the diagnosis itself. Depression, inability to focus, difficulty sleeping, a loss of appetite, as well as other signs of grief may be experienced as the coming death of this important person becomes a reality.
>
> Everyone is different and not all will feel the same type of grief before the death that they will feel after the death. Some will use whatever means possible not to allow themselves to feel the loss before it actually occurs; this may be a necessary way for them to deal with what is to happen.
>
> However, sometimes the grief appears more intense as the family watches the illness progress each day. Interestingly enough, some, in the midst of their anticipatory grief, will come to a place of acceptance for which they often feel guilty. They reluctantly admit that they will feel a sense of relief when the family member or friend is gone. It leaves them with the belief that they have become selfish or unkind or cold. A gentle reminder may be helpful at that time. Rather than unkind, this is the greatest gift of all—a love willing to say "good-bye" and let the suffering person go.

Anticipatory grief should not be minimized because death is the expected outcome. You, who have lived with long-term illness or the slow demise of a loved one, have been burdened in a way none of the rest of us can imagine. Be kind to yourself and forgive yourself for not being perfect—there are no perfect people. Nothing tries the patience or drains a person like living with illness day in and day out. You've had a long path of sorrow and deserve some joy. If that seems like a tall order right now, how about some peace? You certainly merit that.

SUDDEN, UNEXPECTED DEATH

What could be more shocking than the sudden loss of a loved one? Nothing!

Extensive research by Therese Rando and others shows that after sudden death, true grieving cannot take place until the shock and trauma of the loss have been assimilated into the mind and body. If this healing does not take place, the individual is at risk for complicated grief.

If you have experienced sudden loss, your world has been violently shattered. You may feel intense anxiety, like things are spinning out of control. The safety and predictability of your world exist no longer. While the person experiencing anticipatory grief has an overriding sorrow, sudden death carries with it overwhelming anxiety. The mind has trouble absorbing the truth of how your world has changed, all at once. This causes the shock of the death to remain for an extended period of time. All death is traumatic, but because of *who* you are or *how* your loved one died, the trauma manifests in different ways.

TAKE TIME FOR TEARS

As I have reiterated throughout this book, healing takes time. Traumatic, sudden loss often takes more time. If we do not counteract the trend toward the "quick fix," we may bypass the grieving process altogether, with dismaying consequences. In 1988, Scottish scientist James W. Black was awarded the Nobel Prize in Medicine for successfully developing a drug called propranolol, which was used to treat hypertension, anxiety, and panic. It was the first successful beta-blocker and a true breakthrough. Currently, propranolol is being investigated as a potential treatment for posttraumatic stress disorder. Studies have shown that individuals given propranolol immediately after a traumatic experience show less severe symptoms of PTSD compared to their respective control groups that did not receive the drug. But propranolol has been referred to as a "memory dampener," as it may work to inhibit the actions of a neurotransmitter that enhances memory consolidation. In other words, there may be a drug that can alter our memories. This poses many ethical and legal questions.

Imagine a pill for the traumatized person that actually prevents shocking events from being burned too deeply into the brain. On the surface it sounds so wonderful; rape victims and those traumatized by horrific loss deserve to forget the suffering they've endured—don't they? We are so quick to grasp at anything that reduces pain that we overlook the consequences of many cures. One rape center exploring the possibility of helping victims with this pill made the point that if a woman is robbed of the impact of her memory, what is to sustain her through the conviction of her attacker? And what of all those brave souls who have contributed to positive changes in the world based on traumatic events that have motivated them toward creating societal change?

Recently, we learned that the brain may not be the only part of the body in which memory is stored. Should we artificially erase from the brain what our bodies might still remember? How often in session with a patient has a repressed memory been uncovered and together we have discovered how this was negatively impacting on the person's life. In discussion with massage therapists, I have learned that people sometimes hold pain and destructive energy in parts of their bodies. Ailments of the colon or migraine headaches can be the physical manifestations of unexpressed grief. In bereavement therapy we can cautiously bring these memories to the surface, expressing and working through them. Without the memory itself, this would no longer be possible. The questions are numerous and should be studied carefully before the newest magic pill is dispensed to a critically vulnerable population.

One by-product of sudden death is the inability of the griever to finish unfinished business with the deceased. "We had a fight before she went out that night," a grieving sixteen-year-old tearfully explained. "She took my sweater without asking me and I made her change before she left. I didn't give a crap about that sweater! Now I can never even tell her!" She lowered her head into her hands. "Maybe if I hadn't made her change the sweater, she wouldn't have been so pissed. Maybe she would have driven more carefully."

Sudden death causes people to constantly reconstruct the scenario of their loved one's death. They punish themselves with "what if's?" If it was an accident, they wonder if they could have prevented it, replaying over and over again those last days, hours, minutes, and even seconds, looking for clues or answers to explain the inexplicable. The need to blame someone or something for the death may also be a way of making sense out of the senseless. Blame can also serve to alleviate guilt.

People ask questions like "If the medical profession missed something important, how could I have been expected to notice anything?" Perhaps a parent died during a period when one sibling missed his turn to check in on Mom. The other sibling can alleviate guilt by telling herself that it wasn't her turn anyway and therefore not her fault. See how that works?

If only we could accept that death happens. We are vulnerable, imperfect beings who fall prey to many life-ending circumstances. What is the alternative to living our lives—giving up and living like Howard Hughes? Would any of us want that for our loved ones? When one of us leaves this earthly plane unexpectedly, how much better would it be if we could forgive one another our human frailties and help each other through our losses? I have watched so many people waste precious time playing the blame game.

Acceptance is not easy, and in some circumstances it may not be possible to forgive or forget. Certainly when an obvious breach has taken place, it should be acknowledged and may even help a person move on in grief. A loved one's senseless murder may catapult those left behind to fight for justice, understandably. True medical malpractice can be arduous to prove but is sometimes worth the time, money, and energy, if only to keep the practitioner from causing another death.

Far more often, however, death results from causes beyond a physician or hospital's power. These institutions and people, although charged with healing, are no more perfect than those who have died.

Sometimes excessive blame can strangle the process of grief. Individuals and families can fixate on "getting even," with the belief that this will set them free. It doesn't always work that way.

When my sister Cathy's husband died within two weeks of a cancer diagnosis, there were so many secondary losses for her and her two daughters. Although he left his financial affairs in order, Cathy practically needed a financial degree to understand all that would be required by her to manage things; add to this the fact that her world had been torn apart, and the task before her was daunting at best. She had lost her life partner with no warning. Her beautiful daughters, just eleven and seven, had lost their dad and life the way they'd known it.

In her article titled "On Treating Those Bereaved by Sudden, Unanticipated Death," Therese Rando enumerates the issues associated with the loss of a loved one from sudden, unanticipated death:

1. There is not chance to say good-bye and finish unfinished business with the deceased.

2. The death tends to leave the mourner with relatively more intense emotional reactions.

3. Disbelief about the loss interferes with the mourner's ability to come to grips with the reality of the death and its implications.

4. The mourner obsessively reconstructs events in retrospect.

5. The loss tends to cut across experiences in the relationship and to highlight what was happening at the time of death.

6. A sudden, unanticipated death is often followed by secondary losses.

7. There is an intense search for meaning and often the need to determine responsibility, affix blame, and mete out punishment for the loss.

8. A sudden, unanticipated death is frequently associated with other difficulties.

HOW TO HELP YOURSELF AFTER SUDDEN DEATH

If you made it out of bed today, consider it a good day! Every hour you make it through is a victory right now. I can only liken the first days after sudden, unexpected loss to sleepwalking through hell. You may find yourself making funeral arrangements. If others can help you with these things, let them. Don't feel obligated to get everything right. What could possibly be *right* when your loved one is being buried?

Understand that you may not know that you're in shock. Please be careful about driving. The memory is compromised at this time. You may be harboring a terrifying image of the person who died in her last moments or days. If it helps, look at photos or video of that person as you remember him before his life ended. If this is too difficult for you, then wait awhile.

Think about all your memories of that person like a deck of cards— because of the trauma of sudden loss, the most recent and horrifying memories are continually at the top of the deck. Your brain still holds all the wonderful, happy memories, and as time goes by, the deck will reshuffle and the newer traumatic memories will take their place in the deck and no longer be the first cards you see. In fact, eventually they will be only a couple of the cards when compared to the rest of the deck. I know this may be hard for you to believe, but it has been reported to me by many people and I have experienced this "reshuffling" myself. Like everything else about grief, this takes time.

If you are reading this book, you are probably looking for help or helping someone else. Having been through sudden, unexpected death myself, I can tell you that you need all the help you can get! Start by finding a professional—a bereavement counselor, therapist, or spiritual counselor—and seek out friends, family members, and/or a bereavement group. "No," you say, "it hurts too much to talk about it yet." OK, then wait a couple of weeks, but promise to seek an outlet for the immeasurable pain you now face. Because of the shocking nature of your loss, you will need to talk about it and find a way to cope. Maybe you don't care about anything or anyone else right now—down the road, you might.

You may need to ask for extra time off from work if you need it. Some people find solace in the routine of work, but don't be a martyr. If you need to lie in bed with the covers over your head for a while, you are entitled to it. Maybe you need a friend to stay with you, or you just can't think about cleaning or cooking. Ask for what you need.

For those who are family members, friends, coworkers, or counselors to a person whose loved one died suddenly, acknowledge that the stage of shock may be prolonged. The person may seem dazed and confused for a longer period than may seem "normal." Expect the person reacting to sudden loss to display signs of heightened anxiety. Think of it this way: Have you ever been badly hurt, suddenly? Recall any kind of accident you've experienced, maybe a car accident, breaking a body part, or getting slammed in the face while engaged in sports. Perhaps you just missed that last step on the stairs and began to fall. Try to recall the shock that accompanied such an incident—now multiply that a couple of hundred times. Keep in mind what it was like the next time you got behind the wheel of the car or skied down a slope after the accident. Most people talk about feeling a heightened sense of anxiety. This is an encapsulated version of posttraumatic stress disorder. Do not push individuals who have been traumatized by loss to get back up on the horse too soon; you will only increase their anxiety.

After a particularly stressful siege in his life, my husband broke down the philosophy of "one day at a time" to "one task at a time." I have adopted this for my work with traumatized patients. When "one day at a time" is too much to concentrate on, break the day down to those things that must be accomplished, like eating, bathing, or phone calls . . . whatever. Make a list for the tasks you need to accomplish for that day, and in the beginning, keep it as short as possible. What doesn't get done that day is simply carried over to the next.

Have you ever listened to a child who is trying to wrap her brain around something? She repeats the same words over and over again. That is what the traumatized griever must do to accept the reality of the situation. The circumstances leading up to the sudden, unexpected death of your loved one become a well-trodden pathway.

Because it is so difficult to believe that someone you loved and knew so well is actually gone, it helps to see the body of the deceased. Naturally, this is not always possible in unexpected death. Lack of a body is what made the grief work for many patients so complex after September 11. If the griever was not witness to the death and an autopsy exists, it can help to go over the autopsy. Seeing a death certificate or speaking to someone who saw the person before he perished is also helpful.

Literature and education about traumatic loss may be a bit overwhelming at first, but it can help you realize that you're not going crazy. I recommend attendance in a group for sudden loss. Contact your local hospital for listings of such groups.

Expect overwhelming guilt and anger; it often accompanies sudden death. As mentioned previously, guilt can be a powerful, even toxic emotion. Be aware of sabotaging your relationships with people, substance abuse, or partaking in high-risk, possibly self-destructive behaviors. On some level, you may find yourself wanting to escape this world where nothing makes sense anymore. Hold out. As one who has made it out of that dark forest, I know life can be worth living again.

Do you suffer from Posttraumatic Stress Disorder?

On September 12, 2001, I walked outside my home on Long Island and smelled the smoke from the tragedy that occurred thirty-seven miles away. My hometown mourned twenty-three souls after the World Trade Center fell in New York City.

Besieged with phone calls from families and schools, I felt as though I never lifted my head again for a solid year. These good people were dealing with the devastating aftermath. Even my colleagues were calling.

All therapists deal with loss; that's a given. Loss is a part of everyday life, whether it be through divorce, the loss of a job, or just growing older. However, my *specialty* was bereavement, and I could not field the number of cases that were being referred to my practice. So I began counseling some of my therapist friends on how to help patients through the sudden traumatic loss of a family member and dealing with PTSD (posttraumatic stress disorder). What I learned was enlightening to me personally. My father, truly a wise man, once told me that what comes naturally to each of us we often take for granted. For example, a child may be a natural athlete and think that others can do what he does just as easily. It takes time to recognize one's gifts. It took me over twenty years to realize that working with grievers is a gift of mine. Patients would thank me for changing their lives and I would smile indulgently, thinking anyone could have done what I did. What a shock to discover that many very qualified therapists run from bereavement cases.

"I can't help this woman," a colleague told me. "She's just so sad. How do you stand it?" Another well-known psychologist in my area wanted to immediately put all of his September 11 patients on antidepressants. I tried to explain that their sadness was necessary, not pathological, and not *all* mourners should be medicated.

One nice surprise came when a friend and colleague decided to take on a couple of bereavement cases in the wake of September 11. At first she wrung her hands, asking, "How do you have the patience for this work? I don't know what to say, and I don't see any improvement from week to week."

"Hang in there," I told her. "You will."

She did hang in there and worked admirably to assist several widows. In fact, part of the impetus for writing this book was to help create an outline for "how to" work with bereavement patients. Most forms of therapy have a format and structure that seems to be lacking in "grief work." This is understandable, as in the past, so much of this work had been seen as intuitive. While I agree that the counselor must take his cues from the griever and be an excellent listener, just listening alone will not help the suffering individual to move forward.

Good bereavement counselors must be emotionally courageous. To sit in the face of great sorrow takes a special kind of strength. Every good health care professional I know who deals with death and dying has emotional fortitude. Does it hurt to hear the story of the death from a grieving child? You bet it does, but if not me or you, then who?

In my office hangs a poster that reads:

NEW YORK CITY FIRE DEPARTMENT
Members who made the supreme sacrifice
In the performance of duty
At the World Trade Center on September 11, 2001

Under these words are the faces of 344 men and women who perished trying to rescue their fellow human beings on that day. Battalion chief John Newell, whom I counseled for posttraumatic stress disorder, came to his session one day and handed me a palm-sized piece of glass that he had extracted from the rubble only days after the disaster, when larger pieces of glass could still be found. A lot of the firefighters and police took home pieces like this one, as symbols to help them remember what of course they could never forget.

"I didn't know if you'd want this," John spoke uncertainly as his outstretched palm held the small block of glass. The glass felt cool and surprisingly weighty in my warm hand. I studied the three-quarter-inch-thick, two-inch-by-three-inch pale green shard, its jagged edges still holding gray ash in some of its grooves. Tears fell unconsciously from my eyes as gratefully I felt the physical connection to the place where I had been spending so many hours a week with my patients and yet had never seen. It felt like a relic, a piece of history.

I choked out a "Thank you, John." Looking into his troubled blue eyes, I asked, "I thought everything was pulverized down there. How is it that you have this piece of glass?"

"Two theories," John answered in his uncomplicated, truthful manner. "Either this is a piece from the first windows that blew out after the towers were hit, or it's from one of the windows people broke when they jumped."

"Oh." I grasped the glass a little tighter, before placing it down on the coffee table between us. We began where we had left off the week before. Others have held the glass in their hands since John gave it to me, and their reactions fascinate me. Always their faces become somber, as they turn it over and examine the simple jagged shard. More than one person has commented that there are souls attached to this glass.

John Newell's story, like so many of the survivors of that gruesome day, includes the sights and sounds that were branded onto his brain. At the time, John was the captain of 58 Engine in New York City. He had switched shifts with his best friend and partner.

"Taking each other's shifts is a common practice in the department," John explained. "We'd switch all the time." He paused to shut his eyes. "So, why can't I help thinking that it should have been me and not Bobby that day?"

John had been asleep in his bed when he received a call from one of his men: "Cap, turn on the TV." Like many of us, John turned on his television in time to see the second plane crashing into the second tower. Do you remember the horror of watching that first tower fall? Now imagine yourself driving on the Throgs Neck Bridge, toward Manhattan, witnessing great cascading plumes of smoke pour forth from the buildings, as John did on that morning.

"Hundreds of thousands of people were walking away from the city as my buddies and I flagged down an MTA bus and headed in together. It was surreal, like a scene from *King Kong* or some disaster movie."

John looked through me as he spoke. "As we got closer, I was mentally preparing myself for the wreckage I would surely see. I figured there would be bodies everywhere. People in pain, suffering. Blood and guts."

He tilted his head. "Ironically, there weren't any. Everything was completely destroyed. Pulverized." He described the people leaving the area, "They looked like zombies covered by ash, with slits for eyes."

One guy stopped him. "Cap, I think everyone from 58 got killed!" This meant all of his men and women. He had to find out. More of the "surreal movie set" included EMS vehicles on fire, cars squashed.

"Someone told me that 58 Engine was in the Millennium Hotel at the base of the towers. They set up a command post there after the first tower was hit. I ran." Sitting in my office, he stared at the imaginary scene before him. "As I got to the hotel, someone stopped me and said that Bobby had gone in ahead, to check things out before bringing in the guys." At this point, John was informed that his partner Bobby had been trapped inside the hotel, which had been cut in half when the first tower fell.

"At that point, Bobby was still alive," he stated in disbelief. "They heard him! When the first building fell, it cut a 'V' through the hotel from the twenty-first floor down to one of the lower floors. They were trying to dig him out! When the second tower collapsed, it flattened the hotel's seven floor levels into the ground." He closed his eyes and lowered his head. "They never found a trace of him."

There were no tears when John Newell first related this story to me. He was way past tears. His face held the haunted pallor of a corpse itself, as if part of him had been buried in the pile with Bobby and the other thirty-some-odd friends he lost that day. His eyes were sunken and sleepless. He looked ancient in those first days.

There are many theories about how to treat posttraumatic stress disorder. One neurologist, Dr. Robert Scaer, who has been studying this subject for many years, believes that trauma is physical as well as psychological and therefore requires therapy that attends to both. We are learning more each year about the connection of the mind and body. This added knowledge base can only serve to improve our ability to help our patients.

So what is posttraumatic stress disorder? PTSD occurs when a person is exposed to a traumatic event that threatens injury or death to himself or others and he feels fear, helplessness, and horror. As if that isn't bad enough, that person then reexperiences the traumatic event over and over again. Dr. Scaer explains that "the physiology of trauma has its roots in the fight/flight/freeze response." If a prey animal is unable to fight or flee from a predator, it will enter a state of immobility called the freeze response. If the animal survives, it will undergo a "discharge" involving the activation of seizure-like motor responses. He contends that if this discharge does not occur, the animal will tend to retain all the elements of the threatening experience in its unconscious memory.

In far simpler terms, the person who has undergone the trauma cannot move through it or away from it, so she remains frozen. So how do we move through it? Some seek pharmaceutical solutions, others use a technique called eye movement desensitization and reprocessing (EMDR) and somatic experiencing (SE). I work with patients using cognitive-behavioral (talking therapy) methods, therapeutic bodywork, and physical or movement therapy. Other more theory-based therapies may be proven quicker and more effective down the road, but I can only relate here what has worked for my patients—and thankfully worked well.

Let's get back to Captain John Newell's story. In the months following September 11, John's life consisted of the following: "I went through the motions like a mechanical man. We did twenty-four-hour shifts digging down at the 'pile.' After two weeks the memorial services started," he recalled. "When I wasn't at the pile I was attending funerals. It was a sign of respect for our dead brothers and their families. After a while, I couldn't go inside the churches anymore. I just couldn't bear to see the devastated faces of the wives and children. After each service we'd have some beers."

John started drinking more to increase the numbness. He talked about frightened, broken men and women coming to him for counsel when he could barely keep his own head above water. But John did something emotionally heroic and sought help for himself through counseling so that he could truly help those around him.

One of the features of PTSD is "persistent avoidance of stimuli associated with the trauma." In other words, typically, traumatized people avoid that which recalls their trauma. For example, if you've had a tragic car accident, you might avoid driving on the road where the accident occurred. Now imagine these firefighters, forced to return daily to the sight of their trauma and to dig up the remains of their comrades. John became increasingly detached from himself and those around him. It no longer fazed him to dig up body parts. "I remember digging up a shoe with a foot still in it and I felt nothing. I knew then that something was really wrong with me."

Those who suffer from PTSD have recurrent images and recollections of the event. Sometimes John would flash back to the five-story piece of the tower that was left sticking out of the ground. He would visualize the flattened hotel where Bobby lay. He talked about how strange it was to see a couple of square blocks of burning buildings that lay in the wake of September 11 and no one even paid attention to them.

"One forty-story building burned all day long and then collapsed," he recounted. "No one cared. At another time *that* would have made the front page, but after 9/11, it didn't even matter." He spoke about how eerie it was to recall the many triage centers that had been set up by the hospitals. "They were empty because everyone was already dead."

My work with John started with these recollections. In telling his story, he began to remember. Little details that had faded began to emerge, bringing the unconscious into the conscious. Left alone, these memories would have been buried in that pile, only to reemerge in dreams or to distort his reality. John had to feel safe enough to walk through these memories again, and it was my job to create a safe space where he could do just that. He had to build confidence that I was a trustworthy guide for such a journey. As he struggled through the memories, John began to feel the power of being in charge of his own haunting. You must be gentle and patient with yourself after trauma; like all grief, it is a process.

The mind is only beginning to wake up; now it is time to invite the body to join the party (some party!). With John Newell this was not a difficult task. Up until September 11, John had been a jogger, keeping himself in great shape. Losing touch with himself, he also lost touch with his body. In fact, it had been the first time in his adult life when he had not exercised. He began jogging again and thankfully not in a stuffy gym but in a local park with beautiful woods and waterfront trails. It is important for people suffering from PTSD to get in touch with their physical selves. Massage therapy can be helpful, or swimming, or whatever comes to mind for that person.

One fascinating characteristic of John's journey to healing I had never before witnessed. As mentioned previously, over thirty of John's friends and acquaintances perished on September 11. Quite often these kinds of multiple losses do not allow the griever enough time to resolve his grief before mourning his next loss. This can lead to complicated grief and severe depression. But the human mind is endlessly resourceful, and left to its own devices can sometimes find its own form of resolution. During the eighth month of treatment, John reported an interesting phenomenon.

"It's the weirdest thing," he told me. "I'll be driving along or grocery shopping, or whatever, and suddenly I can see one of the guy's faces before me. And then for a few days, I just keep thinking about *that* guy. I remember things, you know? It might be something we did together or a conversation we once had."

Looking up at me he seemed to want an explanation. Then he went on, "I keep thinking about the same guy, and then a couple of days later a new guy's face will pop into my head and the whole thing starts over again. Sometimes I even dream about these guys."

"Is it upsetting?" I asked.

John answered thoughtfully. "You know, it's OK. I feel like I'm giving each guy his due. You know what I mean?" He smiled wryly. "Have you ever heard of anything like this before?"

"Not exactly, but then I've never dealt with people who lost so many friends and colleagues at one time so suddenly before. Perhaps your mind is just working out a way to mourn so many losses."

John nodded his head in agreement. "Yeah, you know I think I am, Judy. Some kind of brain I have, huh?" We both laughed.

Somehow traveling through this unusual progressive mourning seemed to help John. I don't claim to understand it, only to have observed it.

John had all the classic symptoms of PTSD. He became irritable, sometimes with angry outbursts that were uncharacteristic of him. He had difficulty concentrating on things that had previously come easily to him. He lost interest in people and activities he once enjoyed. And he had nightmares.

Through it all, month after month, he never shed a tear in my office. So shut down was this seemingly caring individual that he was only very occasionally able to release his feelings through tears—and in private. In my experience, this is common in PTSD, although I would not make a blanket statement for everyone. In fact, some individuals cannot stop crying, but that has been rarer in my practice.

THE BREAKTHROUGH

In grief there are small victories and occasional breakthroughs. In John Newell's case his breakthrough came through a dream.

"I was in a stadium filled with firefighters who had perished in the towers. I was wielding some kind of a hatchet or sword, and suddenly I began cutting off the heads of the people. It was gruesome with blood everywhere, but I couldn't stop myself! As I was doing this I was crying hysterically. Then I realized that *you* were there, standing next to me with your arm around my shoulder, and together we were watching the 'other me' cutting off the firemen's heads." He looked at me through teary eyes. "I was sobbing so loudly that I woke myself up."

That day John cried in my office. His unconscious mind had worked out what he could not face in reality. I think the dream scared John, and he wanted desperately to understand it. So we set about interpreting the messages he was sending himself. In some way, John felt responsible for the deaths of his friends, particularly that of his partner, Bobby. This was a dream about survivor's guilt, but it was also a hopeful dream in which he viewed himself in two very different ways. Horrified, he watched as his "other self" killed his fellow firefighters, but he was not alone. He was walking through this with a guide—me. Therapy had become a comfort for him, allowing him to distinguish between destructive thinking and reality. John was ready to move forward, to face the secrets he was keeping from himself.

After this session, the waterworks began and John began to cry more often, in and out of therapy. It was a painful time, but his courage was not just confined to the physical realm of his life; he had great emotional courage as well.

In the months to follow, John returned to the land of the living. His complexion went from sallow to ruddy. His lovely blue eyes began to twinkle and the bags beneath them to diminish. Humor began to sprinkle his conversation. I watched the miracle I have been privileged to witness again and again, as a person transforms from death to life. I am convinced that it is a choice made by each individual who faces devastating loss and then fights his way out of the grave and back into the light of day. It is the decision to live again.

During this time, John Newell was promoted from captain to battalion chief. He began returning to his former activities, such as skiing and fishing. He taught local classes to firefighters and worked with an advanced group, training fire departments throughout the country. Often on these trips, other firefighters would ask him about his experiences during September 11, and he began to share appropriately.

John was now able to counsel those who came to him seeking relief from their own nightmares or to guide them to proper help. Before long he even began to write articles for *Fire Prevention* magazine. His life became richer and fuller than it had even been before that disastrous day. Through his worst days, John said he found solace in being around his three lovely daughters and in nature.

EMDR TREATMENT FOR PTSD

Ron Clifford was in the World Trade Center when disaster struck. A wonderfully witty native Irishman, in his past Ron had worked for the City of New York as an architect for the Housing Department. On September 11, Ron was about to enter the elevator when the first plane crashed into the towers. From the elevator emerged a woman who was burned from head to toe. A ball of flame had traveled down the elevator shaft and engulfed her.

"So badly burned, she was," Ron explained in his soft brogue, "that her zipper was fused into her skin. She couldn't even open her eyes."

Ron cried out for help, as panic-stricken people swarmed around him. No one stopped. He found some water and doused her with it and sat her down with him. "Sacred heart of Jesus," the tormented woman whispered beneath her breath.

"I knew then that she was a Catholic, like myself," Ron continued. "So I suggested that we say the Lord's Prayer together, and she was able to do that." Finally a nurse was summoned from the Marriott Hotel, which was part of the Trade Center complex. The nurse hooked the woman up to oxygen. "It was then I felt the rumble and vibration of the second crashing plane; it went right through my body. I remember screaming, 'Let's get out of here!' As I opened the door, everything was gray . . . ashes everywhere! All that was familiar to me had been vaporized."

An officer yelled, "Jesus Christ, run!" So we carried poor Jennieann, oxygen and all, and we ran! Thank God we were then able to get her into an ambulance. During our time in the towers, I had gotten her address and whatever vital medical information she remembered." Amazing how the mind operates in a time of crisis.

Outside now, Ron's hell continued. "I heard the strangest sound around me, like thuds, but the air was thick with the gray dust and it took a while for my eyes to adjust. It was then I realized that there were bodies falling around me. I looked up and saw the people jumping and falling off the building. One woman clutched her pocketbook; two people held hands." Ron's voice cracked as he took a moment to gain his composure.

"I ran toward the ferry to Hoboken. All I could think was that it was my little girl's eleventh birthday and I had to get home. The ferry was full, but I jumped over the partition and just got on it anyway. I turned back and watched the first tower collapse, as I'd known it would. I was also fairly certain the second tower would go down as well."

What Ron experienced was already enough trauma for a lifetime, but his horror didn't end there. He made it home and couldn't wait to shower off the nightmare. His skin was covered with the residue of gray ash, and there were pieces of Jennieann Maffeo's charred skin stuck to his clothing. After he washed off, he received a disturbing phone call from his brother-in-law, who said that his wife, Ruth (Ron's sister), had not called home. She had flown out with her young daughter Juliana to Los Angeles that morning. Ron's heart sank as he began investigating. Sure enough, Ron sister and niece had been aboard one of the planes that was flown into the towers. Ruth's best friend, Paige, had been on the other plane. They were flying out in two separate planes to attend a seminar given by Deepak Chopra.

"My sister Ruth and I were very close, just a year apart; we were Irish twins." He spoke through his tears now. "And my niece and daughter were exceptionally close. Our own family was torn up now, and it was a long time before we would heal."

After that, Ron changed jobs. He could not stop crying. He was plagued by the sights and sounds he had endured, aside from the tragic loss of his sister, niece, and family friend. He suffered with panic attacks and could still feel what he called the "harmonic vibrations" of the buildings as they were struck by the planes. He sought help for his posttraumatic stress disorder through a specialist in EMDR (eye movement desensitization processing). He entered a program of therapy of six hours a week for three months. He also made a conscious decision not to drink for the next year, as he didn't want to use alcohol as a crutch.

"Did the EMDR therapy help?" I asked.

"It saved my life. After September 11, I would scrub my feet in the shower until they bled, and I didn't even know why I was doing it. Through EMDR, I discovered that I was unconsciously scrubbing off the ashes." He paused. "I went to see Jennieann in the hospital, but she died forty-one days later. Her husband thanked me for giving him time to say good-bye to his wife."

And so Ron Clifford healed, as best as one can from such events. He told me that what also truly helped was the support of his wife, Bridgett, family, and good friends. "There is hope for people going through these things," he told me. "You must take hold of yourself and get the proper help. I had to remind myself that it was not all about *me*, that it was about the people around me as well. I could give up and fall apart or I could make it meaningful somehow."

The healing of his family took longer. Ron testified in the trial of Zacarias Moussaoui, the only person charged and convicted in connection with the attacks. At the trial, four years after September 11, Ron's daughter Monica was still unable to speak about the loss of her beloved cousin and aunt. She asked her father if she could attend the trial, and he hesitantly agreed, hoping this might be healing for her in some way. Other family members attended as well. Monica listened intently to her father's testimony and afterward was finally able to speak about her loss. In fact, the trial in some way brought a level of acceptance to the family that Ron felt allowed them to begin to truly heal.

WHAT IS EYE MOVEMENT DESENSITIZATION REPROCESSING (EMDR)?

It is my decision as a psychotherapist to remain open-minded in my approach to helping clients. If I let my ego take over and convince myself that I always know the right answer, then I stop growing. This is why I am constantly trying to learn more about dealing with grief and PTSD. Although I do not personally practice EMDR, I have knowledgeable colleagues that do, and I am grateful for their work with trauma patients like Ron Clifford and many others.

Eye movement desensitization reprocessing was developed by Francine Shapiro, who believed that when a traumatic or distressing experience occurs, the experience overwhelms our usual ways of coping and can be inadequately processed. So sometimes these traumatic events get stored in an isolated area of the brain. Certain triggers can cause these isolated memories to surface unexpectedly, causing the individual to "flash back" to the time of the event. This can result in overreactions.

EMDR uses a structured eight-phase approach to address the past, present, and future aspects of the dysfunctionally stored memory. During the processing phases of EMDR, the client attends to the disturbing memory in multiple brief sets of about fifteen to twenty seconds while simultaneously focusing on dual-attention stimulus.

The therapist asks about the thoughts her patient has about "the incident" and then what new thoughts the patient would *like* to have. Side-to-side stimulus (or sensation) is provided by the therapist, such as the therapist moving her fingers side to side in front of the patient. It has since been discovered that tapping alternate hands or supplying sounds to alternate ears may also be used. How does it work? That's a chapter for a different book, but our friend Ron highly recommends it.

OTHER CAUSES OF PTSD

You don't have to be part of a national disaster to experience posttraumatic stress disorder. When Elisabeth came to me, it had been several years since her fourteen-year-old son, Justin, was found accidentally choked to death with a chain dog collar and leash. This young man was at a friend's house and was fooling around with the choke collar and dog leash, slipped on a staircase, and choked himself. Frightened, his friend called Justin's mother, who ran to the house and tried to perform CPR on her son, most probably already deceased.

We tell ourselves that this kind of thing simply cannot happen! It is not possible! It is a scene from a horror movie. Believe it or not, this is a scene from a real family's life. This is a memory one very courageous mother had to learn to incorporate into her mind and go on living.

Elisabeth suffered from PTSD. Haunted by visions of her son as she last saw him, she wondered if she would ever be able to think of him and not visualize his lifeless pallor and oddly blotched face. She relived that day over and over again, wondering what she could have done differently to have saved her boy. No longer could she drive past the house where it happened. Even seeing the family members of that house was excruciating. To this day, so many years later, Elisabeth avoids the aisle with pet accessories at the grocery store. She turns away from red dog leashes.

Elisabeth was different after Justin's death, as we all are after the death of a loved one. But her grief was compounded by extreme trauma. After Justin's death, Elisabeth jumped at loud noises. The sound of sirens invaded even the yoga class that she attended in an attempt to find some modicum of inner peace.

"I just wanted to shut off my brain. I wished there was a battery I could just remove to turn it off. But nothing would stop the constant torture." After a while she would try to find things to distract or interfere with the steady stream of devastating thoughts.

Always a protective mom, Elisabeth tried hard not to drive her surviving child, Jessica, "nuts."

"I had done everything I could to protect Justin, and look what happened!" she said. "So what's the point? Jessica and Sammy deserve to have their own lives." Sammy is Elisabeth's subsequent child.

In therapy Elisabeth worked through much of the anger that accompanied such a senseless death. She strove to reconcile the death and move on with her life. Over time and with much personal diligence she resumed working toward her teaching degree. An amazing person and mother, Elisabeth and her husband have endured every parent's nightmare of losing a child.

7

How Children Grieve

Most adults share the instinctive desire to protect the young. Pain and suffering on a child's face breaks our hearts. When it comes to the blows that death can yield in a child's life, we are defenseless. It's horrible enough for us to travel through this sunless forest; why are there children scattered about on this treacherous pathway? We don't get satisfactory answers to this question. Nevertheless, the children *are* here—tired, frightened, and confused, trudging along the same cold path. Even in our darkest hours, we must find a way to comfort and guide them. When our own lantern grows dim and our compass is lost, we are still called upon to guide the way and ease their journey.

My work with children and loss has been extensive, and I share now what they have taught me over the years. I do this to provide whatever light and direction I can to those of you who want to help the children who cannot always help themselves.

Children at varying developmental stages can grieve only according to their knowledge and experience of the world. The very young child cannot conceive of the finality of death. Her experience of death may have only been through cartoons, where flattened characters rise up, reinflate, and walk the world again. Permanency is a concept outside the realm of her understanding. Caring adults often ask me how to talk to children about death. There are many fine books on this subject, some of which are included in the "Tools for Use with Children and Teens" section at the end of the book. The rule of thumb is that you speak to the child at the level of his own stage of development. Give only as much information as you think the child can process.

I was seeing a five-year-old girl, Melissa, whose relative lovingly told her that her deceased grandfather "was always with her, right on her shoulder." Before her grandfather's death, Melissa loved to be outside running and playing with the neighborhood children. Her mother brought her to me because she thought she was simply not readjusting to a life without her grandfather. After a session or two it came out that Melissa had stopped running and climbing because she was afraid she would injure or drop her grandfather, who she now believed was permanently fixed on her shoulder. That is how literal young children can be!

We must choose our words carefully. This does not mean that you can't include your family's religious, spiritual, or scientific beliefs in an explanation of death. It is also wonderful for children to be included in healing rituals like wakes and funerals. Contrary to the old belief that children should be kept away from these rituals, children need to feel a part of the family experience. There is no sadder picture than a lone mourner. When we leave our children out of the grieving process, we relegate them to isolated mourning.

Our culture tends to separate children from death and old age. A friend of mine from Costa Rica speaks of her mother's final days as beautiful and peaceful. "Mom was in the bed with the quilt Grandma made, keeping her old bones warm, as the children played on the bed each day until she was tired."

Isn't that a more comforting picture than a sterile hospital room surrounded by strangers? Often children are not even brought in to see a dying relative for fear that they will be traumatized by the image of their ill loved one. In this way we distance our children and ourselves from the truth of the situation. We rob the dying individual as well, a very sacred part of life.

Cultures that embrace death as a natural part of life lessen the fear of the unknown for the younger generation. Sometimes the scariest thing a child carries with her after the death of a loved one is the image that she makes up in her head. Grandma naturally becoming thinner and paler before her body fails is far more understandable and acceptable than one day Grandma is whisked away and then suddenly she is gone forever. Of course not all dying people have the choice of coming home to die, but do we even expect this anymore? Why not?

A comprehensive study at the Barr-Harris Center for the Study of Separation and Loss found 85 percent of children who lost family members to death experienced at least one of the following (many experiencing multiple symptoms): sleep disturbances, nightmares, phobic responses, separation reactions, angry outbursts toward parents, increased tension states, regression, enuresis (repeated inability to control urination), sucking and mouthing objects, attention seeking, confusion, worry, depression, and loss of resiliency. Believe it or not, these behaviors are quite normal under the circumstances. Unexpressed grief may lead to greater numbers of children prone to aggression in schools already taxed to their limits. A lifetime of depression can begin with childhood grief. For a society that espouses to have our children's welfare as a priority, we should not turn our heads from these children in very real need.

Unlike many adults, children grieve in doses. A child may appear very sad one minute and be playing and laughing the next. This is healthy. Adults can find this seemingly erratic behavior disconcerting.

"I think there's something wrong with Derek," a worried father told me. "He just doesn't seem to have normal reactions. I mean, his grandfather lived with us since he was born, and sometimes Derek doesn't even seem to care that he's gone. He asks the weirdest questions about his grandfather's passing without displaying any emotion. Is there something wrong with him?"

Derek just couldn't sustain the kind of all-encompassing grief his father felt at the loss. Derek, being ten years old, was busy accomplishing many of the tasks that are required by a child of his age to develop normally. His peer relationships had become more important than before, so playing and being social had become a priority. His questions, which seemed strange to his dad, were merely a normal curiosity about the biological aspects of death. Children are by nature egocentric. The loss of a grandparent is not the same as the loss of a parent, so in that way Derek's experience was not that of his father's. As adults we should be careful not to project our own feelings about our losses onto our children. Derek's father's expectations of how his son *should* grieve could place undue pressure on Derek, causing him to internalize guilt for not grieving in the "proper" way.

In his article "Helping Children Express Grief Through Symbolic Communication," Robert Segal makes the most profound observations about what happens to communication in some bereaved children:

> Because the troubled child must censor unacceptable feelings related to fear, anger, and guilt, he expends a great deal of psychic energy maintaining a façade of nonexpression. He builds a wall around himself, not permitting free and open communication. The therapist must find a way to break through the barrier to elicit a spontaneous response from the child, a response that more truly reflects the child's genuine feelings.

Play is vital to children, who experiment and fantasize as they try out different personas and situations. They sometimes work things out this way. *Play therapy* is an essential tool for bereavement therapists. You don't need a degree, however, to draw pictures or fool around with a dollhouse. Allow a child open expression through play and watch the magic happen. You will be amazed at the connection you can achieve in this way. An illustration of a young child's anger may show up in the crayoned drawing of flames, or a puppet show may bring a sorely missed family member back to life.

In my office I have a dollhouse that has proven to be an invaluable tool with young children of both sexes. It's not a "girly" dollhouse. It's made of painted cardboard with colorful plastic furniture. I have all kinds of little dolls children can use to make up their families. I never lead with directly asking the child to demonstrate what happened when her family member died. If I did that, her armor might just become more impenetrable. Rather, I ask the child to show me what her room looks like or who lives with her. Incredibly, somewhere along the line, the child usually reveals her feelings. One child whose brother had died brought him magically back to life while excluding herself from the family. It was during that session that I began to appreciate just how guilty this little girl felt for surviving. All play tells us something. I have often thought that this kind of work appeals to the frustrated private detective in me. The clues are all there, if I can just piece them together.

HOW CHILDREN AGES 0–3 GRIEVE

Very young children often cry because they see those around them crying. Although the child cannot comprehend the finality of death, she may indeed miss the person who has died and be sad. A child may regress to an earlier developmental stage and forget his potty training or begin to suck his thumb again. Be patient; he will regain the appropriate behaviors for his age. Very young children are trying to master preliminary separation from parents and in grief may display acute separation anxiety. All children are barometers for the adults around them. When their family members are preoccupied with their own grief, it is not uncommon for children to become very irritable and angry and to display difficult behavior.

HOW TO HELP CHILDREN AGES 0–3

Explain to the child that his loved one has died and will not be coming back. Keep any religious explanations to a minimum at this age. If you mention heaven, you'd better be prepared to answer a lot of questions and be careful with your answers (remember the little girl who thought she carried her grandfather on her shoulder). The good thing about children is that they will demand and comprehend more detailed explanations as they grow older. For now, it is best to keep things simple.

A lot of physical contact like hugging reassures a child that she is safe. Be patient with behavioral changes and regression. Try to keep to a schedule with eating and sleeping, playtime, and so on. Children of all ages are comforted by routine.

HOW CHILDREN AGES 4–7 GRIEVE

The most important aspect of grief for children of this age and up until the teen years is *magical thinking*. This is the belief that just thinking about something can make it happen. An example would be that a child is angry with his father and wishes him dead. If by some tragic coincidence the child's father suddenly dies, he might indeed think he caused his father's death. Young children do not comprehend cause and effect. This kind of thinking can lead children to complicated grief. They may harbor distorted thoughts about why the death happened, how it occurred, and what they had to do with it.

When children face the loss of a loved one, they realize that their parents do not have dominion over death. They may start to worry about their own safety and security. This often shows up as excessive worrying about little things such as asking, "Are the doors locked? Is there enough gas in the car?" Although this can be annoying, try to reassure the child and be patient with this need for safety. It will hopefully lift over time. If the behavior becomes excessive, counseling should be sought out.

Children of this age have not fully developed the capacity for empathy for others' feelings. They probably can't understand how *you* are feeling, and it is unrealistic to expect them to be overly sympathetic to another's losses. They learn empathy and compassion from the adults around them. Show them as much affection and attention as possible during this complicated time. They have no understanding of the finality of death, but they may want to talk about it. Some talk about death being like sleep. You can expect that they may be overly clingy to certain adults for fear of losing another family member.

HOW TO HELP CHILDREN AGES 4–7

Explain to the child that her loved one has died and will not be coming back. If the child has lost a younger family member to some kind of illness, you might want to reassure her that her own body is fine and that people usually die only when they are very, very old. It is important for the child to distinguish between colds and ordinary illness and a chronic or fatal illness, or she might begin to fear illness of any kind. Be honest, but keep the language simple and clear. Speak to the other caretakers of the child to make sure that you are not giving him conflicting messages, as this will only further confuse the child.

Reassurance is also needed for children of any age that they are not responsible for the death. It is vital for them to hear these words and comprehend them: "You did not cause this to happen."

If the child has lost a parent or grandparent, assure the child (if it is true) that the remaining adults in his life are healthy, and should live a long, long time. If the person died in an accident, you may wish to explain that these things do not happen very often. In this way you alleviate some of the fear that it will happen to the child or to another family member. Do not lie to the child, but keep explanations short and factual. Again, be careful about saying things like "Nanny is always watching you from heaven." That is not to say that you can't mention heaven, if it is your belief, just keep in mind that children are literal, and you should always try to imagine how they will receive your words.

You can begin to ask a few important questions to the child at this age to ensure that magical thinking is not distorting her perception of what happened.

1. Tell me, what do you think happened?

2. How do you feel about what happened?

3. What are you afraid of?

If the child answers with one word, follow up with more specific questions:

ADULT: Tell me, what happened?
CHILD: Papa died.
ADULT: What made him die?
CHILD: He had a heart attack.
ADULT: So why do you think he had a heart attack?

The child might say, "Because he was old," or he might tell you he accidentally scared his grandfather and caused the heart attack. The latter is magical thinking, and it is important to hear the story of the death as interpreted by the child to find out if he is carrying around any distortions. Encourage the child to talk about his feelings, for it is these distortions that feed guilt and anxiety.

Sometimes children become preoccupied with thoughts about the person who died. My children's book, *I Miss Matthew*, was inspired by watching my four-year-old son transition through his own grief after the death of his infant brother. The behaviors I witnessed confused and upset me. I would find Carll curled up in his brother's crib or sitting in Jesse's high chair speaking "baby talk." I knew about regression, but his actions seemed to be more about comforting himself than a cry for attention. I've since learned that these behaviors might have come from the longing to have his baby brother back or could even have been an attempt at making Mommy and Daddy happy again by bringing back the baby we mourned so deeply. These are complicated nonverbal messages.

For instance, in the case of Carll climbing into his brother's crib, I might have been able to dig deeper to understand "why" this behavior took place. The surest way *not* to get an answer would be to simply ask "Why?" Most children this age will shrug their shoulders and answer, "I don't know," and that is usually the truth. It is better to explore the behavior together. You might say, "I saw you in Jesse's crib yesterday; were you pretending to be him?" This gives the child a more concrete question. Now comes the important part—sit back and listen. "I miss my baby" tells you *one* thing while "No, I wanted to be a baby" tells you something quite different.

Children are often brought to me after some distortions have taken root. *I Miss Matthew* and other children's books and workbooks are designed to help facilitate communication between an adult and a grieving child to normalize the loss, allow emotional expression, and uncover any distortions in the child's thinking. You will find some children's books listed in the back of this book.

HOW CHILDREN AGES 8–12 GRIEVE

At these ages, children are beginning to become more adult in their thinking yet still maintain magical thinking. They have come to accept that death happens to everyone but are struggling with the idea of their own mortality. This may be a time of nightmares and waking in the night. They may not wish to be alone with their own thoughts. Their questions may become more complex, requiring more in-depth explanations. They may want to know medical explanations about illness and death.

HOW TO HELP CHILDREN AGES 8–12

Even a child of ten may want to sleep with someone else. A sleeping bag on the floor is a good interim measure or temporary lodging in another sibling's room. A fish tank or a pet in his bedroom can work wonders. Good old 1970s lava lamps are restful to lull children to sleep. If insomnia continues after six months, you might want to explore counseling.

Always take your cues from the child. If she is depressed, honor her feelings. Too often adults think that a child should be told *how* to feel about something, as if saying words like "Mommy would want you to be happy" will automatically make the child feel happy. More likely, the child now feels guilty for being sad. Oh, how we human beings love to complicate the simple truth. The child is sad and entitled to her sorrow. Children of this age are beginning to develop more empathy for others.

There is a healthy need for accomplishment. Although all children should be included in grief rituals, at this age it is important to include them in a concrete way. Give them small tasks to carry out, like handing out programs or passing out food when people come to pay their respects to the family. Help them to feel a part of things.

Psychotherapists are taught to "start where the client is," which simply means that we must first ascertain *how* a client is feeling and not transfer our own emotions or beliefs onto that person. This is never truer than when you are working with a bereaved child. Do not assume that you *know* how that youngster feels—you may be wrong. Let him tell you. And here's where it gets tricky—don't *ask* him how he is feeling. Let me demonstrate with an example of this eight-year-old from my practice:

THERAPIST: Hi, Ann.

ANN: Hi.

THERAPIST: I have a workbook here for us to do together.

ANN: I don't really feel like it right now.

THERAPIST: That's fine. But I *would* like to do it sometime, so do you promise that you'll let me know when you're ready? It's kind of fun—you get to draw and stuff. Here, just put your name on the cover so no one else will use your workbook.

ANN: OK. *(She looks briefly through the book and then puts it down.)*

THERAPIST: So you'll let me know when you want to do the book?

(Ann nods yes.)

THERAPIST: Great! How about a card game or a board game?

ANN: Sure.

And so we played a game and talked a bit in between.

THERAPIST: I know your mom used to take you to ballet. Who takes you now?

ANN: Mrs. Davis, the new babysitter.

THERAPIST: Is she nice?

ANN: She's OK, but she doesn't know the other moms or anything.

THERAPIST: Oh, that must be hard that all the other moms know each other and you're with a babysitter.

Ann looked up from the game into my eyes. "I don't want to go to ballet anymore!" The tears were there, but she fought them back—and we were off to the races. The next week she asked to start on her workbook.

Helping grieving children is all about patience and coaxing them gently to come to you. The ages from eight to twelve are difficult. One doesn't have to have a degree in art therapy to use drawing as a means to decipher how a child is feeling. Much can be revealed through a child's artwork. Are the colors vibrant or dreary? Is the subject matter cheerful or morbid? Coloring and drawing together also opens up the door to conversation.

One twelve-year-old boy whom I saw after the death of his mother drew pictures of only his deceased hamster and answered the questions in his bereavement workbook only about the hamster. It took three-quarters of the way through the book and several weeks before he was finally able to transition from hamster to human. Subsequently it was revealed that he had much guilt attached to his mother's death and it was just too painful for him to draw or speak about it. Fortunately, he did work through this and moved out of a depressed state to normal grief.

HOW TO HELP TEENS

As children transition from young childhood into adolescence they have many questions about everything. Their thinking becomes more logical (although if you've raised teenagers that may be hard to believe) and they begin to understand that life is finite. Teens are also better able to think abstractly and are questioning things like religion, the existence of God, and the rules and mores of their cultures. Never is this quite so intense as in the bereaved young adult. Just when he wants to be the same as his peers, an unexpected death thrusts him tragically into the spotlight. This group is most in need of counseling and usually the most resistant to it.

This is the time of rebellion, and emotions are often explosive. Studies have shown that the grieving male adolescent is at risk for drug and alcohol abuse as well as other damaging and self-destructive behaviors. At this age the adolescent is involved in the difficult task of separating from Mom and Dad and forming his own identity. Often this is accompanied by friction and arguing as the adolescent pushes boundaries and limits. To lose a parent at this juncture can be damaging in many ways. The abrupt intrusion of death leaves the more gradual work of separation unfinished, and the young adult may feel guilt for his normal anger toward that parent and even blame himself for the death.

To the bereaved adult, teens often seem uncaring after the death of a close relative or family member. Remember that children grieve in doses, and in this way, the adolescent is still a child. The seemingly self-centered personality so pervasive in teens is really a part of the work he is doing to become an adult. Logically, this carries over into the grieving process.

There is also the occasional teenager who no longer wishes to go out with friends after a loved one's death. She makes it her life's work to care for the surviving family members, making sure everyone is safe. She isolates totally from her peers. If this behavior is still prevalent after a year's time, consider it a cry for help.

Teenagers and younger children as well will sometimes attempt to keep their lost loved one alive by mimicking the behavior and mannerisms of the deceased. This is not necessarily done on a conscious level. A parent might speak to me of certain characteristics emerging in his daughter that belonged to his late wife. As with many characteristics in grief, these changes might lessen as the child fully develops her own identity. Obsessive transformation is an early warning sign for complicated grief, and counseling should be considered.

Teens may become solemn and not talkative about events surrounding the death, almost certainly avoiding talking about the death itself.

This is normal. As parents of teens we must learn to take our opportunities for conversation when they come. Do not judge this behavior, and do not try to force verbal participation. It will only backfire on you, and the teen may pull even further away. It might make it easier to tolerate what we see as abhorrent behavior if we realize that it is not intentional rudeness but simply emotionally excruciating for this young adult to communicate about his loss at this time.

So, how does a parent get an uncooperative teenager into counseling? I am not above suggesting bribery (did I say that?). If you can get him to the first session and the counselor can connect, he may find his own reasons to come back. I suggest a therapist who is used to dealing with adolescents and has some background with bereavement. If your teen refuses to go, back off and try again in a few weeks. Understand that this may feel like an invasion of privacy to the teen who may be defended against uncovering strong emotions, including possible guilt. Sometimes a teacher, family friend, clergy member, or another caring adult might be enlisted to suggest help or to simply lend a listening ear to the hurting teenager. Pediatricians and pediatric nurses can also be helpful. Some doctors go out of their way to speak to children about their losses, and having previously known this adult may add a level of built-in trust. As I've reiterated throughout this book, the mind and body are a connected unit and the list of the physical symptoms in grief are startling, so I suggest that everyone going through grief, including children, have a good physical exam.

It is most important for you to stay as close to your child as he or she will allow. That does not mean talking about the loss at every given opportunity. It is more important now that the young person feel the support of a loving family. That might mean a meal together, watching a movie, or going on a family vacation. Don't expect miracles. Just be open.

Remember, young children grow more inquisitive and demand more detailed explanations as they mature into new stages of development. They will ask about the story of the death all over again and may even experience re-grieving. Many times children come into counseling, work through their grief, and leave therapy doing well. Several years later, a father will call and say something like, "Meagan has locked herself inside her room and refuses to talk to me. She is crying all the time. What do I do?" When Meagan gets back into my office I find out that she just got her period for the first time, which triggered an episode of re-grieving. Meagan is now missing her deceased mother in a whole new way.

Meagan has begun to grieve the loss of her mother at a new developmental stage. She stays in therapy for a few months to regain her footing. Without these important follow-up sessions to original grief therapy, Meagan becomes at risk for many undesired adolescent behaviors that could follow her into adulthood. She needs to be seen and heard.

NORMALIZING DEATH IN CHILDHOOD

A way in which we can help our children is to first realize that they are already acquainted with death. Every time they see a dead flower or bug, they are witnessing the cycle of life and death. If we are to be teachers to our children, we should take early opportunities to help them understand the cycle of life. The death of a pet will bring up many feelings and questions for them. Rather than secretly replacing the dead goldfish for a comparable replica, take the time to go through the grieving process with her, answer her questions, and teach her. When she has to face a more tragic loss down the road, she will have some understanding and coping skills to call upon.

In my opinion, author, educator, and grief counselor Dr. Alan Wolfelt has written the seminal program for working with children in grief. His model includes the concept of "companioning" children going through loss as opposed to "treating" them. Dr. Wolfelt believes, and I agree, that grief requires a different model for treatment than other types of therapy. I like his *Healing a Grieving Heart* series for children and teens.

WHEN A CLASSMATE DIES

The 1999 tragedy at Columbine High School, in which two disturbed students murdered twelve people and wounded twenty-four others before taking their own lives, prompted psychologists and educators to investigate how these young men became angry enough to commit such a massacre. Warning signs were explored to help predict when violence like this might erupt again in other schools. Was it the violent video games or movies that motivated Eric Harris and Dylan Klebold? Maybe it was the heavy metal music they listened to or the pharmaceutical antidepressants that caused brutality of this magnitude. Security increased at many high schools throughout the country after this incident, and the search for warning signs stepped up a notch. After Columbine and so many other tragic school shootings around the country since, educators have started to panic, and who can blame them?

Marsha's backpack was searched because there was a rumor that a group of "goth" kids was going to kill people at her school. Marsha's mother was very upset when she brought her daughter into my office, shouting that she had been suspended. The search turned up a note with a list of her classmates' names and the words "Need to Eliminate" at the bottom. As Marsha's mom ranted and raved, my young friend's lip curled up ever so slightly as she sat back silently watching. Having worked with Marsha for nearly a year, I felt fairly certain that she was not planning a mass murder but more likely trying to elicit the exact reaction she was getting from Mom and the other adults against whom she was rebelling. Still it *was* very disturbing.

After a couple of sessions, it came out that Marsha and her friends had concocted the whole scheme to scare some kids they hated. Freaking out the parents and teachers was just an added benefit. So how do we know when it's the real thing?

According to the American Psychological Association, violence warning signs are the following:

- ⚭ Loss of temper on a daily basis
- ⚭ Frequent physical fighting
- ⚭ Significant vandalism or property damage
- ⚭ Increase in risk-taking behavior
- ⚭ Increase in drug or alcohol abuse
- ⚭ Detailed plans to commit acts of violence
- ⚭ Announcing threats or plans for hurting others
- ⚭ Enjoying hurting animals
- ⚭ Carrying a weapon

So, what do we do for the surviving children when they actually live through the death of a classmate? That depends on the age of the child and the way that classmate died. In the case of the 2012 Sandy Hook Elementary shooting and even in less public cases where violence has led to death, children are dealing with trauma and sometimes posttraumatic stress disorder. Intervention is necessary. Rising violence and suicide rates have caused some educators to institute programs into schools to address these issues. A well-trained staff and guidelines about how to handle the aftermath in such circumstances make for a great deal less chaos after the fact and better outcomes for the kids.

In a growing number of school districts on Long Island, New York, crisis teams made up of school psychologists, social workers, nurses, administrators, and teachers have done training on how to help children after the traumatic death of a classmate. Some districts even establish cooperative ventures with local agencies where mental health professionals train the school staffs. This is also helpful in the case of suicide, where there is always the concern of copycats.

There are effective programs out there today to help schools deal with these kinds of deaths, and some of them are offered free from nonprofit organizations. Some of these are listed at the end of the book.

I was once called into an elementary school to help advise after the death of an eight-year-old boy in an accident. The assistant principal and I worked together to help Raymond's classmates to deal with his death. This was about fifteen years ago, and I was appalled to learn that some parents did not want the issue addressed in the classroom at all. "People are not comfortable with the subject of death," the assistant principal explained. So they chose to ignore the subject completely. I was astonished that things had changed so little. We decided to offer after-school sessions for parents who wished to help their children cope with the tragedy. Many children *did* attend these sessions, which their parents claimed were quite helpful.

These children had questions about what happened to their friend. They had fears that it could happen to them. Many wanted to help Raymond's family to feel better. So we made a giant paper quilt. Each child who wished to participate created one square, on which he colored whatever he wanted in memory of Raymond. During the creation of the quilt, discussion took place. In the end we connected all the squares and decorated the lobby of the school.

Children were encouraged to visit with the school social worker if they needed to during the day. Finally, a memorial service was held during which a tree was planted in Raymond's honor.

HOW TO HELP WHEN A CLASSMATE DIES

As you read earlier in the chapter, the most dangerous aspect of young children and the treatment of loss may be the distortions they create in their minds. Offer an open discussion with your child, and don't worry if she says things you don't expect to hear. Remember, children grieve differently than adults. Be patient and nonjudgmental. If you are not comfortable discussing the subject, let her talk to the school counselor or a bereavement therapist for a couple of sessions.

It becomes trickier with adolescents, who are at risk for isolation from others, aggression, substance abuse, depression, high-risk behaviors, and suicide. If you feel that a classmate's death has seriously affected your child and you have any clout at all, now is the time to use it. If he feels awkward about seeing a school counselor, offer a private therapist. Find out if there are any available resources in the school or the community that cater to this age group. If that fails, any trusted adult may find a way to connect with that teen. You might suggest a book or website that will help inform the adolescent on the subject. Short of this there is nothing much more you can do. Just let him know that you are there if he needs you.

Children do well in groups. Explore any existing children's groups available in your community. You might even start a support group yourself.

BEREAVEMENT GROUPS FOR CHILDREN

I first learned about group therapy from an amazing professor named Herb Schwartz, at Adelphi University in New York. Having worked with violent city gangs, he could deal with just about any kind of group. I guess a group of grieving children could not be farther from those city gangs—or could they? We are all only human and therefore sometimes feel disconnected and isolated. Who is more vulnerable than a child in pain and confusion? Herb taught me to trust the group process and to be patient, allowing things to emerge naturally. They always have.

At Clear Creek High School in Houston, Texas, a grief group has been offered annually since 1985. The school reports that students are receptive to joining the ongoing grief group and even eager to attend. In this program, letters of permission are sent home before the group begins. Teens, who are often uncomfortable opening up with adults, sometimes feel more comfortable sharing their feelings among their peers (at least those who are dealing with the same issues).

Many schools offer groups like "Banana Splits" for children of divorce, but far fewer offer bereavement groups. When I was running a Children and Loss workshop for educators, I even had one elementary principal say, "Death is a touchy subject." You bet it is, especially for the poor child going through it.

If you or an organization is considering putting together a bereavement group for children, or even scouting out a preexisting one for your child, I offer some suggestions. Children should be grouped according to age (within two years of each other). The ideal number of members for such a group is from four to eight members. It is not necessary for children to be gathered according to the type of loss they've experienced. We all know that youngsters have "ants in their pants"—it may not be a technical term, but it's true! Be prepared to mix it up with games, art therapy, and other tactile exercises. One child therapist I know has a sandbox in his office. Whatever it takes!

A child who has lost a sibling or a parent often feels stigmatized and isolated from his peers. He feels discouraged to raise the subject of death. Attendance in a bereavement group can help to normalize the experience in some small measure, provide peer support, and create a safe environment for children of all ages to express fears, fantasies, and feelings. Because these are emotionally draining issues, a child's bereavement group should be no longer than forty-five to sixty minutes.

A great way to begin the first meeting with children under ten is to hand out crayons and blank paper and have each member draw a picture of the person who died. This allows the child to introduce the loss without necessarily speaking. For a child who may have been feeling somewhat ostracized for her loss, it is soothing simply to realize she is not alone. Each child is now given the opportunity to speak about his or her loved one, if the child so chooses.

One wonderful attribute children of this age possess is their candor. I recall one child asking another child if he had more toys to play with since his brother died. The answer was "Yes, but now I have to play with them alone."

There are endless exercises one can suggest for such a group. As they become more comfortable with one another and the subject, the kids may give you a new problem—they won't want to shut up! (That's my kind of problem.) Be courageous and compassionate, and your group may be the beginning of healing for a little person.

In groups for ages eleven to thirteen, you may wish to use one of the workbooks suggested at the back of this book. A topic may be chosen depending on which page the group is working on that week.

Teen bereavement groups should not include younger children. The disparity in their development can cause more harm than good. In fact, early teens are best separated from older ones. Kids in the older group tend to worry about expressing themselves honestly and are thus given yet another scenario in which they have to "watch what they say"—or, equally as destructive, they may express themselves in ways that confuse and frighten the younger teens.

Young adults are analytical. After getting to know one another for a couple of sessions, they might be introduced to a movie in an extended session. Two beautiful films that capture the mind and heart are *Ordinary People* and *An Unfinished Life*. Both films lend themselves to discussions about the emotional roller coaster of grief. Guilt is heavily addressed in both films, and this is an important by-product of grief for the teen population.

As mentioned before, adolescents are best served by professionals who appreciate the complexities of this age group. However, there is no reason why a teacher, parent, or other caring adult can't avail herself of the opportunity to view one of these films with a grieving teenager.

Hospice, in its ministering to the families of the terminally ill, performs a range of therapeutic activities, such as crisis intervention and short-term and long-term therapy. Bereavement programs in which staff members maintain contact with families of the deceased often include counseling for children. Trained hospice workers, social workers, and nurses also educate the public and community organizations about what they do. In this venue, volunteers are often trained to work with families, which brings down the cost.

In the town where I grew up, there was a bereavement center associated with the local Family Service Association. Many such agencies exist throughout the country. Some have "sliding scale" fees for services based on what families can afford. Sometimes they offer groups for children as well as provide some individual counseling services. There are other organizations like the SIDS Foundation, Big Hearts for Little Hearts, Compassionate Friends, and local community centers that may sometimes run children and adolescent bereavement groups as well.

GRIEF CAMPS

Over the past ten years or so, many "grief camps" have sprung up throughout the country. These camps are designed for children and sometimes their families as well. Grief camps allow children who have experienced the loss of a family member to be among other people their own age who have had similar losses. This helps to alleviate the child's loneliness. Some of these camps are terrific, offering fun activities as well as therapeutic ones. We talked before about how children grieve in doses. These types of camps allow for a child's unique grieving journey.

Some camps offer workshops for grieving families. The families are provided with grief education while taught coping skills. Most important, they receive emotional support from adults and peers alike.

Many camps are run by professional bereavement counselors and manned by compassionate laypeople. They assist in normalizing the grief experience but do not belittle the child's loss. The girl whose mother has died may be playing with another who lost her dad. This child might open up to her new friend in a way that wouldn't be possible with her friends back home.

Art and music therapy programs are available at some camps. Recreational activities are offered at most. Camps range in the ages of the campers as well as length of stay. Some camps run only on weekends while others offer longer programs. Some specialize in types of loss. There are camps that specialize in families dealing with cancer, while others handle accidental death, illness, suicide, and homicide.

A good way to look for a camp is to start on the Internet. Look for a camp that will be convenient for your family's lifestyle. Make sure to find out if the facility is run by bereavement professionals. This does not mean that every staff member needs a degree. Some of the most effective help comes from compassionate individuals willing to give of their time and themselves. However, it is important that the facility be managed by experts. I suggest that you even visit the camp before making a commitment to make sure it is a place your child will like.

8

DIFFERENT MOURNINGS

~~~~~~

Remember when we talked about the loneliness of grief in chapter 1? Well, never is this more apparent than when two people are grieving the same loss separately. So, how is it possible for two people to grieve together yet separately?

HOW MEN AND WOMEN GRIEVE

A man and woman arrive separately, from their separate worlds. She wears faded sweats with an attempt at coordinated jewelry. Her brown hair hangs loosely from a red scrunchy, pieces falling over her pale face. Forcing a shaky smile, she glances in my direction before taking a seat at the far end of the blue couch. Still on his cell phone, he arrives, holding up an index finger to indicate he will soon hang up. For a couple of minutes, his clipped, frenetic conversation is the only sound in the room. She puts a hand to her forehead and closes her eyes for a few moments as if to gain her composure. He ends his call, apologizes, and walks over to peck his wife on the cheek before taking his seat on the opposite side of the couch.

Margaret, a teacher, has already been home and changed her clothes, while Don comes straight from his job as the manager of an insurance agency. He attempts to straighten out his jacket. "Mind if I have some water?" As he pours and drinks, I notice the deep circles around his sad brown eyes. She has not moved but continues to stare into space. I breathe in deeply, silently praying for the strength to help these people whose hurt is written all over their faces.

Three months ago, Margaret and Don buried their four-year-old daughter. Only moments after they begin to talk about their week, Margaret starts sobbing. In reaction, Don shifts even farther away from his wife.

"You OK?" I ask Don.

"I just can't take it anymore. She just never stops crying."

This is just the tip of the iceberg for this remarkable couple whose only daughter died of a brain tumor. During her illness they worked as a team around the clock to help her. In her death, they have quickly drifted apart. It isn't that they don't love each other anymore. They have been stricken, suffering from the worst pain a parent could imagine. And to top it off, they cannot seem to grieve together.

This is not unusual. I have seen it so often in my practice, and many studies have been devoted to the differences between the sexes when it comes to grief. There are general differences. Women tend to cry more and have a need to talk about their losses. Men often clam up and throw themselves into work. Of course there are also different individual styles of grief that are not gender specific.

It is my job to encourage each partner to grieve in his or her own way and to teach each of them to make allowances for the other person's individual grieving style. If the couple can make it through the initial year without throwing in the towel, they just might make it. As time goes by, the differences in grieving styles will become less dramatic, and each partner will be better able to comfort the other.

THE PITFALLS

The path of loss for couples is a hazardous one. I encourage counseling. It is not always easy for people to look upon those who grieve alongside them with sympathy. Each person becomes so devastated by the loss that to comfort another seems an arduous task. Yet grieving people need to be reassured. Some people are consoled through their spiritual beliefs. If a couple shares the same religion, this can be helpful.

Maybe you're a woman who wants to talk about your feelings or the circumstances of the death, but your husband cannot bring himself to do so. You might become frustrated and angry, feeling forced to stifle yourself. This will only lead to resentment while constricting your grieving process. It helps to find other people to talk to.

"But why can't we talk about this together?" one partner will gripe. It seems the most natural thing in the world to this person to openly share her loss and heal along with her husband. "Why should I talk to strangers about something so private? Why can't we help each other?"

Men and women typically grieve differently. Accept this as a fact, and don't deny yourself what *you* may need to heal. Also, remember that you have not been appointed to diagnose and prescribe the proper grief process for your partner. Move forward while letting any other adults around you mourn, each in his or her own fashion, and you may save a marriage or another close relationship in your life.

It has been my experience that men *do* share their losses but often in different ways than women. Men cry privately when no one is around. He may talk to another person about his loss but simply does not have the same verbal needs his wife exhibits. In the case of Don and Margaret, Don was obviously grieving. The dark circles under his eyes, his throwing himself into his work, were signs of *his* grief.

When I see grieving couples, I give them literature on how men and women grieve differently. I ask them to be patient with one another and assure them that they will find each other again at the end of this long, dark tunnel. If they can touch each other for comfort through the pain, it is significant. We must learn not to judge each other's grief.

No one person can take that pain away. In our society we don't like pain. We don't always understand that it is a necessary part of healing and must be gotten through to move on successfully. Drugs and alcohol may temporarily dull the pain, but one would have to stay drugged for the rest of one's life to keep such pain at bay. Unfortunately, some people endeavor to do just that. But that is not the answer if you wish to rejoin the world and have healthy, fulfilling relationships down the road.

Blame is often a part of the scenario with couples. This can almost never be worked through without a third party. If finger-pointing is involved in a couple's grief, it is essential to get to a counselor. Blame is the seed of destruction in a relationship. Don't play out a twenty-year vendetta and waste your precious days. Seek help now!

Margaret and Don stayed in counseling, working through their hurt and resentment. They were one of the lucky couples who stayed together. Their underlying love sustained them through their loss and grieving differences. After much counseling, the couple decided to adopt a healthy baby. Margaret did not feel emotionally ready to go through another pregnancy and wanted more of a guarantee that an already thriving child would be healthy. They set about finding a baby through social services, and when offered a little girl who had been given up by her mother, they had the baby tested and brought her home. Hannah was a beautiful addition to their family, but it took some time for Don to accept this child and not feel she was a replacement for the daughter he lost. In some way he felt he was being disloyal to the child who died.

It took about a month before Don allowed himself to get close to Hannah. After that, there was no holding back.

SOCIETAL EXPECTATIONS

Like it or not, society still assigns different roles to men and women, and this certainly carries over into grief. Men are supposed to be strong and take charge. People ask him, "How is your wife holding up?" and neglect to ask how *he* is doing. Being strong is somehow synonymous with being emotionless. These stereotypical societal expectations only reinforce the chasm between husband and wife. A couple can overcome this by making the decision to work together.

Yes—it *is* a decision! *Let's get through this together.*

Grief is not a competition to prove who had greater love for the person who died. If we start comparing our grief and dictating to one another the proper way to mourn, we are doomed to grieve alone. Grief is desperately lonely by nature. If you can at least be kind to one another through your grief, you may be able to share it. A couple must make the decision to honor one another's process. Do not let societal expectations pull you apart. This advice is not confined to heterosexual couples; homosexual couples face the same challenges in a different way.

Listen to each other's story of the death and help one another with issues of guilt and blame. If the loved one who died is a member of your partner's family, understand that it will be felt differently by you. Read the passages in this book about how to help others through their grief. You will want the same compassion extended to you when you lose someone dear.

FAMILY STYLES

This chapter could spill over into a complete book. Families are complicated systems with rules and mores all their own. A family is an intricate network that, even if dysfunctional, balances a variety of personalities and role functions. When one member leaves, the family system will attempt to reach homeostasis in order to continue functioning—or fall apart.

This is not to imply that the family holds a meeting and decides how it will continue to exist without the member who has died. If only things were that organized and simple. The more likely scenario is a fragmented, disorganized attempt to create order out of chaos. Not unlike the restructuring that takes place after divorce—new roles emerge.

I will never forget the O'Hara family. Deidre, the mother, a sixty-six-year-old woman, had died a year before I got the call. It was her daughter, Maureen, who called to ask if I might help her family. I set aside two hours for the initial visit. Maureen arrived with Dad and three brothers in tow, all of whom would rather be anywhere else. I attempted some small talk for a few moments to put them at ease before getting started. They seemed a personable, chatty group until the subject of Mom's death was broached.

"So, I'm glad you all could make it here tonight," I smiled. "Do you know why Maureen requested that you come?"

Dead silence. I waited, surprised that Maureen, who had been so vocal on the phone, was suddenly as quiet as the rest of the family. Finally Dad spoke up. He still carried a wee bit of a brogue from his childhood in Ireland.

"Maureen here thought we should come and talk about her mother."

I wasn't sure if I saw cynicism or a touch of fear in his light eyes. "And what do *you* think?" I asked him. Daniel shifted his large frame uncomfortably in the chair before answering. "Honestly, I don't know what to think about the whole thing. I've never been one for airing my dirty laundry in public. But things have gone to hell without their mother."

"So, how have they gone to hell?"

"Let *them* tell ya!" He waved his large hand at his children and then folded his arms across his chest. His sons said nothing, and Maureen just shook her head. Finally, it was Michael, the oldest, who spoke up. "They're out of control! They're using Mom's passing as an excuse to do whatever the hell they want!"

Patrick, age seventeen, stared daggers across the room at his big brother. "He's an asshole . . . " he began as Dad reprimanded, "Patrick, do not use that language here."

"Well he *is* a damned asshole!" Patrick reiterated.

"It's OK, Mr. O'Hara. I want this room to be a safe place for *all* of you to vent your feelings. Believe me, I've heard much worse!"

"Thanks!" Patrick nodded to me, his wiry young frame tensed with anger as his pitch climbed. "Michael doesn't even live at home anymore and he still acts like he can tell us all what to do! Nobody cares what you think, Michael. You're married and have your own family now. Why don't you just leave us alone!"

"Somebody has to take control of this family; *he* doesn't do anything!" Michael gestured toward his dad, who remained unruffled by this comment. "These kids are running wild. Patrick is skipping school and has no curfew anymore!"

Suddenly Greg entered the fray. "Who are you calling a kid? I'm twenty-three years old!"

"You don't even have a job! You haven't lifted a friggin' finger since Mom died!" Michael spouted at Greg, who resumed his silence.

"This is why I wanted us to come here," Maureen said calmly to her family and to me. "Everything's gone downhill since Mom died. And we don't even talk about it. We just argue all the time."

"Maureen is a nurse like her mother. She likes to talk things out," Dad announced amicably, as though no harsh words had been spoken. "I'm not much for that. Maybe all the years on the police force . . . "

"What the hell are you talking about, Dad? Don't you see this family is falling apart?" Michael asked.

"We're just having our difficulties like any family, Michael. I know I'm no replacement for your mother in the kitchen—"

"You're no replacement for Mom anywhere!" Patrick exploded. Again, Dad showed no reaction.

"Does it bother you, Mr. O'Hara, what Patrick just said to you?"

"The boy is just angry. He misses his mother; we all do."

No truer words were ever spoken in my office. I thank the O'Haras for allowing this window into our session, which demonstrates better than any textbook ever could, the impact of death on a family. Different kinds of losses affect families in various ways. The loss of Deidre O'Hara sent her family into a tailspin. Her husband found denial a nice buffer, while Michael decided it was his job to take on his mother's role as disciplinarian. Young Patrick, who sorely missed his mother, became angry and started acting out, while Greg became depressed, quit his job, and stayed home most of the time. Maureen sought out a bereavement group and was making progress in resolving her grief but saw her family slipping downhill and so decided to intervene on their behalf. As a counselor to the bereaved, it is imperative that I remain respectful of cultural differences. Traditions and belief systems vary widely, and we should all try to be considerate of each other's values.

The O'Haras entered into family counseling with a colleague of mine while I worked with Daniel and Patrick individually. Greg began attending his sister Maureen's bereavement group, and Michael chose only to attend family counseling sessions. We still met as a unit every six weeks in an effort to see how things were going for everyone. These were essential sessions for the family to begin communicating with each other in a civilized manner after the dysfunction of their former communication attempts. We worked at allowing each person to share his feelings without interruption. When each member knew that there would be no interruption, they relaxed their defensive postures and began hearing one another. It was only a few sessions before the family began working toward healing together. Deidre was still terribly missed, but as Maureen said, "Mom would rest much easier knowing her children were all getting along."

If your family member has died, things will never be exactly as they were. Each member of a family is like a necessary piece of a jigsaw puzzle. When pieces go missing, the puzzle no longer makes sense. Sometimes a trained, objective third party can help bring order to the chaos by helping the family to communicate without all the "lashing out" and "family history" getting in the way. And here's what I know; a new puzzle can be created from the remaining pieces.

Bereavement among elders

In a conversation I had with my ninety-year-old father, he said the following: "I can no longer leave your mother for more than a few hours at a time. I do not wish to, nor do I wish her to leave me alone all day anymore. Your mother is more dear to me now than she ever was. How can I put this?" He searched for the words with which to enlighten me. "We are closer now than we ever were; we are like one person now."

My mother is eighty-nine, and neither parent suffers from Alzheimer's. As of the day this book was written, my parents still live in their own lovely little home, taking care of one another. My family and I are truly blessed by their independence and their presence in our lives.

When my father said these words to me, I needed more explanation.

"We used to have our separate lives, when we were younger," he explained. "I went to my business, your mother was always busy with you girls and her many projects, and we would come back together in the evenings."

I also remember my parents as being fairly social with a great many friends. Since they moved closer to my sisters and me, we have been worried that they had stopped being as outgoing as they used to be. We wondered if they should have moved away from their friends, even though it was their choice to do so. And yet they seem happy. Amazingly, my father has completed writing three novels, on which he worked for two hours a day, every day!

"Any more than two hours of work, or a nine-hole round of golf, is too much of a commitment for me anymore," he told me, "I miss your mother and she misses me. Can you understand that?"

I tried, but I wasn't entirely sure I *could* understand what it was like to be in my parents' well-worn shoes, so I did some research and was astounded with my findings.

In a study published in the *Annual Review of Gerontology and Geriatrics*, it was shown that older persons may narrow their social involvements to avoid especially challenging events and to reduce their social networks by focusing on emotionally rewarding relationships. All that means is that in their wisdom, our seniors have adapted to the aging process by decreasing their social circle to those who count the most to them. Hence, my dad's circle narrowed to golfing buddies, family, and his Rosey (my mom). In another study, published in *Psychology and Aging*, the seniors scored higher than younger persons on measures of "emotional control" and "mood stability" and were shown to be increasingly effective in using coping strategies in regulating emotions.

This research made me increasingly curious. If older people are smart enough to limit their stress and show greater emotional control and mood stability, how do they deal with loss? Everything I was reading suggested that they would cope better with loss than most of us, so I continued to investigate.

It turns out that as a group, seniors *have* better learned to cope with loss than the rest of us. So I guess that means they have a more effective grieving style. Certainly our older family members are constantly coping with changes in physiological functioning and must deal with the many losses that accompany aging. They do become more physically and mentally fragile and more dependent on others for their day-to-day existence. However, with these losses comes a level of acceptance that can be gained only with age.

Multiple loss is prevalent among our elders. The most frequent losses are those of friends and siblings. Although there seems to be a need for more research on this subject, seniors are often relegated to the periphery when their brothers or sisters die. It seems that this population, often negated in life, also tends to be neglected after a death. For example, when an elder sibling dies, who makes the funeral arrangements? In most cases, the surviving spouse or children of the deceased make all the choices. Siblings are rarely consulted on these matters. Yet who's known the deceased the longest? While the spouse and children are comforted and cared for, the aging sibling is often ignored or left to console others. We seem to overlook the fact that this person has suffered a monumental loss as well.

My hope is that we become more aware of the surviving siblings of our older relatives and include them in the mourning process. Perhaps we can have them help with funeral or wake arrangements in some small way. I have seen elderly siblings share a few words about their brothers or sisters at the funeral service. Let's not forget to console them as well.

To lose your husband or wife in these late years—to find yourself without the reassuring presence of the *other*—can be unimaginably painful. We may tend to underestimate this kind of loss because it is expected. Families tend to be more spread out geographically these days, which can mean that older parents are not living near their children when they suffer the loss of a spouse. It may take time and assistance to aid the widow or widower in adjusting to his or her new life. It may require family members to travel and take time off from work to help set up their surviving parent during this transition.

According to MetLife, as many as one-quarter of all women over the age of sixty-five can expect their son to predecease them. Loss of an adult child tests even our seniors' ability to adjust. A mother or father of any age suffers untold agony from the loss of a child, but our elders experience persistent, intense grief, monumental survival guilt, and severe yearning. They are at risk for complicated grief. In one study, the health status of the elderly after the loss of a child declined at a more rapid rate than the rest of the population.

This type of loss may be best helped in a group setting among other grieving older adults. I once sat in on such a bereavement group at a senior center and witnessed a very effective session. There was no leader for this group, so each member took a turn running the group each week. Beatrice led the group that night. Her son had died of cancer.

Beatrice instructed the group: "Next week, I'd like everyone to bring in two pictures of their deceased child: one when they were little and the last one you have of them when they were healthy."

The next week I attended again and was astonished by what I saw. Every member followed Beatrice's instructions and, in turn, displayed the two photos of each beloved child, at the beginning and end of life. They spoke about when the photos were taken, passing them around to one another. They laughed, cried, and talked all the while. It was one of the most healing groups I'd ever seen. For one hour, their children were alive again. Someone was interested in the life that had graced these parents and the world. I was truly touched.

Haven't we all experienced the need to speak about our children? John made the baseball team; Mary just graduated law school. How must it feel to have nurtured your child through all of these things, watch her blossom into an adult, perhaps raise a family of her own, only to have her prematurely snatched from you? If you are an older adult and have experienced a devastating loss, don't hesitate to reach out for help. Senior centers are a good start. Many older people even share with one another during other activities like cards or sewing groups.

What can *we* do for those who have lost adult children? We can listen. How we care for our seniors is a reflection on our humanity. Let us not neglect this wonderful group in its need for bereavement help.

9

—

WILL IT
EVER END?

UNTIL

We are here
but for a short while,
Let us leave a light behind.

I am here
but for an instant,
in the cosmic glow of time.

See me shine
for just a moment,
in this mystic realm sublime

We shall meet
in other doorways,
I will call your name again.

We shall touch
beyond together,
Heaven keep you until then.

—*Judy Heath*

—

ACCEPTANCE

The term *resolution* in conjunction with grief can be misleading. Although we have clearly discussed the meaning of unresolved grief and how individuals get stuck in grief, the resolution of grief is not so cut and dried.

I prefer the term *acceptance* to *resolution*. Acceptance means to come to terms with something—the realization of a fact or truth resulting in somebody's coming to terms with it. For our purposes, acceptance means that the griever has found a way to incorporate the loss into his reality.

In a recent study on the "stage theory of grief" published in the *Journal of the American Medical Association*, "acceptance" was found to be the most frequently endorsed item by the study's participants. This seemed astounding to me until I further investigated the study to find that the mean age of the participants was 62.9 years of age and that over 83 percent of the participants had lost spouses to natural and not traumatic causes. As discussed in the previous chapter, older people are obliged to do a great deal of accepting along the way, as they have weathered many of life's challenges and usually some prior losses. Acceptance comes more readily to this population.

Acceptance does not imply that you have stopped missing the person who died. Let me illustrate with an example:

Beth and Peter lost their son Greg to leukemia at the age of eight. Being the parents of two other children, they were determined to heal and move on, so that they could "be there" for their surviving son and daughter. Devastated by her loss, Beth took a six-month leave of absence from her job. She entered into therapy with a grief counselor and also attended meetings for parents who've lost children. Beth was blessed with a supportive extended family, and she and her husband had an incredible group of friends—in other words, the best-case scenario.

Peter also had a supportive family but was unable to take time from his job. Trying not to ignore the agony of his loss, Peter also joined the group and occasionally attended counseling individually. Both were actively involved in helping to raise money for continued research for the study of the disease.

I saw the couple three years after the death of their son. "We have done everything we're supposed to do," Beth assured me, "but I'm not better. We're not better!" Peter sat silent as his wife continued to run down the litany of what they had done to resolve their grief. Finally he spoke.

"I feel like a robot going through the motions of life," he stated simply.

It struck me that this couple was like the perfect poster couple for how to deal with grief, but they were "trying" so damn hard to do things properly that they really weren't listening to their own hearts or each other's words. Certainly they had made progress since their son died, yet in their own ways they were stuck.

"You don't get a report card at the end of this," I said gently. "There *is* no true resolution of grief."

This angered Beth so much she stood and told me I was incompetent and stormed out of my office. Peter apologized and excused himself to follow his wife, but not before turning back to me and saying, "I want to learn more about this. I'll call you tomorrow." I nodded and the session abruptly ended.

The next day I spent some time on the phone with Peter. "Beth is really sorry for the way she acted," he explained.

"It's OK, that's how she felt."

"She has been hysterical ever since last night, like when our son first died."

I was not really surprised. "How do *you* feel?" I asked.

"I'm confused. Beth has been great about gathering all the information she could about grief so that we could move through this thing and still be there for our other kids."

I noted that Peter had euphemized the death of his son into "this thing" in an attempt to distance himself from the real feelings. Freud called this "intellectualization." Peter went on, "She read about resolving grief and how important it is. We did everything they tell you. It didn't work. It doesn't work! I am so sad, Judy." And now he cried. He sat on his phone at work, muffling his tears, and my heart went out to him.

"Peter, the resolution of grief does not remove the sorrow completely. We have loved deeply and will always miss that person in our lives. You can't force yourself to resolve the irresolvable."

"But then what do I do?"

"You learn to live with it, to move on despite the pain. You continue to work toward funding for future victims, if that gives you satisfaction. You let yourself grieve without the timetable."

"I want to set up another appointment for Beth and me."

"Of course, but are you sure Beth wants to come back?"

"She does. She asked me to make the appointment."

Two nights later Beth and Peter returned to my office. Beth had the bloodshot eyes of early grief. I went through with her what I had previously explained to her husband. She was very angry: "Well then why do the books and articles tell you that there's a resolution to grief?"

"Because, in a sense, there is." She looked questioningly at me. "Not counting these past few days, how many bad days do you have versus good days, now, three years after Greg's death?"

"I don't know. It's not really whole days anymore, so much. I mean I still have days where I pull the covers up over my head and see no one, but that doesn't happen often. Mostly it just comes and goes."

"Would you say you have accepted the reality of your son's death?" I asked.

"Well, it's not what I expected, and it sucks," she replied. "I wanted to be better! When will I be better?"

"You *are* better. You are better than you were. But, Beth, this is not a medical condition."

At this point we listed all the ways in which Beth had returned to a more normal life. This is helpful to do toward an understanding of acceptance. We concentrate on progress, not resolution.

Beth is a perfectionist; she was like that before her son died. The way she grieves includes the characteristics she possessed before her loss. Working on her need for perfectionism in sessions to come carried over into Beth's progress toward acceptance.

INTERNALIZATION OF A LOVED ONE

As I sat on the staircase, the sun poured in through the skylight illuminating and warming the space around me. It was the very staircase I had traveled up two steps at a time on the night that Jesse died. As the warmth encompassed me, there was an oddly comforting sensation in my chest as I felt Jesse's small heart blending into my own. It was a moment of enlightenment, in which I knew that my son Jesse had become a part of me in a whole new way. It is impossible to relate the peace that fell upon me, for it was in this moment that I knew Jesse was a part of me forever.

What is *internalization*? Famous French novelist Marcel Proust said, "You will not be cured, but . . . one day—an idea that will horrify you now—this intolerable misfortune will become a blessed memory of a being who will never again leave you." As always, my patients have taught me more about this than any textbook ever could.

My patient Judy had been down the path of grief before with her mother and was granted the wisdom to transition quickly after her sister's death. "I feel her with me now," she told me. "I laugh and tell her things. I know she's there. People probably think I'm crazy, but I don't care. I'm happy again."

My dear friend Sue, whose infant daughter Kelly died, once told me, "She's with me in a way my other children cannot be. I worry constantly about Chris and Taylor, but Kelly is safe—and she's always with me."

So, what is internalization? Is it wishful thinking and denial? I don't think so. If that were the case, I believe people would experience it much sooner after their loved one's death in an effort to soothe themselves. But it doesn't happen that way. It seems to come about much later, when a person has found some acceptance of her loss. In an amazing old pamphlet I was given by my first supervisor, John Erskine describes it this way: "I know by personal experience that the dead whom we have loved do not leave us, but in some fashion continue here as faithful companions, sustaining and inspiring us. We find them in familiar places, in the home, in the garden, on the street. This constant resurrection of the dead is for me a simple fact, a part of my human acquaintance with the daily mystery and beauty of life."

Beth, although initially angry with me, continued to come to sessions and, true to her perfectionistic nature, demanded to know "What is this *internatization*?"

"Beth, I can't really explain it. It's just that sometimes, usually well after a loss, people seem to find a new sense of peace. Some have even restructured their lives because of their loss and become happier, more fulfilled individuals. You have certainly changed your life since Greg's death. Doesn't it reflect more of your beliefs than your old life did?"

"Yes," she nodded, "but, I don't have this 'peace' you're talking about. I am not peaceful!"

"Give it time."

She huffed and puffed a bit but kept coming back. A few years later, after she had left therapy, I ran into Beth and Peter at a local restaurant. I couldn't help but notice them across the room. They were with another couple, and I had never seen Beth looking better. There was a serenity about her I had not seen before. On their way out, they spotted me and swung by my table for a quick hello. Beth was radiant. I smile now, remembering what she whispered in my ear: "I'm at peace." That was it.

Internalization does not have to come like a bolt of lightning. "I feel like every year, my dad becomes more and more a part of me," Lou explained. His dad had been gone for three or four years.

As I have tried to emphasize throughout this book, your grief experience will not necessarily follow an exact pattern. That does not mean that you're not normal. Not everyone will experience the sense of internalization, but to deny its existence would be a disservice to all those who have voiced this very essential manifestation of grief.

Believing what you don't see: spirituality

Certainly whole books have been dedicated to this topic, regarding grief. Never is one's spiritual resolve more tested than after a loved one's death. Your world is rocked, and consequently your belief system is as well. We human beings are fascinating creatures; we ask the question "Why?" Why am I here? Why is he gone? We look for answers and don't always get them.

The concept of spirituality here is not meant to be synonymous with religion. Some people who do not attend any organized religious services are surprisingly spiritual, and I have known a few religious people who weren't very spiritual at all.

Many of us have read or heard of the famous book *When Bad Things Happen to Good People*, in which Rabbi Harold Kushner faces his own child's fatal illness. This book, written more than twenty years ago, has lost none of its resonance. People continue to ask "Why me?" when presented with losses of this magnitude. Somehow it helps to know that even rabbis question God.

Although it happened many years ago, I can remember one rainy night like it was yesterday. The roads were slick, and I was winding down a curvy section in my car. The tears were streaming down my cheeks when suddenly, in less than a second, all that sadness exploded into rage. Banging the steering wheel with both fists, I screamed out futilely into the night, "Why the hell did you do this to me? Why? Why? What did I ever do that was so goddamned bad?"

My car aimed at a massive oak tree on the front lawn of a Methodist church. I skidded uncontrollably toward it. It seemed a simple solution at the time: just let the steering wheel go and end the torment. At the last possible moment, I took the wheel in my hands and veered away from the tree.

Afterward, I pulled over to the side of the road in disbelief at my own actions. I thought about my dear little boy at home and wept. Strange to say, but from that day forward I no longer felt alone. I somehow knew I would see my Jesse again. That is not to say I was at peace; in fact, I had only just begun to realize the depth of my anger at God, but my *relationship* with God changed that night on that slippery road. In the days to follow, he allowed for my anger and loved me anyway. No longer was God the powerful figure of my childhood, doling out punishment from his mighty throne. Instead, he became a much closer and comforting figure in my life. I came to know him not as the unforgiving being of my catechism days but as a loving parent. Just as we as parents cry when our children are hurting, I felt God's tears for me on that day.

Each of us has to make peace with our losses in whatever way we can. Anger can be a motivator as much as it can paralyze. Many people have been fueled by loss to make changes in this world; just look at organizations like MADD (Mothers Against Drunk Driving).

That cold forest path can get pretty lonely without an occasional ray of light peeking in among the trees. The divine touches each of us in some way, whether it be through the smile of a child, a fine work of art, or perhaps just a moment, however fleeting it may be, when everything seems to make sense. Many of us travel rapidly through our lives, rushing from work to home, from chore to chore, juggling bills, meals, and obligations. In between, we try to find time for meaningful relationships, hobbies, and relaxation. So, who has time for a spiritual journey? We all do.

As discussed in previous chapters, the death of a loved one slows us down. In her beautiful poem "Parting Drapes," Janet Buck expresses it this way: "Where every clock has lost its dial." Time moves differently for the griever. This seemingly altered state of time allows for thoughts, ideas, and activities previously disregarded or never considered at all. Some people find a sudden interest in spiritually based books with broader, more esoteric themes; some discover time for meditation, even if it's only to sit for a while on a park bench and study the flowers.

I encourage you in the pursuit of spirituality, whatever that may mean for you. Religious or other forms of spiritual services may make you feel closer to God, to your community, or to some universal life force. There are amazing faith communities of all denominations that gather around their hurting members and help them through their losses.

We can choose to become bitter and stagnate or find a way to accept reality and move on. Those who get stuck in the anger and unfairness become bitter. Can one reconcile loss without a belief in God? Of course! A person can choose to go forward simply as a caring human being invested in this world.

I have watched grievers, unable to find true consolation in their religion, find new avenues for their spiritual growth, and I have seen others turn away from the notion that the divine exists at all.

So how does a believer reconcile belief in God and the seeming evil that goes on in this world? If I could answer that, my book would have a different title. I will, however, pass along an explanation some greater minds than mine have espoused. If we were created to have free will, then it stands to reason that God would not intervene at every given opportunity. Humans have made a mess of this planet, even as they attempt to make things right. We pollute the environment and our bodies and wonder why heart disease and cancer have decimated our population. Certainly, we are not to blame for natural disasters and all disease. Unfortunately, we are mortal and fallible. We are a vulnerable, fumbling lot, but there is certainly goodness within us.

Spirituality as it relates to mortality is baffling. Our connection to those who have gone before us is intensely personal. My best friend's mother, who was like a second mother to me, would never say "good-bye" because she found it too final; she preferred "so long" with the addendum "until we meet again." Spirituality is like that for me. We are here but for the blink of an eye yet tied to the infinite through one another. Revere your own interpretation of spirituality and trust the bonds of love. Respect and honor the spiritual beliefs of others.

It has always amazed me how many people report having signs from their departed loved ones—some have moments of feeling their presence while others connect with them in dreams. Are all these people crazy? Or are life and death still beyond our knowledge?

VISITATIONS

At a Loss of Parent bereavement group, Meredith told her story. "I was talking to my mom about cleaning the house," she began, and then corrected herself. "I was complaining loudly, actually." Twenty-year-old Meredith and her mom had lived together before her young mother's untimely death six months earlier. She continued, "Since my mom died I have to do all the housework myself! The other day, I was cleaning dishes, when suddenly I heard a crash upstairs. I ran up to find my mother's favorite book on the floor. It had fallen out of the bookcase, but the weirdest thing was that nothing had caused it to fall and no other books had fallen. It really freaked me out. 'Cut it out, Mom!' I screamed. 'You're scaring me!'" Meredith laughed. "Would you believe, I put the book back, and when I got home from work yesterday, the same book was on the floor again!" She smiled her broad white smile, "Only for some reason it didn't scare me anymore. I just said, 'Hi, Mom!'"

Signs can come in many shapes. Here are two amazing stories that actually occurred. Sue's baby Kelly died in infancy. "Everywhere I go I find these feathers," she told me. "Most of the time they are small feathers, like from baby birds. I never found these feathers before. Now they are everywhere, on my car at work, in my driveway. The other day this woman handed me a feather for no reason. Its Kelly's way of telling me she's all right. I can't tell you how I know this—I just know."

My sister Cathy became astonished when after the death of her husband, her two daughters Ashley and Greer kept finding four-leaf clovers. My brother-in-law Gregory was of Irish descent and had quite a wit. Now I don't know about you, but I have looked long and hard for four-leaf clovers with very little success. These girls found them everywhere. In fact, we were at my son's baseball game one day when the girls found one. "Look!" my bright-eyed little niece exclaimed. "It's Daddy again." Upon inspection, I was mildly shocked to see that it was indeed a true four-leaf clover. I looked for some myself that day but once again came up empty. "We keep them in a jar at home," Ashley informed me.

You can accumulate all the scientific explanations you like, but it won't stop people from believing what they feel in their hearts. And do we really know?

Hallucination is defined as "an apparent perception of an external object when no such object is present." In most cases, this seems pretty simple—if you're seeing things that aren't there, it's not a good sign. In bereavement work, counselors need to consider a broader interpretation of perception. Judging the griever who experiences smelling the soap that was used by his dead grandmother may be detrimental to his grieving process. Better to let a griever talk about how it felt to inhale that fragrance, to feel his loved one's presence. This is called an olfactory hallucination and may be brought about by the intense yearning to have that person back.

DREAMS

The dreams of the grief-stricken fascinate me. Nightmares and erratic sleep tend to follow the death of a loved one. People speak of disembodied images, confusion, and destruction like plane crashes, earthquakes, fires, and the like. At times dreams of voices screaming, sirens, and loud noises jar them awake. As they try to make sense out of the disarray in their lives, these nightmares reflect their unrest.

Traditionally, as the griever comes out of shock, her loved one may appear in her dreams. My own theory about why the deceased doesn't appear right away is that it's too painful for the mind to be with that person during the night and without him in the waking hours. The griever sometimes talks about knowing his loved one was present in his dream, but he couldn't actually see her, or perhaps he hears her imageless voice. I even had one teenager who talked about her deceased father "being in the wings of a stage while the rest of the dream was taking place *on* the stage." She would hear his voice but could not see him or find him. Wow! At first, it may be too painful for the griever to see the deceased, so she works her way up to it.

Professor T. J. Wray and psychoanalyst Ann Back Price of Newport, Rhode Island, have researched grief dreams and believe in the healing power of such dreams. In their book *Grief Dreams*, they break down the dreams people have after the loss of a loved one into four main categories: the visitation dream, the *message dream*, the reassurance dream, and the trauma dream. If you wish to study this information more thoroughly, I have included the book in my bibliography. The following is *my* experience with patients in grief who related their message dreams.

THE MESSAGE DREAM

"I finally saw my sister last night in my dream," one woman told me. "She looked beautiful, like her old self before the cancer. I felt relieved." If you did your own independent poll about how many bereaved people have a version of this dream, you would be astounded. Native Americans believed that their ancestors could communicate with the living through dreams, and early American folklore speaks of this as well. Some believe that we are giving ourselves a message with these dreams. All I can tell you is that people talk about these dreams as being "more vivid." They feel that they have truly been visited.

Recently a young woman named Ashley, whose ex-husband committed suicide, came to see me. Understandably she had great pain over this loss. There were many unanswered questions that continued to disturb her. Her ex had tried to make his death seem like an accidental drowning, tying weights to his body and positioning himself in such a way as to drop off a boat after he shot himself, never expecting his body to resurface. Tormented with a plethora of emotions, Ashley could not make peace. This one day, she arrived at our session filled with a visible energy.

"I had the most amazing dream," she told me. "Greg came to me! It didn't feel the same as other dreams I've had. He was there. I felt his body and it was real! We were on a boat," she continued, "not *his* boat, but a sport fishing boat like the one he sometimes worked on. We were down below talking, and I asked why he hadn't come to me like this before. He told me he had to get special permission from God and that it was hard for him to do this. He had been with his parents and other family members until now. He had his bike with him." She laughed, "Anyone who knew him knew that he rode that bike everywhere. He was never without it! When I asked why he brought it with him, he told me that he needed one more ride." The tears welled up. "He had a message for me. He told me to do what's right and to stand up for myself, like he told me to do." A peace came to her lovely features. "I knew it was him."

Sometimes other people have these dreams *for* us. "I had a dream about my nephew last night," another woman explained. "He was riding on a golden bicycle with wings, and he wanted me to tell my sister that he was at peace." Did this sister's mind create the dream to soothe the boy's grieving mother, or did her nephew send a message through his aunt's dream? I may tell the aunt that she unconsciously created this dream out of longing to ease her sister's pain, but she may still believe that her nephew visited her. Visitation dreams are intense, and message dreams can be startling. They can also be peaceful and soothing. "When I woke, I could feel my mother's arms around me," a teen told me, "and I could smell her perfume. She *was* there. The whole rest of the day I was happy."

RECONCILIATION OF GRIEF

The resolution of grief, in many ways, is only a myth. Although you may never feel your grief is completely resolved, you may come to terms with, or *reconcile*, your loss. The chart on the next page is simply a way to measure your progress along the way.

Keep this chart to refer to along your path of grief. Eventually you will take notice of the progress you have made as you mark off another milestone on your journey. There are no shortcuts out of this dark forest, but you do not have to walk alone.

I have discussed obstructions to reconciliation. We know too well that guilt and anger will tangle us up like thorny vines and keep us from proceeding further on this seemingly endless trail. Many have walked where you are walking now and have survived to step out into the daylight once again. This of course is little concession, but at times all you get is a hand to hold or a kind voice to whisper in your ear.

Our world is drifting further from the elegant and simple truth of life and death. We medicate ourselves like some futuristic species that has outgrown the need for feelings. We replace lost loved ones as though they were as interchangeable as Stepford wife replicants. But

RECONCILIATION OF GRIEF

- ∽ Healthy eating and sleeping patterns resume
- ∽ Integration of happy memories about the deceased
- ∽ More good days than bad
- ∽ Focus and organizational skills return
- ∽ Any trauma associated with the death has been significantly reduced
- ∽ The ability to form new relationships
- ∽ Fewer feelings of loneliness
- ∽ Reduced guilt and anxiety
- ∽ A return to former self-esteem and self-confidence
- ∽ Significant reduction of any self-destructive behavior
- ∽ Growth from the loss
- ∽ Thoughts toward the future
- ∽ Enjoyment of activities again
- ∽ Acknowledgement of passage through the grief process
- ∽ Renewed interest in the world
- ∽ Renewed purpose in life
- ∽ Acceptance of new reality
- ∽ Internalization of loved one

we *can* choose differently. It takes emotional courage to walk the path of grief, from which one emerges changed and hopefully healed into a stronger, wiser human being. You may always be lonely for *that* special person yet move on to make new relationships; this is reconciliation. Just having more good days than bad ones is a form of acceptance.

How are you getting along with other family members and friends? Part of your reconciliation may be to find answers to some of these relationships. Even if relationship problems preceded the death, they may become exacerbated through grief. You may work to mend these relationships or decide to end some of them. Either solution may be interpreted as reconciliation.

I am constantly amazed by the butterfly that emerges from the cocoon of grief. The self-assured person stepping into my office barely resembles the stoop-shouldered individual who first came in for counseling. This is a gratifying miracle to behold. As individuals reconcile their grief, they begin to get back out into the world again. They start to participate in activities that had dropped off and sometimes even add some new ones, as they acknowledge their own growth through the grieving process.

Ryann, a warm and lovely young woman who lost both her younger sister and her father within a short time period, said it this way: "I'm not exactly happy all the time, but sometimes I find myself playing with Aiden [her son] and laughing, and it actually sounds strange to hear myself laughing, you know? But it feels so good to feel normal, even if it's just for that moment. I know I'll never be the same, but I'm coming back to life."

I think about the first time I saw Ryann. She was pallid with circles under her eyes. And how one day, much later, she bounced into my office, her beautiful strawberry blond hair flying behind her, her skin luminous and eyes twinkling as she displayed for me an assortment of gorgeous glass jewelry she had designed and crafted in honor of her sister. It was truly breathtaking. Always an artist, Ryann used to make pottery, but the desire to create lay dormant under her grief. Suddenly as she began to awake from this heavy slumber, so did her need to create, only now it had transformed into something new and amazing.

I have been blessed to see this startling metamorphosis many times. All at once, a person starts talking about life again. In many cases there is a renewed sense of purpose. Some people find a lasting shift in priorities and make insightful decisions about the direction of their lives.

After awakening from the dread of this occurrence, people frequently change their life paths. A new career seems more fulfilling now, a fresh cause emerges, or one just has an altered perception of life's meaning.

Each of us faces mortality in our own way. Saying good-bye brings you closer to the sense that life is ever-changing. Those of you who are able will incorporate your loss into your world. You may hear a widower tell of talking to his deceased wife or a mother mention that her child is always with her now. You may listen as a sister laughs about what her brother would say "if he were here" or a man jokes about asking his dead father for advice on the golf course. What you are hearing is acceptance and internalization; what you are hearing is hope. Henry Wadsworth Longfellow puts it this way:

> *Tell me not, in mournful numbers,*
> *Life is but an empty dream!—*
> *For the soul is dead that slumbers,*
> *And things are not what they seem.*
>
> *Life is real! Life is earnest!*
> *And the grave is not its goal;*
> *Dust thou art, to dust returnest,*
> *Was not spoken of the soul.*

10

ADULT LOSS OF A PARENT

~~~~~~

If you have suffered the loss of a parent, you have probably parted from the person who has known you the longest in this world. This is a profound and painful loss. Yes, it is in the natural order of things, but that doesn't lessen the pain. As a young counselor, I was charged with leading many parental loss bereavement groups, and it was the devastated members who taught me so much about this significant loss. Our identities, like it or not, partially come from our parents.

SOCIETY: Well, at least he had a good long life.
GRIEVER: Yes, and he was a part of *my* life for as long as I have lived!
SOCIETY: He would want you to be happy.
GRIEVER: I am not happy.
SOCIETY: I'm sorry she had to suffer.
GRIEVER: She was my mother, and I couldn't take her pain away!
SOCIETY: You have to be strong for your family.
GRIEVER: My parent was my family too, and I am not feeling strong!

Early bereavement is not the ideal time to be presented with the many choices that follow death. All decisions should be reached collectively, taking into consideration any wishes the parent voiced prior to his death. Far too often, the most dominant sibling makes decisions for the group while the others have been rendered vulnerable by grief. It is often the person least in touch with her emotions who stays level-headed. Remember this and find your voice no matter how shaky it may sound. An elder-law attorney or a bereavement counselor can be helpful in guiding families toward caring and equitable solutions for everyone.

When a child dies, compassionate people offer condolences about "what a tragedy" you have suffered. After the loss of a parent, clichés abound. Most of these clichés negate the feelings of the griever, as if to say, "Hurry up and get over this. You knew it was bound to happen someday."

When a person becomes a widow or widower, society allots him or her several months to "get back on your feet again," although this person, too, is subjected to patronizing clichés. Certainly not afforded the same kind of compassion shown to those who lose children, the widow and widower are still emotionally embraced to a greater degree than the adult whose parent dies.

"What's wrong with me?" people ask themselves. "My mother was old and sick. Why is this so hard for me?"

Let me tell you why. In some cases the relationship with your parent may not have been an easy one. Sometimes the death of a parent leaves a person feeling that he will never be able to "fix" what was unsatisfactory about that relationship. Let's face it, one may have traveled through his most tumultuous years with this person. Some grievers still carry guilt and resentment while others have finally worked through their difficulties, attaining a wonderful bond.

The parent-child relationship is fraught with a spectrum of emotions. Unresolved issues and negative emotions tend to complicate grief. Some parent-child relationships are filled with resentment and anger, leaving the person to mourn what never was. Others deeply grieve the loss of a parent they truly loved and respected.

One group that is particularly hard hit by parental loss is women aged twenty to forty suffering the loss of a mother. This is true primarily because Grandma is often intricately woven into the very fabric of the lives of her daughter and grandchildren. Many grandparents are part of the caretaking of children in today's families. Women with young children may rely on their mothers for advice on child care. The loss of Mom at this age leaves women bewildered and lonely.

"I don't know how I'm going to do this without her," Mandy cried. "My husband works long hours, and Mom was my other set of hands." Her tears held the sorrow of the very close relationship she shared with her mom. "No one understands my kids like her! No one will ever care about them like she did."

Many women whose mothers die young speak of feeling envious when they see mothers and daughters shopping together or enjoying other activities, like taking the grandchildren out to lunch. It's a piercing reminder of what they've lost. "My mom will never see my children grow up and my children will never know my mother," one young mother, Sheri, told me. "I'm not sure the baby will even remember her at all."

We talked about how Sheri could make a photo album for her children and talk to them about their grandmother. It's not the same, I know, but it's what we *can* do.

As mentioned earlier, the grief process is influenced by the age of the griever and at what point in his life he loses his parent. Childhood loss of a parent is obviously devastating, but adult loss of a parent is still pivotal in one's life. Why? Think about it: no one has known you as long or shares the same history. We may be fathers, husbands, mothers, or wives, but we are always "children" to our parent. When both parents die, we are no longer children to anyone. In the ideal sense, no one cherishes you unconditionally the way a parent does.

Although we do not *all* experience this ideal relationship, parents still influence who we become. Whether we are emulating our parents or rebelling against them, our thoughts, morals, and even our physical beings began with them. Whether their influence has waned over time or we have chosen to part from their teachings, they are a part of our history. Perhaps a parent was abusive and responsible for a poor self-image; still, that parent held a position of power in the life of his child at one time, thereby profoundly influencing her. The loss of an abusive parent may bring with it a feeling of relief or may surprise you by conjuring up sorrow for the things you truly loved about that parent. You may even find yourself grieving the parent you never had. Grief is multifaceted and sometimes baffling.

Secondary loss issues readily surface after parental loss. Issues of inheritance and money may become paramount. Sadly, I have witnessed families torn apart after the death of a parent. Many times this plays out through financial matters, but if you delve into the history of the family, the seeds of destruction have often been growing for years.

In one case, Sarah did most of the caregiving for her elderly father. Her three siblings could barely find time to visit him with their "busy" schedules. Mother to three children, Sarah had her hands full with her own family, and in his later days, her father demanded quite a bit of care. Although her siblings *did* contribute to the home health care, Sarah and her husband bore the bulk of the day-to-day responsibility. She uprooted her family, sold their home, and moved in with Dad. Excessive? Perhaps, but at the time no one else had a better plan. In fact, they were more than happy to let Sarah disrupt her life to temporarily solve their mutual problem.

It was only one week after Dad died that the siblings started clamoring to put his house on the market so that they could all get their fair share of the proceeds. Exhausted and shell-shocked, Sarah complied. It was then she came into therapy.

What a horrible family, you say? Believe me, this kind of thing happens more often than you would imagine. Unfortunately, this scenario had been set up many years ago when Sarah was just a little girl and used to help Mom cook dinner while the others were out playing or when she would thanklessly cover for her brother when he had too much to drink. Does Sarah deserve this kind of treatment? Absolutely not, but this world is not fair, and Sarah let her caretaking go too far.

To avoid this kind of thing, family members may want to sit down with a reputable elder-law attorney. These attorneys are knowledgeable about dealing with the death of an elderly parent. If the family's financial affairs can be put into order before crisis strikes, they might escape this kind of agony. To all you wonderful "Sarahs" out there, I offer these words of advice: it is right to help your ailing parents, but you must also learn how to take care of yourself. This may mean seeking therapy, legal advice, or group support. If you do not heed this advice, you run the risk of becoming an angry, resentful martyr or an easy target.

Family dynamics often play out after a parent's death. People act out old roles and aren't even cognitively aware of what they are doing. Many families unravel during these difficult times, never to be mended again. It is sad to witness and tragic to experience. A family counseling session can be helpful at such a time or just a good old-fashioned "sit-down" with everyone included. Just set some ground rules about name calling and finger pointing. It may help to have a trusted family friend or objective onlooker to referee. Many lifetime grudges start with insignificant occurrences that get blown into full-fledged wars.

Sometimes men come into counseling after parental loss. Dave comes to mind. He appeared one night at one of my groups. This was a man whose ducks were always in a row. An accountant by trade, he spoke of a well-ordered life. He was manicured and impeccably dressed. Dave explained that now that his kids were older, he and his wife had begun to vacation and dine out more often. What I remember most about Dave was how embarrassed he was by his tears whenever he spoke about his dad. Inevitably, he would start to share with the group and when the tears started, he stopped. "I'm sorry," he repeated to us. "I'm sorry."

I expected him to run from the group, mortified by his display of emotion. Thankfully, Dave kept coming. After several weeks, he was finally able to tell us his story.

"My dad and I never really had much in common. He was a man's man, into sports. He made his living with his hands, in construction. He used to take me to the sites where he worked, but I really didn't have much interest. I liked numbers and was always a good student. Dad was proud of me; he supported all my endeavors. I respected his work and the way he treated my mom."

He choked up a bit. "When I was young, I looked down on him." His head lowered and he spoke quietly. "I didn't like that he had dirt under his fingernails or that he dressed like a slob. I had no right to judge him!"

Dave choked back the tears, anxious now to get his truth out. "Just the past couple of years I came to realize what an exceptional human being my father was. My kids loved him so much. He was never too tired to throw the ball around with them and never missed their games." He closed his eyes for a moment. "More recently we began to hang around together. He'd come over and watch football or I'd meet him for lunch. We got close—really close, you know?"

When Dave's eyes met mine, it wasn't guilt I saw, just sorrow. "I wish I had gotten closer to him, younger. I just wish I had more time."

It is natural, as we grow older, to become more attached to our partners and children, but that does not negate the special place that parents hold in our hearts. No one can fill that place. Dave continued to express his great sorrow for the next couple of sessions, and then a transformation happened. The good memories began to surface.

Firefighter Tyrone was devastated when his elderly father died of pneumonia. In fact, he came into counseling for this loss. "I know it's ridiculous," he said. "The man was eighty-six years old—but he was everything to me." Tyrone and his wife helped to care for his sick father for a number of years before his death. "He was my mentor. It was because of him that I went into the department. Everyone knew him. He was so good to everybody." The tears streaked down his face. "My father and my grandma raised me and my brother after our mother died. He helped care for my children when my wife and I worked. He was always there for me—always! I can't believe he's gone."

Tyrone's father was the rock on which he'd built his life, his foundation. With that foundation gone, Tyrone felt shaken, unstable.

A testament to his father, Tyrone had truly grieved the passing of his mom in childhood. Before the benefits of including children in grief rituals were understood, Tyrone's dad made sure he and his brother were a part of everything. "Dad framed pictures of my mother for my brother and me and put them in our rooms. We talked openly about her and would tell lots of stories about her. I think that's why I remember her so well, even though I was only eight when she died."

Losing the first parent is different than both parents having died. After one parent's death, you are still someone's child. After the second parent dies, people feel completely alone. If you have no partner or children, you may experience "a disconnect" from your past, your ancestors, and your history. People speak of feeling orphaned, no matter what their ages. You may feel as though you've lost the ties that bind you to the rest of humanity, like part of a broken branch from the family tree. It can be disorienting and terribly lonely. Your spouse doesn't totally get it—because he still has his tree intact. You may love his family, but they are not your flesh and blood.

You may find yourself jealous of others who still have their parents and then guilty for those feelings. This is normal! "I don't want to be around my husband's parents right now. They haven't done anything wrong, it just makes me miss mine more!" one woman explained.

As stated often in this book, you are entitled to your feelings, and right now that may include jealousy. You are not an evil person just because you can't handle your in-laws at the present time. Explain to them how you feel or give them this chapter to read to help support your position. This *will* lift in time, but you must honor your needs right now.

Parental relationships are complicated and change over time. In the ideal sense our parents are our first teachers. They provide guidance and direction. When both parents are gone, your sense of security can vanish. There may no longer be a "home base." A role that you have fulfilled your entire life is gone. At eighty-nine years of age, my mother still introduces me as her baby. How I used to cringe when she'd say, "This is Judy, she's the baby of the family." Now I smile, knowing that one day I won't be anyone's baby.

Parental loss also brings us psychologically one step closer to our own death. Although we may find a way to bury the reality of our own mortality, unconsciously we grapple with this eventuality. If my parent is still living, I have a barrier between this world and the next. When Mom and Dad are gone, theoretically, I'm next. Aside from that, we have become the elders of the family, changing our roles yet again.

11

LOSS OF A CHILD

NIGHT

Oh night upon my heart does fall
As cries into the stars, I call.
Come back, my sweet cherubic boy,
Who takes with him my every joy.

But for the twinkle of your eyes
The laughter of your sweet surprise
Like fluffy clouds are parted now
How does this sin my God allow?

Like howling birds my face to scar
While stuck within this blackened
*   tar*
No light to warm the darkness here,
Or Angels to my night appear.

And now a small hand touches
*   mine,*
With warmth upon its fingertips.
I struggle for his face to see
He kisses me with softest lips

Oh God send forth your heavenly
*   light*
To lessen my unending night
And free me from "what might have
*   been"*
To let me live and love again
*   —Judy Heath*

In a sense, this is the most difficult chapter for me to write, as it is
the reality of this loss in my life that eventually led to this book.
Let me start by saying that the death of a child may be the single most

devastating event that can occur in a person's lifetime. It goes against nature and what we perceive as the natural order of life. However, many people are forced to accept this grievous injustice and go on.

If you have suffered the loss of a child, my heart goes out to you. You will never be the same—no matter what they tell you. To have a limb ripped from your body would be easier. But please stay with me, for it is here that I will share personally in a way I have not done before, in an attempt to reach you honestly. Although self-disclosure is somewhat controversial in many aspects of the therapeutic process, most bereavement counselors will tell you that this policy does not always hold true for grief therapy. When you have looked into the eyes of those who have lost children, the book goes out the window.

"How can you possibly understand?" they want to know.

MY STORY

It was January 1985, and I decided to go to dinner and the movies with my best friend, Jeannie, and her mother. I remember the movie, *Starman*, and the English pub–like restaurant in Huntington, Long Island, where we dined. I had left my three-year-old son, Carll, and my five-month-old son, Jesse, home with their father and the young girl next door who babysat for us. Upon my return, between eleven thirty and midnight, the house was dark and quiet. The moment I stepped through the front door, I knew something was wrong. I moved quickly toward Jesse's room and found his crib empty. Propelled by an inner dread, I took the steps two at a time up to my bedroom. There I found Jesse, cold and with a pale bluish pallor to his skin, on the bed next to my husband. I screamed and shook Jesse, but he did not respond. I vaguely remember blood on the sheets. The rest of the story I have pieced together, although I'm not entirely sure how accurate it is, because I had entered into a state of shock from the extreme trauma of the events.

My husband attempted to perform mouth-to-mouth resuscitation on Jesse as I called 911. What I heard next were the haunted cries of a wounded animal in anguish as my husband hollered out my name. He had discovered what I already knew: our son Jesse was dead.

The paramedics arrived and attempted to revive our son to no avail. From the back of the house, my son Carll and the babysitter emerged. I remember seeing them through a haze. The paramedics worked on Jesse, but I knew he was gone and I didn't want to see him that way. I went away—far away to a place in my head from which I did not return for a very long time.

The trip to Huntington Hospital, where they took our Jesse, was a blur. Some doctor was muttering to us details that didn't seem to matter. Jesse was gone. My beautiful, chubby baby was taken from me. There was no point in listening to anything or anyone ever again.

After that, the memory fades into endless hours of gray with a stray bit emerging here and there. I recall my beautiful friend Terry standing in the snow like an angel waiting for our return from the hospital. She handed me a hot toddy. I remember needing to hold my little boy, Carll. I remember calling my dear friend and therapist Pirkko and asking her for the words to tell Carll that his brother was dead.

I was treading water in limbo, moving weighty arms and legs in an effort to keep from sinking into the murky abyss. I was numb, but beneath the numbness beat a painful throb that threatened to explode. The only presence that penetrated this hellish limbo was Carll. He was the lifeline for me now; his sweet face and voice were all that kept me from plummeting irretrievably downward.

My husband was there in his own hell, but we were separate. After a couple of days of not sleeping, his eye began to twitch. A phone call came that echoed through our separate limbos. Jesse had died of sudden infant death syndrome. Now we had a name. Later, a very kind woman from the SIDS Foundation called and answered our questions. Barbara told us that there was nothing we could have done to prevent such a death and explained to me why there had been blood on the sheets, an aspect of Jesse's death that haunted me. She said that when a body of any age shuts down, it automatically gets rid of all fluids that are drained from the internal organs. Although it was tinged with red, this was not just blood. This was not comforting, but we needed to know, to understand. After that, my husband's eye stopped twitching and he was able to grab some sleep.

I do not recall making any decisions about the funeral except that I wanted little Jesse's coffin closed in the church. There was an outpouring from the community, and thousands of dollars were collected for the SIDS Foundation in Jesse's name. I floated through the funeral aware that the church had standing room only and that my father, always my tower of strength, was there next to me. I grabbed onto his hand to keep from drifting away from a world that seemed so unreal to me now. The sermon, given by Pastor Michael Lindvall, provided some of the most touching and profound words I had ever heard spoken in any church, and they will live with me forever. But nothing could touch the pain—nothing. Not my parents, nor my sisters, who lay on my bed with me and surrounded me with love; not my best friend, Jeannie, who moved into my guest bedroom for two solid weeks. They tried, but there was nothing anyone could do.

My sister Robin, who did not live locally, called daily and just talked to me. Her voice was soothing and calmed me down. She constantly sent me cards and small gifts of love. Sister Cathy made the drive from Manhattan to Long Island and back home again, every day, a major effort that I will never forget. Sister Bonnie knew Jesse best of all my siblings, and she would speak to me of her memories of him, while providing support for my son and husband as well. No person on Earth could have been more blessed or supported, but it couldn't touch my pain.

I am endlessly grateful for all who were there as I emerged from this purgatory, because although treacherous, the muck I had been floating through kept me buffered from the reality of my personal hell. Once I surfaced, the pain tore at my very being. Gratefully, I'd drift back into the fog for a while longer, but the clouds of my denial were growing thinner and less able to cushion me from the truth. My baby was gone . . . my beautiful, precious baby. . . . This is how it is when shock and denial wear away.

Ridiculously, we took the February vacation to Florida we had previously planned. I remember staying at my parents' home, and my mother, also devastated by the loss, did her best to help me. Just being in her lovely home was comforting and familiar. How I clung to poor little Carll, playing games with him and watching him in the pool with his father. My husband was grappling with his own demons, which pushed us further apart.

During this time, my stomach constantly ached and I ate next to nothing. I remember looking at myself in the mirror and thinking that I appeared like pictures of people I'd seen at concentration camps. In the subsequent year, I got down to 107 pounds (I am 5'6½")! The anxiety and relentlessness of the grief eventually led to a diagnosis of Crohn's disease and an emergency operation to remove the ulcerated portion of my colon. Crohn's disease is a chronic disorder that causes inflammation of the digestive or gastrointestinal tract.

I went to therapy and began attending SIDS meetings, but I could not begin to grieve properly until the trauma was gotten through. Because I lived this nightmare, I know what one's brain and body can do in grief. Thank God I had some enlightened professionals who intervened to help me learn to begin to accept my loss and to process anxiety differently.

I got better. No, I will never stop missing my son, but he has become a part of me in a new way. Ever thankful to have traversed this horrific passage and finally enter back into the land of the living, I came to see it as my honor to help others to do the same. Just as a social worker named Pirkko Montner, a former surgeon turned author named Dr. Bernie Siegel, and an innovative gastroenterologist named Dr. Alan Toffler, among many others, helped put Humpty Dumpty back together again, I now had the desire to pass along their combined wisdom of mind and body to others.

SHOCK AND HORROR

I've heard it said that when a child dies there is a rip in the universe. No parent is ever prepared for such an event. There is no rehearsal for this. I feel that often fathers are neglected when a child dies. What is the saying? "Every mother's worse nightmare"? What about Dad? He carries the outdated role of "provider" and is traditionally the *one* in charge of guarding his family and keeping them safe. We all know that societal roles have changed, but men still talk about letting their family down when they fail to keep them safe.

Both mothers and fathers often speak of failure when a child dies. Just as I blamed myself for being out the night Jesse died, his father was left with the guilt of being *there* and still not being able to prevent the death. Guilt takes on new meaning for parents of a dead child. And where there is guilt, there is blame. Sometimes when a person's guilt becomes too much to bear, he may shift the blame onto somebody else. There is nobody more convenient for this than one's partner. If a marriage is to survive the death of a child and be anything besides a bitter coexistence, counseling is often mandatory. In some cases blame is not a component of the scenario, and in ideal cases, couples bolster each other up and work together, but this may not happen right away or at all.

Recently, it has been my privilege to counsel a couple who suddenly lost their adult child. The excruciating pain that entered my office with Connie and Ted was overshadowed by the awe-inspiring bond of love and commitment they shared for one another and their surviving son, Ryan. When Connie came she talked about her husband and asked how he was doing with his therapy, while Ted was more concerned for his wife. Ryan attended college in another city but made the trip home often, to grieve along with his folks. A former US Marine, Ted had faced his own hardships in life and had to keep a brave face on at work. But he was unafraid to cry, and he took the opportunity to do just that on weekends and in my office.

As a trauma respiratory therapist, Connie had worked in hospitals dealing with trauma, and life and death, every day. She described her vocation as "never staying in one location but all over the hospital saving what lives I can and being with people when they take their last breath. I consider it an honor to be present when a person leaves his body and makes his way to heaven."

Another person might not have been able to return to such work after the devastating loss of an adult son, but Connie did. Less than a year after her son Christopher's death, she had already decided to put together a continuing-education-credit talk for health care workers to hopefully help them be better managers, coworkers, friends, partners, siblings, and family members.

"It blows my mind," she explained, "that death is a part of life, yet no one ever talks about it—and, even worse, no one knows how to handle it, even when it's right in our face at work."

I am continually amazed at the human spirit and fortitude. So much is made of our frailties and base nature, in the press, books, and movies—everywhere. I am truly blessed to witness the beauty, vulnerability, and strength of the human being daily.

You have already read in chapter 8 about how men and women grieve differently. This is most evident when a child has died. To ignore this reality or regard it as sexist is foolish. It is best to acknowledge these different styles and not to judge one another. If you have just lost a child, your marriage may not seem important to you right now; probably nothing does. That is no reason to throw it all away. Remember that your partner is the only other person who shares this loss as a parent, and although that may not matter to you right now, it may have meaning for you someday. Therapy may allow a couple to traverse this perilous time and find one another again.

"Being around my wife just reminds me of my little girl and what I've lost." Scott said, miserably. "I just don't want to go home anymore. So I stay later at the office and then I go out for a couple of drinks after work. It's deadly at the house. Kim is always crying, and I can do nothing to soothe her."

Kim said, "I've lost my daughter and now I'm losing Scott. He comes home smelling like booze every night and then just passes out in the bed. We have nothing to talk about anymore. Nothing left between us."

Obviously this couple chose therapy. It doesn't always work. Scott continued to drink heavily and eventually left the marriage. Kim continued counseling and reconciled her grief. She is a happy, productive person today with a new husband and two subsequent children.

If you have lost a child, you may be having great difficulty moving past the grief. It is such a profound loss. Not only have you lost the face, the touch, the sound of your child (of any age), you have lost his or her future. You have been cheated out of every change or growth you should have shared with him or her. You may have been robbed of his missing teeth or his first school play. If your child was older you will never see her prom or her wedding or enjoy your grandchildren. Each birthday marks another year that has been taken from you. No wonder you're angry and so remarkably sad.

When a child dies, people stop talking about him. To the parent whose identity has been linked with a child, it is strange. "How's your daughter?" friends and coworkers constantly ask, and parents proudly share the latest news about their children. Now nobody asks anymore. It's as though that child never existed.

If you've lost a young child, well-meaning people will tell you, "You'll have more children," as though your child was as interchangeable as a goldfish. But you cannot fault people who are as baffled by the incomprehensibility of this occurrence as you are. What could anyone say that might make sense of such a thing? So, they stay away. People whose children have died talk about feeling stigmatized. I learned this from people I counseled and I experienced it firsthand.

I was once in the ladies room at a tennis club when I overheard some women talking about me. "She looks so thin," one woman said. "I heard her baby died," said another. I didn't know whether to step out of the stall to end the whispers or just hide in there. Luckily, the conversation ended abruptly when one woman checked her watch, and they hurried off. Looking back and trying to honestly assess my feelings, it was a profound vulnerability, humiliation, and anger. It was as though my heart were exposed for all the world to see and poke at. Naturally, I hold no malice toward those women, who were simply human beings, doing what we do; we wonder, we question, we gossip. It is all natural and normal. The sensitivity of a grieving mother or father is greatly amplified.

Another time I was invited to a woman's home for a luncheon. Seated at her table, I realized that her dining room window overlooked the cemetery where Jesse was buried, and I could actually see Jesse's grave. Although I did not know this woman well, a good friend of mine was also at the luncheon, and she never even considered my position. Needless to say, for a woman who never takes a drink during the day (I fall asleep), I downed a couple of glasses of wine that afternoon before crying my way home in the car. Should I have spoken up? Those of you who have lost somebody *know* what that would have cost me. First, I would have disrupted the luncheon, and second, it would mean exposing my tears to people I didn't know well. I share these personal experiences in the hope that you grieving parents and others will better understand the emotional turmoil that exists in mourning.

When a young child dies, you lose his future and his loving acceptance of *you* as the center of his world. When an older child dies, you lose that human being you've nurtured and kept safe through illness, helped through school projects, and cheered through accomplishments. You lose the friendship and unique bond that has formed through all your years together, and so along with the future, you lose the past.

Many losses stigmatize the griever. People who have lost a family member to suicide have the worst of it. People tend to act like some forms of death are contagious. Grief can also estrange you from others. When other mothers and fathers are discussing their children's new swing sets, verbalizing a dilemma about what words to put on your child's gravestone seems unspeakably bizarre.

SURVIVING AND SUBSEQUENT CHILDREN

If your child has died, the children that remain living are known as surviving children. I've always hated that term. It sounds as though they managed to escape that which annihilated their sibling. Whenever a child of any age dies, there is guilt. It is not surprising that brothers and sisters often feel responsible for their sibling's death. If conflict existed in their relationship, which is often the case, brothers and sisters regret the animosity after the sibling's death. They feel guilty for not treating that person better.

As adults we tend to negate or trivialize the true impact of death on young children. I might have been tempted to do the same but for my son, Carll. When his baby brother Jesse died, he was about to turn four. Carll anticipated the coming of his brother as siblings do, through the actions and words of the adults around him. He was excited about the arrival of Jesse, though quizzical about how it would change his life. He embraced his baby brother immediately, feeding him bottles and driving his minicar to make deliveries—as the much-acclaimed superhero "Diaper Man"! Carll was a natural big brother. Along with his father and I, he watched his brother grow in size and abilities. Soon Jesse was enthralled with his big brother's every move—his best audience.

Jesse was a lovely, chubby baby who liked to coo and laugh. Every night, Carll would kiss his brother goodnight and look for him in the morning. On that tragic morning, Carll awoke to find Jesse's crib empty. I had learned the words to say to my sweet, blue-eyed boy about the death of his brother, but his heart could no more be healed than my own. I witnessed his grief firsthand. Always full of questions, Carll had many about his brother. The suddenness of a seemingly healthy baby's death was incomprehensible to any of us. Imagine this young child's fear that this could happen to anyone. Consequently he began to worry about all kinds of things. It wasn't enough to convince him item by item that everything would be OK. He needed to relearn how to think like an innocent child, to trust the world again.

Of course I would like to think that I handled the situation flawlessly by spending inordinate amounts of time trying to overcompensate for Carll's loss. But I'm quite certain that a hidden camera from that period in my life would reveal a ghost-like creature (me) trying to force a smile on a troubled face. I was probably often preoccupied with my own grief and certainly only a facsimile of the parent I had once been. But Carll's father and I did our best. I am grateful that I sought counseling, which helped me to move through my grief and taught me how to help my son.

In grief, surviving children also seek to console their parents, and Carll was a born caretaker. He would lie by me, clutching his yellow blanket and snuggling. He brought me goodies from the kitchen and drew me pictures. One day he drew the most beautiful picture of a little boy in a colorful scene of rainbows and flowers. I was astounded when he announced that it was his brother, Jesse, in heaven. I knew he had begun to heal, and this gave me the courage to do the same.

I became pregnant only six months after Jesse's death. I probably wasn't emotionally or physically ready, but it happened. Nine months later, our beautiful Abby was born. She was perfect, achieving a nine out of ten on the Apgar test of health given at birth. But unlike the prior two pregnancies, this one was filled with fear. Her father and I obsessed about whether or not to have a baby monitor attached to the infant when sleeping, despite the fact that at the time there were no known preventative measures to stop sudden infant death syndrome.

Parents today are asked to have their babies sleep on their backs and to avoid fluffy bedding or large stuffed animals in their babies' sleeping area. Bed sharing or bringing one's baby into bed is discouraged, as is smoking during or after pregnancy. These are risk factors that can be minimized, while the infants' abnormalities are still not fully understood. Research shows that SIDS is not hereditary.

After learning I was pregnant, I found an extraordinary obstetrician who was one of only 250 qualified in high-risk pregnancies in this country. Dr. Wilson's kindness, humor, and compassion were invaluable to me.

"Don't forget to bring the M&M's," he instructed when I called to tell him I was on my way to the hospital.

"What?" I cried in a frenzy.

"They're for me!" he chuckled.

I stopped along the way and arrived for delivery, M&M's in hand.

With Jesse gone only a little over a year, I was in ragged shape. I hired Maureen to help me with my daughter, and she was like an angel. Anxiety is a very real part of all death. I didn't know then, but I do now, what a smart move it was bringing Maureen into our lives.

The fear of those first few months was overwhelming. If you have ever seen the movie *Terms of Endearment*, there is a scene in which Shirley MacLaine's character crawls into the crib next to her sleeping baby. I all but did this every night. With the amount of times that Abby's father and I woke her up to see if she was breathing, I am amazed that she never developed a sleep disorder.

What I am about to admit is difficult for me but essential if you are to understand my state of mind in grief. I was afraid to bond with my daughter. This magnificent ray of sunlight that streamed into our family's life in the form of a dear baby was the source of my greatest fear. I would hand her to Maureen or to her father, often with trembling hands.

"Not to worry," Maureen would assure me in her lovely Irish lilt, "Abby will be fine. She is a strong child, and look at how she smiles."

One day it lifted. I simply could not stand on the outside of this child's life, waiting for the other shoe to drop. What is the old saying— "In for a penny, in for a pound"? There was no holding back from this adorable baby. My sister Cathy used to say that Abby was born with a sense of humor—and it was contagious.

HOW TO HELP YOURSELF AFTER THE LOSS OF A CHILD

Time. How often have we heard it—time heals all wounds. *This* wound doesn't mend easily or completely. There is more of a chance for complicated grief after a child's death, because it is simply less acceptable to us. When a badly mangled limb heals, it might come back together misshapen, different. Sometimes too much tissue has been lost, scar tissue forms, or the bones of the limb have been shattered beyond repair. The connection of the mangled limb to the body must be made artificially. So it is with a child's death.

You will need time—time to process your loss, to believe the truth of it. You might need "escape" time. You might not be able to care adequately for your remaining family members for a while. That's all right. You might sleep for long periods of time or just sit, dormant. The mind is working on processing this truth even if it seems blank.

Spend whatever time you can with your loved ones, even if you are not yet ready to carry on conversations. Be around your other children, and don't worry that they won't understand if you're not "yourself" right now. Remember that they too are experiencing a loss and are comforted by your mere presence—even if you don pajamas and just watch them play. We are so used to mindlessly "going" and "doing" that we've lost the art of just spending time together quietly.

Maybe you have no other children. You are denied the comfort children can render, but you have a spouse. It may be uncomfortable to be around each other right now, but do it anyway. Don't make yourself weary by engaging in endless conversations of what might have been; instead just *be* together. A touch can be comforting, a shared meal, a cozy fire. Leave some of the heavy discussions until therapy, where a trained professional can help you to navigate through any mutually negative patterns. Please put yourself in the company of a competent therapist with a background in bereavement, as well as a group, if you can handle it. You need to start building up a link back to humanity, like the limb that may need help to function again. Give yourself silence and time.

Hold society accountable. This means letting others know that you and your family are struggling through the most difficult time possible. We, as a civilized nation, need to step up to the plate when it comes to grief. That means teachers, bosses, neighbors, and so on should be helping one another through these tragic events. It is not acceptable for adult human beings to utter phrases like "It's not my job" or "We simply can't make exceptions" at a time like this. It is unconscionable and unkind. It is our humanitarian duty to acknowledge and help each other through our losses. Each of us will face loss of some kind in our lives; would we not like the favor of compassion returned to us in kind?

Don't worry about being a burden to your friends. Ask for help! A friend of mine suggested that I pray to feel safe in God's plan, and I did, even though I was sure I would never really feel safe again. Pray or meditate for strength and guidance. Ask for divine healing light and listen for a loving voice. If you don't trust your higher power anymore, that's OK; unburden yourself anyway. Tell God, or whatever your higher power may be, how you're feeling.

It is hard for me to put into words how to help yourself through the loss of your child. Love yourself through it, somehow. Don't abandon yourself to guilt or hopelessness. You deserve to live out the remaining days you have been given. Choose life, just a little bit each day, whether it be to wash your face, cook an egg, or to call the dentist about that nagging toothache. Each day you choose life, you heal a tiny bit more, until one day your mangled, wretched limb is restored. Do it for the child whom you lost or for those you must still parent on this Earth; do it for the love of your partner and family. But mostly do it for yourself, my sweet friend, because you deserve it.

How to help the family with loss of a child

I have already emphasized the serious need for counseling when a child dies. Surviving children and parents alike need help. Families can fall apart without it. Mothers and fathers may have to work out guilt and blame in couple's sessions. We can be helpful friends and neighbors by being respectful. This family has been through hell on Earth and does not need to be further ostracized. It never hurts to ask people what makes them comfortable. Don't exclude them from an event or party just because you don't think they're up to it. Sometimes the grieving family may just want to feel normal and at least to be asked.

Be aware of the extreme vulnerability of the grievers at this time. Unhealthy dynamics can emerge when so much guilt and blame are involved. Parents might idealize the dead child, causing the surviving siblings to lose self-esteem. Acting out is common among children of all ages after sibling loss. There is a heightened risk for self-destructive behavior in all family members. Look for these behaviors and address them. Respect one another's grieving styles and find a way to come together in your grief. A husband and wife who mourn the loss of their child might try reading the same bereavement book, so that they might find a common ground on which to share.

Setting up some kind of fund in lieu of flowers may unite your family in a cause. Recently, I learned of a family who lost an adult sister. A softball tournament in her name raised money for her young son's education. This family came together in their grief and produced a touching memorial to their loved one.

Don't be afraid to share memories about the child who died or to ask about what he or she was like. A mother and father are always the parents of all their children—living and dead.

12

——

Loss of a Spouse

〰〰〰〰〰〰〰〰〰〰〰〰〰〰〰〰〰〰〰〰〰〰〰〰〰〰〰〰〰

As a young intern, one of my duties was to do "intakes" on clients, meaning I interviewed new clients, gathered information, and directed them toward the appropriate bereavement group. Late one evening, a large, gruff-looking older man sat across from me, suspiciously eyeing the tissue box. His impassive face sported a couple of days' stubble, his flannel shirt was faded, and he appeared to me like a big impervious block of a human being. Nervous and inexperienced, I forged ahead with my list of questions.

ME: What brings you to the center?
MAN: I don't know.
ME: Are you here for one of the bereavement groups?
MAN: Maybe.
(I could see this wasn't going to be easy.)
ME: Did someone close to you die?
MAN: My wife.

It was then I saw the merest crack in the cement facade as his lip began to quiver. He breathed in deeply while glaring at me, almost daring me to ask another question.

Me: I'm so sorry. How long ago did you lose her?

That was as far as I got with the questions. You know what they say about grown men crying? This was the saddest thing I'd ever seen. His massive shoulders began to shake as the pretense melted away and my stoic friend broke down completely. Not daring to hand him a tissue from the box he so disdained, I waited for him to reach for one himself. Eventually he did, and he went on sobbing for what seemed like an eternity. The agency had allotted me only fifteen minutes an intake, but even as green as I was, I knew this man's grief could not be confined to such a limit. An hour later he left, both of us wrung out like dishrags. Before he left, he took my hand in his giant calloused ones and thanked me for listening, promising to return next Thursday night for the bereavement group. This was my first brush with this kind of grief.

This man was truly alone, the depth of his sorrow palpable. His wife of forty years had died. He had no children and, to hear him tell it, no close friends. He had only his dog, whom he loved. "My wife was my whole world," he explained between sobs. "I have nothing left to live for."

I have since learned that society expects widowers to be strong and silent and that the death rate among widowers is three times greater than it is among widows. If you have lost your husband or wife, you have, in a sense, lost your world. When we become a couple, we often join every aspect of our lives together—physically, emotionally, and financially. In marriage, spouses' identities become intricately linked together. When one dies, the other usually feels a crippling loss of self. This is because in many ways the "self" has expanded over time to accommodate two people.

In a marriage, decisions are often made based on conversations with one's partner. Everything from "Where shall we live?" to "What do you want for dinner?" is up for discussion. The "other" is always *there*, to bounce ideas off of, to argue with, or just to share a laugh over something your child did. In death, the other has been taken from you. Your life companion is gone. The loneliness is tragic, and there are constant reminders throughout the world you shared together. Grief looms around every corner. There's his voice on the answering machine, bits of her hair in a brush, the family photo over the mantel.

The longing and pining to have your partner back may also be magnified by expectations. The future you dreamed about together is shattered. I have often thought about the "life of words" spoken between two people. Ideas take on a mystical reality as we go from day to day creating them with another soul. When one person dies the other is left alone with the hollowness of all those words, as they collapse around her like a house of cards. Yes, it can be rebuilt, but it will never be quite the same.

After the death of my sister's husband, people began suggesting she "get back out there" right away. Thank God she ignored such advice. Moving at her own pace, Cathy began the burdensome ordeal of grief. When eventually she began to heal and face the world again, she even attempted dating. These first excursions were disastrous, producing such anxiety that she was incapacitated for days after each outing. This was not due to horrible dating scenarios, although there were some of those; Cathy simply was not ready to completely accept her changed world. This, combined with a great sense of loyalty to the man she had loved so deeply, caused a heightened sense of anxiety.

In our disposable society, Cathy's behavior might be viewed by some as abnormal, while "normal" behavior has widows and widowers remarried within a year of their partner's death, long before true healing has taken place. Unresolved grief is then carried into the next marriage. Combine this with whatever other issues these two people face, and is it any wonder most of these marriages eventually fail?

Together you shared a "couple identity" with friends and relatives. Widows and widowers sometimes talk about not being invited to couples gatherings anymore. Suddenly, after everything else, they are forced to revamp their social lives, much like individuals going through divorce.

When I asked my mother-in-law, Maggi, what she missed about her husband, Bill, she said, "I miss having someone to talk to at the end of the day." These two individuals led rich, full lives, raised four children together, and had successful, busy careers while traveling extensively. Maggi still travels and loves to meet people, but it's different. "Even though Bill and I weren't always interested in seeing the same sights," she explained. "I might go to a museum, while he sat outside people-watching, but we would always meet up afterward and discuss our meanderings. I miss that!"

With every loss comes a redefinition of one's role, and loss of a spouse can leave one wondering, *Who am I?* and *Where do I fit in?* Widows and widowers may no longer feel comfortable socializing with old friends they've known for years. True friends are sensitive to this, but inevitably there will be some friendships that need reevaluating.

When a spouse dies, the secondary loss is tremendous. You might be thrust into single parenthood while the children are still at home. This is a daunting task under any circumstance, but during grief when one's capacity for organization and focus may diminish, it is further complicated. By necessity we share responsibilities with our spouses. Perhaps Dad did all of the outside work while Mom prepared the meals. Whatever the scenario, when one major component is gone, the whole thing falls apart, leaving the grieving parent to put it back together again. This takes time.

Widows and widowers report reexperiencing the loss over and over again. "I never realized how many things my wife got done in a week!" one widower exclaimed during a bereavement group.

"My husband used to fix the cars himself," a widow chimed in. "I don't even know how to talk intelligently to a mechanic. They're probably ripping me off!"

"The word *widow* still sounds foreign to me. How did I become one of those?" The label is unnerving and with it goes a lot of stereotyping.

We have discussed that men and women grieve differently, so it's no surprise that widows and widowers do as well. I have heard it said that "men replace," meaning that after the death of a spouse, men often remarry, sometimes quickly. This seems to make everyone uncomfortable. But is it so difficult to understand when you think about it? On the one hand, society encourages the male to "be strong" and hide his emotions, and on the other hand, he is expected to endure the devastating pain of grief. I don't think so. It's so much easier to bury the pain and start a whole new life. My advice to the widower is to take your time. Consider talking to a counselor, a clergy member, or a friend. Running doesn't work. You have to *stop* sometime, and when you do, grief will be sitting there waiting.

The age at which your spouse died will also affect your grief. Young widows and widowers are often asked to face life as single parents. They mourn the dreams of a future together with their spouses. Middle-age loss leaves people wondering what their life together meant. Their identity as a couple had been fine-tuned, and they may have worked hard to raise their families only to have the years of savoring grandchildren and relaxing a bit snatched from them. Elderly widows and widowers are no longer looking so far toward the future, but *they* have lost the partner that will reminisce with them, as well as the person they depended on to take care of them through the last part of their lives. They despair as they face the additional losses of friends and relatives. Those who shared their history are vanishing, and they face the very real dilemma of loneliness.

HOW TO HELP YOURSELF AFTER THE LOSS OF YOUR SPOUSE

Guilt and anger may be prevalent after the death of your life partner. You might think there was something you could have done to prevent the death or something you overlooked. Perhaps you feel you should have dragged your spouse, kicking and screaming, to the doctor. This is one reason bereavement groups are so helpful. Members learn that they are not alone. Everyone seems to have guilt and anger at his or her spouse's passing. People are angry for their husband or wife abandoning them, even though it may not make logical sense. Who says feelings always make sense? They simply *are*. Talking out your guilt and anger is the most healing thing you can do for yourself.

Physical activity like walking, running, biking, and swimming can help to release anger. It is a normal reaction to feel angry when something is taken from us; just watch a child when someone takes away his toy. As adults we sometimes imagine we should no longer feel these basic emotions, but unless we've learned to detach from our true feelings, grief carries us through emotions in great tumbling waves. Like rag dolls we are helplessly churned and tossed. But the wave will end, if we can just endure it.

Give yourself time to heal. Too many bad marriages and relationships are forged from the embers of grief. Don't carry your loss into the next relationship. Better to heal first and then move on. If you find yourself already in a relationship that is going downhill fast but would like to salvage it—get into therapy. Some lucky people do in fact find love again but then unconsciously sabotage the relationship. Guilt and disloyalty can be powerful adversaries.

Marital relationships, like all bonds, are complicated. Who among us does not understand the nature of the "love-hate" relationship? Some spouses report relief at the passing of their partner and then suffer terrible guilt because of these feelings. We can miss the person and yet feel liberated at the same time. "I never really cared for her family," one man told me. "Now I don't have to see them every Sunday and I feel good about that. Is that wrong?"

It is neither wrong nor right—it's just a feeling. Try not to judge your feelings, just watch them. Just because this man realized he didn't like spending so much time with his in-laws didn't mean he had to completely write them out of his life. It was just an awareness that surfaced after his wife's death. You can love your spouse but not like some of what he or she brought to the marriage. Maybe you didn't like a gambling habit or the television on all the time. This does not mean you didn't appreciate other things that you will dearly miss. Why are we so invested in judging our thoughts? We do not ask for them—they simply come. Allow that there was good *and* bad about this person and try not to idealize him in death.

We have been brainwashed not to "speak ill" of the dead. This is dangerous thinking and can hold us hostage after the death of a spouse. We are coerced to sculpt the perfect figure of a being who unquestionably had flaws and faults, just like the rest of us. What happens when Daddy displays the perfectly sculpted figure of his deceased wife for their children to admire?

"Oh, your mother never used a curse word."

"But I remember she used to say 'Shit!'" the daughter might say.

"Oh no, she never used language like that!"

This leaves the young woman scratching her head and wondering if she remembers correctly. It's OK for this daughter to remember her mother as she truly was, because when you idealize someone in death, in essence you are saying that this person wasn't good enough just the way she really was. It also makes for a hard act to follow, if indeed you would like to find another companion at some time in the future. Neil Simon's play *Chapter Two* addresses how idealization of a dead spouse can hinder a person from moving forward with a new love relationship. This was also made into a movie, which might prove worthwhile viewing if you feel yourself or somebody else is stuck in idealization.

There are also relationships that were not working before the death of one partner. Maybe the spouse was incredibly difficult to live with or unfaithful, or you just didn't love that person anymore. This kind of loss can be accompanied by guilt as well. *I wished he was dead*, and oh, the horrible self-blame for such a thought. Unless you took out a gun and put a bullet in your spouse's head, you did not—I repeat—you did not kill your spouse! We are mortal; we die. Not all people are loveable or even likeable. Forgive yourself for maybe not liking your spouse, and if you can't do that, seek counseling. You deserve your life.

The loneliness we spoke of in a previous chapter is particularly prevalent in the loss of a life partner. Perhaps spending time with family members and friends who knew and loved your spouse is comforting. Loneliness is another good reason to join a bereavement group; nobody understands this like those going through it.

Choose ahead of time how you would like to spend your birthday, your spouse's birthday, and your anniversary; these and other holidays can be very difficult. Think about what would be most consoling to you on these days. Would you like to be with your favorite friend or relative and talk about your husband or wife? Would you like to be alone and just get through it? Some people like to keep busy. Plan ahead.

Ask a friend or family member to accompany you to events where you might feel out of place alone. Maybe you can channel this energy toward the positive.

Help yourself with secondary losses. Learn how to barbecue or hire a housekeeper, if those were your spouse's specialties. Don't go to couples parties for a while, unless it is a gathering of dear friends who can allow you your grief. Ask for help when people offer it and even when they don't. You'll need it.

When you are starting to emerge from the darkness, add something new to your life. Take a cooking class, or skiing lessons, or Italian classes—anything you've thought about over the years but never did. "How can I even think of such a thing right now?" you may ask. *Now* may not be the time, but the time will come when you are ready, and if you don't push yourself to step outside of that comfort zone—you may never. Don't bury yourself while you are still alive! Rather, live for those who no longer can.

Leaning on family and friends may be inevitable for some of us, but there comes a time when you must make a life for yourself, wherever that may lead you. Ask for courage from the God of your understanding, or from within, to help you in this endeavor. And give yourself time.

As in all grief, don't mask it by consuming alcohol, sleeping around, or engaging in whatever may be your personal destructive comforting behavior. Face your grief, even if you don't think you can. It will pass and you can eventually move through it. I promise there is an end to the tunnel you are in. If you are a spiritual person, pray. Read inspirational books that center you. Choose positivity when you are able.

HOW TO HELP THE GRIEVER WITH LOSS OF A SPOUSE

Don't push the griever because *you* want her to be better. There is a tendency for people to want the person they love to feel good again, and they may try to fulfill that need for us by hiding true feelings. If you really want that individual to be restored to a happier life, let her travel through the process of grief and truly heal. Be patient and supportive while she is on this most difficult path. If this makes you uncomfortable, you might want to look at your own need to suppress feelings. Emotions are a normal healthy part of being human—just ask anyone under the age of four!

Be a good listener. Expect anger and don't try to talk the person out of his anger to make yourself feel better. Loss of spouse requires a lot of sorting out of one's life. You can provide a much-needed service by being a sounding board. He may need to get finances in order or figure out how to organize his life as a single parent. Friends and families can pitch in by temporarily filling the void created by the loss. Be a partner at an event for the widow or widower. Go with him to his child's school play or back-to-school night. He will get used to doing these things alone, but it might take time.

If the griever is open to it, talk about memories of her partner. Just as in the loss of a child, there is the need for a spouse to remember her loved one. It is overwhelming to endure the silence and the loneliness of this time without the comforting salve of memories. This person *did* exist, and that presence was a *constant* in the spouse's life. To act as though the physical lack of presence erases the life that was so real to the surviving partner is like saying that person never existed. It is unconscionable.

Couples without children are even more open to isolation after they lose their partners. A support system is very important for them.

Loss of a Former Spouse

America watched as Cher eulogized her former husband Sonny Bono after he died during a skiing accident in the late nineties. Tearfully she called him "the most unforgettable character" she had ever met. She spoke of how they'd met when she was very young, stating that he was like a father as well as her husband. What I saw in Cher's sad eyes was true grief. Just because a marriage ends does not mean that you do not mourn your former partner's passing. This is complicated, so bear with me.

Justine joined a Loss of Spouse bereavement group and was extremely upset when another member told her she didn't belong there. She met privately with me after the group meeting. "There are no groups for me," she cried. And there weren't.

Justine's ex-husband had died months ago, and she was "blown away" by the depth of her grief. This woman taught me a great deal about loss. Justine was not just mourning the passing of this man, whom she typically saw only a couple of times a year at their grown children's special events. She was mourning a time in her life that she and her former husband had shared. In our sessions together, she talked constantly of the ten years they had been married, when her children were still young.

It was a messy breakup; he had left her for another woman, and she was angry and bitter. But over the years she had moved on. Justine co-owned a local bakery, and her grown daughter lived nearby with her two beautiful grandchildren. There was no love interest in Justine's life, which may have also made her more vulnerable to the loss, but not necessarily.

"I don't love him anymore, but I just can't stop crying."

In subsequent sessions Justine realized that she had been so bitter over what he had done to her that she never allowed herself to mourn the loss of this man in her life when they had divorced years before. Fueled by anger and hatred, she forged forward with her life. Over the years, the anger had mellowed and she was even able to admit that the marriage had many flaws before her husband began his affair.

"Did you go to the funeral?" I asked, and she looked mystified. "Of course not! I'm not going to show up where I'm not wanted!"

"So you never got to say good-bye."

She softened her tone. "No, I guess I didn't. I didn't want to make it awkward for my children."

"How would you feel about paying a visit to the cemetery?" This was met with an icy stare, but, amazingly, she did it. The next week she reported going to her ex-husband's grave and talking to him. And what she said astonished me.

"I told him I wished we'd talked more over the years. I would have liked to talk about our kids. They turned out to be such wonderful people, and they always loved him. He was a good dad. A lousy husband, but a good dad." She reached for the tissues, tears streaming down her face. "You know, I still love that son of a bitch! Not the way I used to, but some other way. Do you understand?"

I did. Relationships are complicated. We can love and hate at the same time. Many thoughts and feelings make up a marriage. Divorce is fraught with bereavement, which mirrors many of the same symptoms as death. With all the divorces we are living through these days, one wonders how many people are plagued with unresolved grief issues due to divorce. How many people just turn their feelings of love into hatred but never acknowledge the loss of that love?

Family structures are ever-changing. As families become more complicated, grief changes as well. Children bind former marriage partners together, through finances, special events, and family members who stay close even after marriages end.

You may think you will celebrate on the day your ex is buried, and perhaps you will; however, you may be unexpectedly sad. Attend the funeral, if you feel it will help. You deserve the same closure afforded to others. Hell, if Cher could get up there and speak, why can't you just sneak into the back of the room and take your place? You were a part of this person's life on Earth and you warrant a part in his or her passing. If that is not necessary for you, at least give yourself time to grieve. Talk about your feelings.

One day when Justine was visiting her daughter Beverly, Beverly asked if Justine would mind watching the grandchildren while she went to place flowers on her father's grave. It was his birthday.

"Why don't we all go?" Justine asked, to which a surprised Beverly responded, "Why would *you* want to go?"

"Because I once loved your father and I would like to wish him a happy birthday—wherever he is!" Beverly's jaw dropped, and off they all went to pay their respects. Justine stopped coming to counseling after that. She had finally made peace.

13

WHEN A FRIEND DIES

〰〰〰〰〰〰〰〰〰〰〰〰〰〰〰〰〰〰〰〰〰

The loss of dear friends seems relegated to secondary status beneath the death of blood relatives. Many companies do not even grant leave. But who are these individuals we choose to call our friends? Unlike family members, friends reflect our *choice* in companionship. We connect in some special way with these people, among all others walking this Earth. Wouldn't that make us closer to our friends than some relatives?

One of the saddest women I ever saw was an elderly woman whom I met on a home visit when I was interning. We spent our time seated in the sunny living room of her lovely Long Island home. There were pictures scattered about the room of various moments in Martha's life. Mostly, they were of her son, Martin, who she told me had moved across the country years before.

Martha's world had become quite small. Each day, she ate her meals on a little metal tray table in front of the television. The house was relatively well kept, and she explained that Martin paid to have a woman come in and clean weekly but that she also still liked to putter around herself.

"All of my friends have gone now. First my husband and then all the rest of them, one by one." She smiled sadly at the memory. "I had quite

a lot of friends, you know. I once had a card group, and I used to go to
the senior center with Bea."

"Does your son come to visit?"

"Oh, yes, every year in the fall. He checks on me to make sure I'm
doing all right."

Being the neophyte I was at the time, I called Martin and tried to
persuade him to see his mother more often or perhaps to have her come
to visit him and his family, but he was not interested at all. He really
didn't want to know anything about his mother except that the housekeeper was doing her job and that the senior center was still providing
home visits.

"I really miss my friends," Martha said sadly. True, Martha was
luckier than some of our elderly, who have no family and languish in
institutions. Yet I will never forget the pain in her dark eyes when she
spoke about outliving her friends. I have never run a Loss of Friend
group, but I venture to guess that if I did, there'd be some takers. Certainly the older members of our populace have had to face this kind of
loss regularly.

Chances are that you confide in a friend differently than you do with
family members, even with your spouse. This person may have known
you since childhood and therefore knew your family dynamics and history. You may have been able to laugh with this person and share good
times. So in the loss of your friend, you have lost a large part of who
you are. Part of how we define ourselves is through the relationships
in which we engage on a regular basis. When a friend dies, people talk
about losing a piece of themselves. Losing a contemporary also causes
one to question one's own mortality, as we closely identify with friends.

HOW TO HELP YOURSELF
THROUGH LOSS OF A FRIEND

Expect to be devastated. There is not a great deal of literature out there
on loss of a friend, and it isn't always taken as seriously as other losses.
But you need only to see the faces of those overcome by grief after a

friend dies to know how significant their loss can be. Don't apologize for your grief—you are as entitled to it as anyone!

You might take comfort in helping the family of your friend in some way. Perhaps you can assist with funeral arrangements—with child care, or cooking, or putting a photo display together. If this is too difficult, do not feel obligated. Only help if you want to.

Give yourself time. Being around other mutual friends who can share stories about the deceased might ease the pain. Explain to your boss that you may need a couple of days off, if that might help. Everyone knows what it is to have a dear friend. If you wish to join a bereavement group, there are some available that do not specify type of loss but are more general in nature.

14

COPING WITH SUICIDE

∞∞∞∞∞∞∞∞∞∞∞∞∞∞∞∞∞∞∞∞∞∞∞∞∞∞∞∞∞∞∞∞∞∞∞∞∞∞∞

The Centers for Disease Control and Prevention (CDC) collects data about mortality in the United States, including deaths by suicide. In 2011 (the most recent year for which data is available), 39,518 suicides were reported, making suicide the tenth leading cause of death for Americans. In that year, on average, someone in the country died by suicide every 13.3 minutes. Yet it remains a quiet killer. People don't like to talk about suicide. The study of suicide itself presents difficulties in that no one can question the victim after the fact. Information must often be obtained through the "psychological autopsy" or by questioning those who are left behind to pick up the pieces.

Alfred was introduced to me two weeks after his wife completed suicide through asphyxiation in their garage. He was tall and thin; his visage seeming almost specterlike, with a pale white complexion and hollowed-out eyes. Chilled, he kept pulling the collar of his sweater tighter as he sat bolt upright on my couch. His eyes bore the signs of shock, and his words came so slowly that they sounded distant, as though he was speaking through some invisible barrier. I have never seen anyone more affected by death, more haunted. Never having dealt with suicide before, I learned along with him.

Alfred taught me of the intense guilt that permeated his every cell. How my heart goes out to all of you who are forced to deal with a loved one's decision to end his or her own life. It took Alfred years to let himself off the hook, even after it was determined that his wife, Sally, like so many suicide victims, suffered from severe depression. I have learned that a vast majority of people who commit suicide suffer from acute psychiatric disorders, whether or not they have been diagnosed.

As we have discussed previously in this book, with guilt comes blame. In an attempt to ameliorate some portion of the guilt that Alfred carried with him like an anchor around his neck, he looked to blame Sally's boss for "piling too much work on her," or the family doctor for "not diagnosing her depression," or his children for "putting too much pressure on their mother." He never spoke a word of blame for his wife's own decision—till years later.

"The strange thing was that Sally seemed so happy the week before she did it," Alfred explained. "She helped my daughter redecorate her room and had so much more energy than usual."

I have learned that most people actually feel relieved after they've made the decision to kill themselves; they enter into an almost euphoric state prior to the suicide. This just further confuses those left behind.

Alfred spent untold hours rifling through Sally's belongings, looking for answers, for some kind of clue—as though the discovery of such a clue would somehow ease his pain. It reminded me of those patients who search tirelessly for another clue to support their already confirmed suspicions that their partners are indeed cheating on them. Why do we human beings torture ourselves in this way? Maybe we're hoping against hope that in our mad search we'll discover that the worst has not really happened, that he isn't really having an affair after all or that she is still alive and this has all just been some monumental hoax. One colleague suggested that the search is just to break through the denial and allow the person to acknowledge the truth. With Alfred it was more like he was looking for a trail of clues that might lead to absolution from his guilt. But no clue was uncovered that led him to a satisfactory conclusion, and in the end he finally stopped asking why.

Families that deal with suicide are isolated in their grief. People fear what they cannot understand, and most of us can not truly understand the taking of one's own life. So the desolate, confused family must also face the stigma of suicide, an act disdained by our culture and deemed a sin in many religions.

The term *rational suicide* refers to a suicide that was planned as a way of dealing with a terrible situation like terminal illness. Although no less painful for family members, it is sometimes more understandable to them.

In suicide, the family often agrees upon the story of the death together and may even use the very same words to tell it. "He was driving, and his car spun out of control" might be the words they use, while the truth might be very different. Often when people take their own lives there is room for doubt. It's not like the family members get together and conspiratorially discuss the story of the death, although occasionally that does happen. More likely an explanation emerges and others pick up on it. It's easier to explain an accident to others than to go into the complicated circumstances that led up to a person's choice to end his or her life. Family members may believe that it is "nobody's business" and that the details of a loved one's death are private. The family itself may be confused about where the truth lies or might feel an obligation of loyalty to the deceased loved one.

One by-product of suicide is the looming issue of abandonment. After an earth-shattering event such as this, thoughts can include questions like "How could she have abandoned me?" You may be left with fear and uncertainty about those you love and yourself. But suicide is not about leaving people behind; it is about a need for release from desperation. In the wake of suicide, survivors may doubt their interpretation of the world and those around them. Fears emerge in the form of questions: "Do I really know anybody?" or "What if someone else leaves me this way?"

Singer Judy Collins wrote a poignant book called *Singing Lessons* about surviving the suicide of her thirty-three-year-old son. It remains one of the most helpful guides for a parent whose child has taken his or her own life. In this book she mentions that most people cannot believe that their child could make such a shattering choice and instead convince themselves that their son or daughter was murdered or that it was an accident. She said that nothing was more helpful to her than talking to others who had gone through the same thing. "The world was suddenly the enemy, the place where this could happen, where it had happened. My knees wouldn't hold me, nothing could—but my loving family held me," she wrote.

HOW TO HELP YOURSELF AFTER SUICIDE

You do not owe anyone an explanation! Decide what your standard answer will be and dole it out to those you wish. Save any deeper clarification for the people who matter most in your life. However, you should let yourself say the words you *need* to say to a professional or to someone you trust. Remember, we are only as sick as our secrets, and this is a large one for your psyche to handle.

Do what you need to do for your variation of acceptance. You may not ever get the answers you seek, but it is human to try. When should you stop searching? We do not live in a perfect world. Some say suicide is not a choice but comes to those who are hopeless as a way to end their suffering. Studies show "at-risk" characteristics that sometimes accompany suicide, and the most prevalent feature is acute depression, among other psychiatric disorders. Depression may stem from a chemical imbalance that may have nothing to do with the life circumstances of the individual. Let yourself off the hook: you did not cause this. In the end, no matter why this person chose to end his life, it was his choice, not yours. You may have tried to help that individual in your own way, but a person intent on suicide usually accomplishes it.

You may find the need to talk about "what might have been" in terms of lost possibilities for the future and ways you might have done things differently in the past. This is common. After all, none of us lives entirely in the present.

When anger finally descended upon my patient Alfred, he was close to exploding. This placid, almost timid man started fighting with everyone, even me! One night he threw a stapler through the window of his office because his computer malfunctioned. I may have been the only person relieved to see this side of Alfred—although I hoped it wouldn't last too long. His daughter was horrified as she watched her formerly mild-mannered father give some man "the finger" on the highway. What *I* saw was life pouring back into the skeletal figure that nearly buried himself along with his wife. Alfred eventually worked through his anger.

One night we role-played—I played Sally—and he was able to tell her how angry he was that she went off and left him with two teenagers to raise. Once he got started, he really let her (me) have it! Afterward he kept apologizing for the names he called me (Sally), and we had a good laugh. What a joy to watch people come alive again. Believe me, you *will* live again someday. Let yourself be angry at the person who left you, if that is what you need to do. Scream, throw things—whatever it takes.

If you have flexibility in the workplace, you might want to ease back into work a few hours at a time. Be careful about overuse of alcohol or substances that depress, interrupt sleep, or mask feelings. These will inhibit your grief process.

A support group pertaining to suicide can be most helpful, because it is such a unique loss and others really can't understand. People don't know that you might even feel a sense of relief, like a weight has been lifted off your shoulders, after that person is gone. Depression is draining to be around, and you may have even felt like you were trying to keep your loved one alive and happy. This might add to your guilt, but guess what, many people feel this way. Certainly you would do anything to have that person back again, but that doesn't mean that you are not relieved. Remember, conflicting feelings can coexist after suicide.

HOW TO HELP THOSE DEALING WITH SUICIDE

If someone you know is trying to cope with such a loss, don't ask too many questions. People have a morbid curiosity about this kind of death, and it is unfair to constantly place grieving family members in the position of explaining the death. On the other hand, if the person opens up voluntarily, just listen and give support.

We have all heard the saying "There but for the grace of God, go I." Imagine the horror of enduring a loved one's decision to end his or her own life. Do not judge or think that this could never happen to you—it could. Offer your hand and anything else this person or family might need.

When a griever is in "search mode" looking for answers after a death, allow her the time and space to do this without added guilt. Part of this hunt takes place in the mind and in talking with others who are engaged in probing their own thoughts, trying to consider every little detail that the suicide victim did or said in the past. Here you might remind her not to sift through just all the negatives but to also recall the positives about the person. Although the positives won't help the searcher find the reasons for the suicide, they *will* provide a more realistic picture of who that individual was.

Be a patient listener. You might suggest books and websites on suicide or a good support group.

When talking to children about a family member who committed suicide, speak as truthfully as you can. As always, keep it simple and tailored to the developmental age of the child. If you don't tell this child, he may hear it from someone else. Alleviate guilt by explaining that no one *caused* this to happen and that it was a decision made by the person who died. Children are naturally self-centered and often feel responsible for the death of a loved one. It is very important for the child to understand that this person's thinking was flawed and that suicide is not the answer to anything.

A child whose parent has committed suicide may blame herself for not being "good" enough. She might think she is unlovable and not worthy of happiness. These kinds of distortions need to be explored or the child might become self-destructive as well. Children worry that other adults might commit suicide. They need to be assured that this will probably not occur. Suicide is baffling to adults as well as children, and it's OK to admit that you don't really understand the whole thing either. It's not necessary to always have the answers.

Do not judge the child's reactions to the death, as children grieve differently than adults. Older children verbalize less and are affected differently than younger children. This child should have a venue to express his emotions and vent his anger. A group for children or individual counseling is important. Any communication is valuable. Perhaps she trusts a friend or relative or a teacher. Let her satisfy her need to work things out verbally. Inform the child's teachers or important adults regarding the suicide; you never know when the opportunity for communication might present itself. Any additional support is helpful.

IMPORTANT FACTS ABOUT SUICIDE

According to the CDC, suicide is the third leading cause of death for those aged fifteen to twenty-four. Male adolescents complete suicide at five times the rate of females, even though females make more attempts. Typically males use firearms, which have a 78 to 90 percent chance of causing fatality. Attempted suicides should be seen as a cry for help. Some contributing factors to this high number are depression, peer pressure, self-esteem issues, and believe it or not (added recently), the stress of getting into college.

Suicide prevention in young adults hinges on several factors. Troubled teens need to talk out their problems with someone they trust. Depressed kids may need medication as well as cognitive/behavioral therapy to help modify self-destructive thoughts.

Don't try to talk them out of it or make them feel guilty, or they will stop talking to you. Be aware of copycat suicides; these are duplication suicides after a friend, classmate, or someone in the media completes suicide. Teens are impressionable and sometimes influenced by the glorification of a suicide or the idea that there is a way out of their painful existence.

The largest number of people who commit suicide in our society are sixty-five and over. The factors that put them at risk are illness;

depression; substance abuse; panic attacks; being divorced, widowed, or unemployed; having relatives who commit suicide; mental disorders; stressful life events; and possession of a handgun.

15

COPING WITH MURDER

Sitting across from my former patient Paula Keener, I try to envision the horror she was forced to face when her sister Kathy was murdered. I too have a sister named Cathy. How would I have felt had it been my sister? I watch as her pretty face darkens at the reiteration of her tragic tale, knowing that the murder of a loved one simply cannot be imagined.

A noted scientist, marine biologist, and ocean science educator for NOAA (National Oceanic and Atmospheric Administration), Paula is a dynamic, articulate woman. "My sister was forty-nine years old. They shot her in the head and threw her in an alligator-infested pond, hoping the evidence would be eaten." Her abandoned and burned vehicle led the police to the pond. Divers worked for several days to find Kathy's badly decomposed body, with only her clothing and teeth to identify her.

The nightmare began when Kathy went missing. "I knew it was bad," Paula says, puting her hand to her head. She had the premonition that so many speak about before a loved one's death. "I still remember the term the officer used when they searched the pond—*cadaver dog*—what a horrible image." Three years later, the memory still transforms her face, and I am reminded of how people look watching a horror movie.

"When I got the call that they found the body, I remember collapsing on the floor with my head buried in the sofa cushions, banging my fists and shouting over and over, 'They killed my sister! They killed my sister!' I wanted to escape, to run out of my house and down the street screaming. It took two men to hold me back." She looks at me. "And then *I* had to deliver the news to my mother that her daughter was dead. I felt violated, and certain things about Kathy's death will haunt me forever. I will never know what her very last thoughts or words were. These things were stolen from me! This is not like any other losses I've gone through. Family should be with family when they die." Her words pierced my heart as I thought about the helplessness Kathy must have felt and the powerlessness her family experienced at having been robbed of the ability to comfort their dying.

In what ways does this differ from all other losses? "Murder is senseless and disconnected. It is unforeseen and incomprehensible," Paula explains. "This was my own flesh and blood; we shared the same genetic material. It was a violation of my *own* being. At first it was a struggle just to breathe. This was not one day at a time; it was one *breath* at a time."

Another aspect unique to murder is that at a time when grievers are most vulnerable, they are often asked to face the legal aspects of the death. As a loving sister and a scientist, she could not stop looking for answers from the beginning. "My mother, my twelve-year-old son, and I all had a determination to bring the perpetrators to justice," she tells me. "Suddenly I found myself connected to a whole new group of people—people whose loved ones had been murdered. This was not a club I wanted to belong to." She smiles sadly. "But we all find each other somehow."

Because Kathy's case was newsworthy, this family also dealt with the media. Paula would catch a news report mentioning her little sister's name linked with the words *murder victim* and it seemed "unreal" to her. A picture of Kathy would flash on the screen and she would have to look away. Meetings with the police and media interviews became a weekly part of her life—a life that had become anything but normal.

The secondary losses were also mounting. She began to wonder if she could ever feel the same about her hometown of Charleston, South Carolina. For survivors of murder there is always more than one victim. Privacy often goes out the window, not to mention the whispers behind their backs.

Posttraumatic stress disorder is a pervasive problem when a loved one is murdered, and as stated in chapter 6, the trauma must be dealt with before true healing can begin. Triggers all over Charleston can propel Paula back to that fateful night, even after the work she's done to move on in her life. Another major characteristic of murder is anger—no, make that rage! How could anyone avoid rage when her loved one has been snatched from her? And sometimes there's anger at those we love. In Paula's case, Kathy had been addicted to drugs and was attempting to put her life back in order when once again she succumbed to her addiction, and it was this tragic flaw that left her vulnerable to murderers.

"Were you angry with her?" I ask.

"Honestly, no, not after she was killed. I was more angry with Kathy when she was alive and hurting herself and my mother with her behavior. But she was finding her way out of all of that. We were so hopeful."

Paula's anger belongs to those who killed Kathy, "these terrible animals that do this to our loved ones. They can take away the physical body, but they can never touch the love, the memories. Their spirit is always with us."

After three years only one perpetrator has been placed in maximum-security prison for twelve years. When I ask who paid for this crime, Paula is ready with her answer: "My sister, my mother, my son, and me."

So how do you get through it? For Paula, her faith was essential. "I believe that Kathy is at peace and in a better place, that I will see her again," Paula says. "Bereavement counseling helped a lot. Family and friends were a big support. You never completely resolve this kind of loss. It's not natural; it is a breach of nature. You kind of become three people: the person you were before the event, the person who was affected by the event, and the person who tries to grow from the event, the one who asks, 'What good can I take from this?' We get through it by celebrating our loved ones. We put their pictures out, we talk about them. It's our responsibility never, never to forget them."

Others have shared with me that physical labor and exercise can help make you stronger and temporarily take your mind off things. Getting involved in a cause where you can redirect your energy toward a positive outcome assists many family members.

What about those murder victims who are never found or whose bodies were destroyed in death? One of the women whose husband was killed in the terrorist bombing of Pan Am Flight 103 has written about the denial she and others experienced while waiting for notification of death. Driven by a deep sense of loyalty to the victim, she held out hope that he was still alive. Upon reading this, my mind shifted to scenes of Natalee Holloway's mother searching for her missing daughter in Aruba. The pain of loss can color logic and make giving up hope seem like giving up on the person herself.

HOW TO HELP THOSE COPING WITH MURDER

If ever there was a need to tell the story of the death—murder would be it. Because of the traumatic impact linked with sudden, violent death, loved ones may have a need to retell their story many times. We must be patient listeners as they attempt to make sense of the senseless. On the other hand, there are those so traumatized that they simply cannot mention their loss and do everything they can to avoid the topic. These are the folks who probably have the greatest need for counseling. Because so few individuals truly understand this type of loss, a bereavement group specific to murder is most effective.

Because he may be dealing with gossip and curiosity seekers, we should understand the survivor's need for privacy. He may not wish to go out much anymore. This kind of recovery may be slow, and a great deal of "room" should be granted, socially and in the workplace. The usual disorientation of sudden loss is magnified by its violent nature.

Expect focus and concentration problems and sometimes extreme distractibility. Imagine what it would feel like to no longer trust your safety in the world or the safety of those you love. Anxiety and depression are common after a murder, and survivors may require medication to function for a while. This is one of those types of loss when we say "Whatever it takes" to comfort our mourners through their grief.

16

PET LOSS HURTS TOO

~~~~~~

Every six weeks or so, a big truck pulls up to my house and my friend Bobby pops out. A bubbly little woman with auburn hair and twinkly blue eyes, Bobby collects my Glen of Imaal terrier, Murphy, who happily follows her to her truck to be groomed. A quirky breed, these stocky dogs were bred in Ireland to help eradicate badgers and foxes from the countryside. Murphy's head is disproportionately large, causing him to look a great deal like a stuffed animal, fluffy and cute. That's why I bought him. I knew nothing about the fact that his oversized head allowed him a jaw large enough to eliminate vicious animals a hundred years ago. Consequently, I own a dog who does not like other dogs or small animals. He is, however, a brave and true lover of human beings and keeps us all laughing with his endearing antics. Having withstood public humiliation on more than one occasion, my husband and I have opted not to bring Murphy among other dogs anymore, hence our traveling dog groomer.

A few weeks ago I answered my front door to find Bobby, leash in hand. Gone was her usual enthusiasm and lovely smile. Her shoulders were stooped, and the sparkle had left her eyes. I knew the telltale signs all too well. When I asked her what was wrong, she spoke of her friend, Bett. Bett was sick and dying: the very bones within her were disintegrating. Bobby's friend was her beloved pet. It was touching to witness

221

how she cared for that dog in the weeks to come, tending to her every need. Do we have any doubt that we grieve when our pets are ill and when they die? We know that they are part of our families and hold a special place in our hearts. And yet many of us apologize for feeling this way.

Bett truly was a special dog. She was a champion Chinese crested show dog. I came to learn that Bobby owned twelve dogs and that besides being a groomer, she bred and professionally showed her dogs. In her soft southern twang, she told me, "I love all my dogs, but Bett was my heart."

Bett was given six months to live but went on for another two years. She would be hurting for a while and then suddenly snap back into health for days and even weeks at a time for no apparent reason. She had the vets stumped. So amazing was this dog that at age fourteen she was the oldest dog in a veterans competition dog show and took first prize one month before the decision was made to euthanize her.

Bobby's eyes welled up as she talked about those last days. "She was with me every second that last month. I carried her in my truck during the day. Finally the pain got so bad . . ." Bobby dissolved into tears. And there it was—the guilt, evident even in pet loss. On top of everything else people go through at the end of their pets' lives, like carrying them outside to urinate and defecate or listening to them moan in pain, people are expected to make the decision to end that pet's life—after which they must bring their beloved pet to its own execution. Talk about guilt!

After a bad experience with an unfeeling veterinarian, Bobby switched to a new vet. This man said some very wise words to my friend, which I would like to pass along to you. He told her that the only gift she could still give Bett now was to let her go. Maybe that is good advice for all of us when it comes to those we love: sometimes we must just *let them go*. Although it may not seem to be the right thing for us, it may indeed be the right thing for them.

"The hard part for us *both* was the giving up," Bobby explained. "We couldn't fix her."

Let's face it, we are mommies and daddies to our pets. We feed them, train them, and care for them. Parents are supposed to keep their children safe. We feel responsible for their well-being. It is natural to feel guilt and even a sense of failure when our pet dies, even if he was old. Animals' life spans are so short in comparison to our own that in some way we feel short-changed.

So, what emotion does Bobby feel most of all?

"Lonely," was her simple, poignant response. There's that word again. Even with eleven other dogs, Bobby is lonely. No other dog or person can fill that spot in her heart where Bett belongs. This is true grief.

To help those who are grieving pet loss, we can remember that they may experience many of the same symptoms as anyone in grief. Be kind and caring and do not belittle their loss. There are pet loss websites and chat rooms available on the Internet. There are even bereavement cards available to send to someone whose beloved pet has died. If children are involved in the loss, let them talk to you about their feelings. I have seen miniburials for all kinds of animals, including hamsters. Let the child come up with the ritual, and don't laugh at the idea. Even a goldfish flushing can have pomp and ceremony. Encourage the child to draw pictures or frame a photo of her deceased friend. This may be the first opportunity for a child to learn about the natural order of life and death. If children can incorporate this knowledge into their psyche, perhaps they will learn to deal with loss better in the future. No matter what you or I try to do to protect our children, we cannot shield them from loss. Assisting our children through their losses and teaching them to reconcile and move on with their lives will make a difference that can last a lifetime.

DO ANIMALS GRIEVE?

I believe so—I have seen it firsthand. When our old dog Sullivan died, Murphy lay on the couch for three days straight, just moping. That's right, we had dogs named Sullivan and Murphy; my husband said it sounded like an Irish law firm. A friend of mine who is a true dog lover suggested taking Murphy with us when Sullivan was to be euthanized, and I responded by looking at her as if she were nuts. She went on to explain that if dogs know that an animal or person has died, they will not spend several weeks looking for or waiting for the animal's or person's return. Although they mourn, it will shorten their mourning period. See that—even dogs like to have answers! Knowing that it is often necessary for humans to see their loved one's remains to truly believe that person dead, this suggestion should not have seemed so strange to me.

So, when the time came, we took Murphy along with us to the vet on poor old Sullivan's last day. I was astounded by Murphy's reaction after Sullivan passed away. As the old dog lay on the ground, no longer living, Murphy stepped right over him as though he wasn't even there. It was quite odd, really. Murphy in no way even acknowledged the other dog's body, not even to sniff him. Normally he would have snuggled or jumped on the larger older dog. Instinctively Murphy knew that his old friend was gone. Once home, Murphy mourned for three days and then popped back up and resumed his life as though nothing had happened. He never looked around for Sullivan.

After Bett's death, Bobby witnessed an interesting behavior with her other dogs as well. At night, Bobby and her husband (who should be sainted) sleep with four small dogs on their bed. After Bett's death, although there is barely enough room on the bed for everyone, none of the other dogs would sleep on the spot that Bett's death left empty. Were they honoring their missing friend or grieving her? There are many more qualified people than me on this subject, as my life's work has been with human beings and not animals. Yet it is something to think about.

17

AN ENDING AND
A BEGINNING

Many years ago I buried a part of me along with my beautiful son Jesse. Left behind was an empty shell that other people seemed to recognize as me but whom I no longer knew at all. Friends and family spoke to this being, who looked like Judy, about memories we had shared together or something that had happened just a few short months ago, but it might as well have been a lifetime ago. How could they know that I was gone? Judy had left the building.

In my place was the mere trace of a human being, someone who neither ate nor slept anymore. A million miles away, I was aware that people were talking, but I was never really sure what the words meant. I'd forgotten the language. I could talk now only to small children and old people. The other ones seemed like they were hurrying around with a sense of purpose that had no meaning to me.

Hours would go by as I sat on the floor playing with my son Carll. He made me feel safe. We sat in the sunlight so I wouldn't feel cold all the time. That's where I felt God, I guess—in the sunlight.

Others came and went in this new world, people I once loved—still loved. They comforted me with their smiles, their touches, their warm hugs. I wanted to make them feel better, to tell them I was all right inside this shell, but it was hard to remember the words, and I was so terribly tired.

So it began, my relearning of the world. It was slow and painful. Looking back, I am grateful to my ex-husband that I was able to stay at home with my son at that time. I would have been lost out there in "the real world." I needed time.

It would have been so much easier to stay gone. I can understand why some people choose that option. But I wasn't raised that way. I had been taught to find my way home no matter what, and when that didn't work, to fight my way back. And besides, I had the big, blue, innocent eyes of a child before me, like a beacon showing me the way.

And so I returned, in bits and pieces, and even though I looked the same, I never would be.

Each of us has a story, and these stories have given me great hope for the human spirit over the years. I tell mine only because I have lived it and thus know it truly. We are complicated creatures, we human beings—fraught with imperfections, and yet also noble in many ways. Re-created by our losses, or perhaps forged into a stronger metal, we endure.

So, *who* emerged to inhabit my old skin? It was just me, only altered. Once I returned to the land of the living, over time, my life changed. Some of these changes would never have happened if Jesse hadn't died. Would I give up my life to have Jesse here? Yes. But it doesn't matter—we don't get that choice in this world. Our life is revealed and altered because of what has occurred. My own life was transformed, in some ways for the better and in some for the worse.

My marriage did not make it, and I'm sure that the death of our son contributed to the eventual end of the marriage in some way. There were some happy years before we parted, and we were blessed with a third child—Abby, our glorious daughter.

When my marriage ended, I moved to a smaller house in the same town. I had begun to volunteer and work in the bereavement field when I decided to return to college and become a psychotherapist. Having written and published before my loss, I now began to do so in the field of bereavement. Jesse taught me a sense of purpose, and I had so much more to learn.

For many years I had internalized anxiety, and after Jesse's death I ended up in emergency surgery with Crohn's disease. If I did not wish to follow Jesse to my own young grave, I needed to make some new life decisions to go with the new person I was becoming.

This led me to a healthier lifestyle. I began exercising on a regular basis, eating better, and finding ways to relax. I made friends with God again, although he had never left me even when I was so angry at him. Feeling closest to God in nature, I began taking daily walks and feeling his touch on the breeze. It was as though I'd been reborn with better senses. The colors of the beautiful flowers and trees that surrounded my neighborhood appeared more vivid than ever before, and I would literally stop and smell the flowers. It was as though I'd given myself permission to live again.

Joy began to turn up in my life. My children amazed me by adapting to all the changes in our lives, and they taught me how to keep my heart open. I allowed myself to audition for a play in regional theater, a passion I had let go years before. It was nearly impossible to juggle being a single mom, going to school, and working, but I felt I needed an outlet just for me. I got the part, but the commitment proved more than I foresaw. Ready to quit and feeling basically inadequate at the time, it was a fellow cast member who talked me out of throwing in the towel. "Trust the process," he told me, and his words touched my heart. Wasn't that what I'd been trying to do—to trust again? So I stuck it out and had a good time playing a bitchy gossip columnist every night on stage. What a great way to release my anger!

That handsome, blue-eyed gentleman became one of my best friends as we would meet weekly for lunch at a local Japanese restaurant for what we called our "Miso-rendezvous." Thomas proved kind and patient, as he taught me how to trust again. I fell in love—another testament to the healing heart.

And so the unfolding of my life and what Jesse's legacy has given me endures as I continue to teach and learn about grief. Loss is part of life, and those of us who can accept this are destined to help others through their pain. For on the other side of loss is a new beginning. I have seen it; I have lived it.

There is hope for each and every one of you who is trapped in a world that no longer makes sense. *Trust the process.* When you find your way out of the fog, you'll know what matters. Maybe it will be to hold those around you a little bit closer or to realize a dream you tucked away years ago . . . you'll know. My heart goes with you, and I hope that you might find some words in this book helpful. May you find healing and learn to live again.

FREQUENTLY ASKED QUESTIONS ABOUT GRIEF

CHILDREN AND LOSS

How do I talk to my child about death?
Keep all explanations simple; complicated answers leave too much room for imagination. Gear your words to the developmental stage of the child. (Chapter 7)

Do I bring young children to a wake?
If the person who died is someone important in their lives, children should be included in all rituals to feel a part of the mourning process. Some wakes go on for long hours and several days. Children grieve in doses. It is not necessary for young children to remain at wakes for the full amount of time. (Chapter 7)

Should all grieving children go to counselors?
If the child has lost a significant person, like a parent, sibling, or someone with whom he is in a close relationship, consider counseling. It is not always necessary if surviving caretakers are well informed and can spend the time helping the child. (Chapter 7)

WHAT DO I SAY?

What do I say to a person whose child has died?

Obviously there is no blanket answer to such a question. My suggestion is to keep it simple. A heartfelt "I am so sorry for your loss" and "Your family is in my thoughts" (and/or prayers—if so inclined) are enough. Don't avoid comforting a person because there are no magic words. Acknowledge the griever and be a good listener. (Chapter 11)

Then what?

If it's a good friend, learn to listen. A kind touch goes a long way. Sharing memories about the person who died may be appropriate only if this kind of conversation is positively received. (Chapter 11)

What about suicide or murder?

These people need you most of all. There are no better words than "I'm so sorry for your loss." If appropriate, you might also mention that you will indeed miss this person. Don't say, "I don't know how you're handling this." A statement such as this only further stigmatizes the griever. Remember it's not contagious, and there are no words that can take *this* kind of pain away. (Chapters 14, 15)

What about when no body was found or salvaged?

Hopefully the family will see fit to have a memorial service of some kind. Nothing changes. You should attend and send flowers or donate to the designated fund.

TERMINAL ILLNESS

Do I talk to a terminally ill person about dying?

If you are prepared to do so, you might just go ahead and ask the person if *she* would like to talk about it. It's not like you're bringing up something she hasn't thought about. Too many people end up feeling guilty because they ignored this eventuality while their loved one was trying to reach out. It takes true emotional courage to broach this subject. (Chapter 6)

Isn't talking about dying giving up hope?
The old saying goes "Hope for the best, but prepare for the worst." And sometimes, when your loved one is suffering, death doesn't even seem the *worst* alternative. Dying people sometimes want to resolve issues or put their affairs in order. Talking about the possibility of death doesn't mean you've given up hope. (Chapter 6)

Is it normal to feel relieved when a terminally ill relative dies?
We Americans have an interesting misconception that people experience only *one* emotion at a time. This makes it all the more confusing when a loved one dies and we are flooded with conflicting emotions. If you have watched a terminally ill relative suffer, or perhaps even been his caretaker, one of the many conflicting emotions you will experience is relief. This does not make you a bad person, only human. (Chapter 6)

WHEN A PARENT DIES

How do you prevent the family from falling apart?
This is a complicated question that I have heard often. Of course family counseling can help, but unfortunately with a grown family, emotional issues often get worked out through material things. Family feuds can arise over a pair of cufflinks. Better to have all material goods itemized before death is imminent and allow parents to decide to whom they wish to leave their worldly goods. Does this sound cold? Not if you have watched a family tragically unravel because members are emotionally charged after a parent's death. (Chapter 10)

What if you're the only one in a family who wants to talk about death?
People grieve differently. In grief, you should respect your siblings' choices. That does not mean that you can't bring things up from time to time, in an attempt to reconcile your grief as a family. Wait awhile

and maybe play a video or look at photographs of the family the next time you all get together—that might start the ball rolling. But if they are not open to it, you will have to find another outlet. You might seek a bereavement group, individual counseling, or even friends who have lost their parents and are more open to sharing feelings. (Chapter 10)

Who speaks at the funeral service?
The family should discuss the service as a whole unit. If this fails, there are some times when one family member is more comfortable taking on this responsibility. Do what is helpful for all involved, not just trying to please the member who is the most aggressive. If there are too many siblings and everyone wants to share about their parent, there are other sensible solutions. You might write some words about your parent, together, and then choose a representative to deliver those words, or you might choose another family member or dear friend to speak. (Chapter 10)

What do I say when an elderly parent of someone I know dies?
Far too often I think this kind of loss is minimized. It *is* in the natural order of life, that is true, but hasn't that person still suffered a terrible personal loss? Rather than jumping on the bandwagon with the overused "Well, he had a good life, didn't he?" how about sharing a fond memory about his mom or dad with the griever or a heartfelt "I guess you will really miss your father." (Chapter 10)

DEATH IN THE WORKPLACE

How do we show our respect to coworkers?
There is no one right answer to this question. It depends on how well you know the person experiencing the loss as to whether or not you choose to attend services. It is not always necessary to know the person who died, as these rituals are to comfort the living. Sending flowers or contributing to a chosen charity may be done as a group. (Chapter 5)

Should I avoid or bring up the subject after the person returns to work?
Quietly mentioning that you are sorry for the person's loss is enough. Most people do not wish to go into details or break down at work. However, ignoring the subject completely is not appropriate unless the person has requested it. If the griever wishes to discuss his loss and indicates such, then it is up to you to find the appropriate time and place to listen. Always take the griever's cue. (Chapter 5)

What if an employee is having trouble focusing and getting work done?
If your employee has suffered a recent loss, it may take time for him to readjust to the workplace. Perhaps other employees can help fill in the gap for the time being. If things get really bad, you can suggest counseling. (Chapter 5)

WHEN A CLASSMATE DIES

What do I tell my elementary school child about the death?
Be honest and keep it simple. If your child was close to the child who died, allow her to participate in appropriate mourning services and rituals. Understand that even if your child did not know the child who died well, she may still be affected by the loss. Let your child join in to any help offered through the school and any memorializing that takes place. Ignoring the death will not shield your child from her thoughts or feelings. (Chapter 7)

What if my explanation of death differs from what is being said at school?
Remember that children are much more open-minded than we adults. Generally, a broad, secular explanation is provided by the school. If you wish to fill in with your own particular beliefs at home, that is your prerogative. The more chances the child has to speak about his thoughts and feelings, the better toward resolution of his grief. (Chapter 7)

What do I do when an older classmate dies?
Children of all ages should be allowed to participate in mourning their classmates. (Chapter 7)

What if the person died of a drug overdose or suicide; doesn't it condone these behaviors to mourn for the deceased?
This is a common misconception that could not be further from the truth! If young adults are not given the chance to participate in community mourning rituals, it may lead to further isolation. At the same time, they may need some group or individual counseling. They *must* hear the message—loud and clear—that suicide and substance abuse are not the answers to their problems. (Chapter 7)

What can we do for families who have lost a son or daughter?
Recently my friend's son had a classmate who died at college. She didn't know this young man's parents and wondered what was appropriate for her and her son to do. Sometimes a well-meant condolence card with a heartfelt message is enough. It is always appropriate to respond to the loss of someone's child in whatever way makes sense to you and reflects how well you know the family. (Chapter 11)

THE RITUALS

Is it appropriate for people to be laughing at a wake?
People are forever wondering what proper decorum is for funerals, wakes, and other loss-related rituals and ceremonies. Traditionally, wakes have been held to mourn the person who died, support the family who lives, and to celebrate the life of the deceased. Uproarious laughter while family members are grieving is not supportive; however, quietly remembering and speaking about the person who died is very appropriate, and if subdued laughter is a part of that reminiscence, it is fine.

If the family has requested contributions to a particular fund, are flowers still appropriate?
If donations have been requested "in lieu" of flowers, then you should probably save the flower money for the fund, but there is nothing saying you can't make a donation *and* send flowers. If donations are only "suggested," you make your own choice.

Is it seen as an insult if I do not pay my last respects by kneeling before an open casket if this makes me uncomfortable?
Absolutely not. If this is not a part of your own faith-based ritual, or you simply find it uncomfortable, it is not necessary to pay one's last respects in this manner. Just being there to support the family is fine. (Chapter 2)

Should those not of the Jewish religion wear yarmulkes at a Jewish funeral?
It is a sign of respect but not mandatory.

Should I be aware of the difference in ethnic rituals?
Many previously differing ethnic mourning rituals have been watered down and adapted to a more universal American tradition, but it doesn't hurt to be aware of cultural diversity. It is simple enough to learn more on the Internet or read one of the books included in the bibliography. (Chapter 2)

WHAT SHOULD I DO?

If I suspect a person is stuck in complicated grief, should I intervene?
Many people are not informed or educated about bereavement and tend to hold on to outmoded beliefs. You might give this or another book or pamphlet that includes an explanation of complicated grief to the griever herself or to a family member. In some cases the denial is just too deep to reach a complicated griever. We can only make the suggestion for counseling, but she may not follow up. (Chapter 3)

What should I do if someone I love displays symptoms of PTSD but refuses help?

This is a tough one. We cannot force other adults into therapy. You can give the person literature, but that's about it. If you find that your loved one's symptoms are affecting your life, find a group for yourself that deals with PTSD. If you have no luck, try a website dealing with this subject. (Chapter 6)

BEREAVEMENT RESOURCES

GENERAL ORGANIZATIONS

Center for Grief, Loss & Transition
www.griefloss.org
(651) 641-0177
A nonprofit organization that provides specialized therapy and education in the areas of complicated grief, trauma, and life transition.

National Hospice and Palliative Care Organization
www.nhpco.org
(703) 837-1500
Enhances quality of life for people dying in America, as well as their loved ones.

LOSS OF A CHILD

National SUID/SIDS Resource Center
www.sidscenter.org
(866) 866-7437
Provides informational services on SIDS and related topics with assistance for reference and referral services.

The Compassionate Friends
www.compassionatefriends.org
(877) 969-0010
Assists families toward positive resolution of grief following the death of a child at any age.

GRIEVING CHILDREN

Rainbows
www.rainbows.org
(800) 266-3206 or (847) 952-1770
An international not-for-profit organization that fosters emotional healing among children grieving a loss from a life-altering crisis.

The Dougy Center
www.dougy.org
(886) 775-5683 or (503) 775-5683
Maintains a directory of programs across the country that serves grieving children and teens.

LOSS OF A SPOUSE OR SIBLING

Daily Strength
www.dailystrength.org/c/Widows-Widowers/support-group
Support for those who have lost a husband, wife, or partner.

The Compassionate Friends
www.compassionatefriends.org/home.aspx
In addition to helping those dealing with the loss of a child, this site can help those dealing with with sibling and grandparent loss as well.

Twinless Twins Support Group
www.twinlesstwins.org
(888) 205-8962
Mutual support for twins and other multiples who have lost siblings.

SUICIDE

Friends for Survival
www.friendsforsurvival.org
(800) 646-7322
An organization of people who have been affected by a death caused by suicide.

American Association of Suicidology
www.suicidology.org
(202) 237-2280
Provides referrals to support groups for survivors of suicide victims.

HOMICIDE/MURDER

National Organization for Victim Assistance
www.trynova.org
(800) 879-6682
Provides crisis intervention and counseling for victims and survivors of violent crime and disaster.

National Organization of Parents of Murdered Children
www.pomc.com
(888) 818-POMC or (513) 721-5683
Provides support and assistance to all survivors of homicide victims.

MILITARY DEATHS

Society of Military Widows
www.militarywidows.org
(800) 842-3451
Serves widows of all branches of the uniformed services. Offers support, guidance, referral services, and chapter development guidelines.

TAPS (Tragedy Assistance Program for Survivors)
www.taps.org
(800) 959-8277
Support for persons who have lost a loved one who served in the armed forces.

PET LOSS

Pet Loss Help
www.petlosshelp.org
Maintains a list of pet bereavement support groups, counselors, and hotlines.

TOOLS FOR USE WITH CHILDREN AND TEENS

~~~~~~

Over the years, I have discovered many useful tools to help open up a dialogue with a grieving child. I have tried numerous workbooks and games and found those listed here to be among the more useful catalysts for communication. Marge Heegaard's series also has useful workbooks for children experiencing divorce, remarriage, and substance abuse in their families, but I have chosen to list here only those dealing with grief.

I have already mentioned my handy dollhouse (made by IKEA) with full complement of dolls. Puppets are also invaluable. A child is sometimes more comfortable hiding behind a nice furry bear who is acting out the story about how his "sister" bear died, rather than explaining how he feels about his own sibling's death. This only works for young children (ages three to seven); after that, the connection becomes too obvious.

We who work with children are blessed with patients whose imaginations are endless. A sketchpad and crayons are sometimes all it takes. Teens are tougher! In more recent years, I have begun to use the computer as a tool for communication.

Many books, coloring books, workbooks, games, and DVDs are available today to help in this endeavor. Here are some suggestions that can be useful for children and teens:

CHILDREN

Books

Grollman, Dr. Earl A. *A Scrapbook of Memories: A Workbook for Grieving Children*. Batesville Management Services, 1996. (Ages 5–10.)

Heegaard, Marge. *Facilitator Guide for Drawing Out Feelings*. Woodland Press, 1988.

————. *When Someone Has a Very Serious Illness: Children Can Learn to Cope with Loss and Change*. Woodland Press, 1988.

————. *When Someone Very Special Dies: Children Can Learn to Cope with Grief*. Woodland Press, 1988.

————. *When Something Terrible Happens: Children Can Learn to Cope with Grief*. Woodland Press, 1988.

Powers, Lynn, and Laurie Van-Si. *A Keepsake Book of Special Memories*. Compassion Press, 2012. (Ages 4–12.)

Shapiro, Lawrence E., PhD. *55 Favorite Healing Activities for Children*. Childswork/Childsplay, 2010. (Ages 6–12.)

Coloring Books

Stickney, Doris. *Water Bugs & Dragonflies: Explaining Death to Young Children*. With illustrations by Robyn Henderson Nordstrom. Pilgrim Press, 2009.

Wolfelt, Alan D., PhD. *How I Feel: A Coloring Book for Grieving Children*. Batesville Management Services, 1996.

Game

Doggone Grief. Board game designed by grief expert Brenda Brown. 2010. (Ages 4 and up.)

TEENS

Books

Gootman, Marilyn E., EdD. *When a Friend Dies: A Book for Teens About Grieving & Healing*. Free Spirit Publishing, 2005.

Hughes, Lynn B. *You Are Not Alone: Teens Talk about Life After the Loss of a Parent*. Scholastic Paperbacks, 2005.

Wheeler, Jenny Lee, and Heidi Horsley, PsyD. *Weird Is Normal: When Teenagers Grieve*. Quality of Life Publishing, 2010.

DVD

When a Loved One Dies: Walking Through Grief as a Teenager. Paraclete Video Productions, 2006.

CHILDREN AND TEENS

Book

Schwiebert, Pat, and Chuck Deklyen. *Tear Soup: A Recipe for Healing After Loss*, 5th ed. With illustrations by Taylor Bills. Grief Watch, 2005. (Ages 8 and up.)

Websites

Compassion Press has a wonderful website with a variety of very good materials for children and teens, including the DVD *Grief & Loss: A Child's Perspective*. For these materials go to www.compassionbooks .com.

Childswork/Childsplay is another website with books, workbooks, and games for children and teens: www.childswork.com.

NOTES

1. THE THINGS THEY DON'T TELL YOU ABOUT GRIEF

This is a strange by-product . . . Holly Prigerson and Paul Maciejewski, "An Empirical Examination of the Stage Theory of Grief," *Journal of the American Medical Association* 279 (February 2007): 716–23.

2. IN THE BEGINNING: THE ROLLER COASTER OF EMOTION

The mood swings . . . Margaret S. Stroebe, Robert Hansson, Wolfgang Stroebe, and Henk Schut, *Handbook of Bereavement Research: Consequences, Coping, and Caring* (Washington, DC: American Psychological Association, 2001).

The griever who cannot . . . Ibid.

A recent study . . . Holly Prigerson and Paul Maciejewski, "An Empirical Examination of the Stage Theory of Grief," *Journal of the American Medical Association* 279 (February 2007): 716–23.

"Who the hell" . . . Beliefnet.com, www.beliefnet.com/search/site .aspx?q=death%20rituals.

3. GRIEF INTERRUPTED

An article titled . . . Parker-Pope, Tara. "For Some Bereaved, Pain Pills Without End," *New York Times: Health and Science*, October 10, 2007; see also Brian Garavaglia, PhD, "Avoiding the Tendency to Medicalize the Grieving Process: Reconciliation Rather than Resolution," *New Social Worker*, Summer 2006, www.socialworker.com/feature-articles /practice/Avoiding_the_Tendency_to_Medicalize_the_Grieving _Process%3A_Reconciliation_Rather_Than_Resolution/.

Along the same lines, more recently . . . Loana Lordache and Nancy C. Low, "The Over Diagnosis of Bipolar Disorder," *Journal of Psychiatry and Neuroscience* 35, no. 3 (May 2010): E3–4.

What is unresolved grief . . . Sidney Zisook and Lucy Lyons, "Bereavement and Unresolved Grief in Psychiatric Outpatients," *Omega: Journal of Death and Dying* 20, no. 4 (1990): 307–22.

Clinical psychologist Therese Rando . . . Therese A. Rando, PhD, "The Increasing Prevalence of Complicated Mourning: The Onslaught Is Just Beginning," *Omega: Journal of Death and Dying* 26, no. 1 (1993): 43–59.

4. THE LANGUAGE OF LOSS

For instance, if your spouse . . . Jane Loretta Winsch, *After the Funeral* (New York: Paulist Press, 1995).

5. COMFORT

If you are headed . . . Helen Fitzgerald, "The Bereaved Employee: Returning to Work," American Hospice Foundation official website, accessed October 8, 2014, http://americanhospice.org /the-bereaved-employee-returning-to-work/.

I am happy to report . . . Kathryn Tyler, "Giving Time to Grieve: Compassionate Bereavement Leave Policies and Procedures Provide Support to Employees When They Need It Most," author's official website,

accessed October 8, 2014, www.kathryntyler.com/giving_time_to_
grieve.htm.

It pays—literally—for companies . . . Susanna Duff, "Unresolved Grief
Can Be Costly," *Employee Benefit News*, July 1999.

A very unusual type . . . Kristen Gelineau, "For Some, a Blue Christmas
Is Enough," *Post and Courier*, December 21, 2006.

6. HOW DID YOUR LOVED ONE DIE?

The National Cancer . . . "Types of Grief Reactions," National Cancer Institute official website, accessed October 8, 2014, www.cancer
.gov/cancertopics/pdq/supportivecare/bereavement/HealthProfessional
/page3.

In another article, I read . . . Nina Millett, "Hospice: Challenging Society's Approach to Death," *Health and Social Work* 4, no. 1 (February 4,
1979): 131–50.

A leading figure . . . Joy Buck, PhD, "Policy and Re-Formation of Hospice: Lessons from the Past for the Future of Palliative Care," *Journal
of Hospice & Palliative Nursing* 13, no. 6 (November–December 2011):
S35–S43.

My friend and colleague . . . Alan Poe, interview by the author, February
9, 2011.

In her article . . . Therese A. Rando, "On Treating Those Bereaved by
Sudden, Unanticipated Death," *Psychotherapy in Practice*, February
1996, 59–71.

There are many theories . . . Robert Scaer, *The Body Bears the Burden:
Trauma, Dissociation and Disease* (Binghamton, NY: Haworth Medical
Press, 2001).

What is eye movement . . . Francine Shapiro, *Eye Movement Desensitization and Reprocessing (EMDR): Basic Principles, Protocols, and Procedures*, 2nd ed. (New York: Guilford Press, 2001).

7. HOW CHILDREN GRIEVE

Children at varying . . . Darlene E. McCown and Betty Davies, "Patterns of Grief in Young Children Following the Death of a Sibling," *Death Studies* 19 (1995): 41–53.

A comprehensive study . . . Sol Altschul and George Pollock, *Childhood Bereavement and Its Aftermath* (Madison, CT: International Universities Press, 1988).

Derek just couldn't . . . George H. Pollock, "Process and Affect: Mourning and Grief," *International Journal of Psychoanalysis* 59 (1978): 255–76.

In his article . . . Robert M. Segal, "Helping Children Express Grief Through Symbolic Communication," *Social Casework: The Journal of Contemporary Social Work*, December 1984.

Very young children . . . Altschul and Pollock, *Childhood Bereavement and Its Aftermath.*

Sometimes children become . . . Judy Heath, *I Miss Matthew* (Charleston, SC: Book Surge, 2007).

In my opinion . . . Alan D. Wolfelt, *Healing the Bereaved Child* (Fort Collins, CO: Companion Press, 1996).

The 1999 tragedy . . . American Psychological Association, "Demand Continues for APA's 'Warning Signs,'" *Monitor on Psychology* 32, no. 1 (January 2001).

According to the American Psychological Association . . . Ibid.

At Clear Creek . . . Julia Moore and Barbara Herlihy, "Grief Groups for Students Who Have Had a Parent Die," *School Counselor* 41 (1993): 54–60.

8. DIFFERENT MOURNINGS

and many studies . . . Margaret S. Stroebe, Robert Hansson, Wolfgang Stroebe, and Henk Schut, *Handbook of Bereavement Research: Consequences, Coping, and Caring* (Washington, DC: American Psychological Association, 2001).

In a study published . . . L. Carstensen, J. Gross, and H. Fung, "The Social Context of Emotional Experience," *Annual Review of Gerontology and Geriatrics* 17 (1997): 325–52; C. M. Aldwin, K. J. Sutton, G. Chiara, and A. Spiro III, "Age Differences in Stress Coping and Appraisal: Findings from the Normative Aging Study," *Journal of Gerontology: Psychological Sciences* 51, no. 4 (July 1996): 179–88.

According to MetLife . . . Stroebe, Hansson, Stroebe, and Schut, *Handbook of Bereavement Research.*

9. WILL IT EVER END?

In a recent study . . . Holly Prigerson and Paul Maciejewski, "An Empirical Examination of the Stage Theory of Grief," *Journal of the American Medical Association* 279 (February 2007): 716–23.

What is internalization . . . *Letters of Marcel Proust*, trans. and ed. by Mina Curtiss (New York: Vintage Books, 1966), 313.

In an amazing . . . John Erskine, *On Being Alone* (Commack, NY: Suffolk Community Center, 1996).

Many of us . . . Harold Kushner, *When Bad Things Happen to Good People* (New York: Avon Books, 1981).

"Parting Drapes" . . . Janet I. Buck, "Parting Drapes," *My Favorite Bullet* 4, no. 1 (January 2003).

Professor T. J. Wray . . . T. J. Wray and Ann Back Price, *Grief Dreams* (San Francisco: Jossey-Bass, 2005).

Henry Wadsworth Longfellow puts it . . . Henry Wadsworth Longfellow, "A Psalm of Life," collected at Bartleby.com, accessed October 8, 2014, www.bartleby.com/102/55.html.

10. ADULT LOSS OF A PARENT

To avoid this . . . Linda Norlander and Kerstin McSteen, "The Kitchen Table Discussion: A Creative Way to Discuss End-of-Life Issues," *Home Healthcare Nurse* 18, no. 8 (September 2000): 532–39.

12. LOSS OF A SPOUSE

By necessity we share . . . Elisabeth Berg, *Talk Before Sleep* (New York: Delta, 1997).

Marital relationships . . . John Erskine, *On Being Alone* (Commack, NY: Suffolk Community Center, 1996).

14. COPING WITH SUICIDE

The Centers for Disease Control . . . Centers for Disease Control and Prevention, "Suicide and Self-Inflicted Injury," official website, accessed October 8, 2014, www.cdc.gov/nchs/fastats/suicide.htm.

Singer Judy Collins . . . Judy Collins, *Singing Lessons: A Memoir of Love, Loss, Hope, and Healing* (New York: Pocket Books, 1998).

According to the CDC . . . Centers for Disease Control and Prevention, "Suicide: Facts at a Glance," official website, accessed October 8, 2014, www.cdc.gov/violenceprevention/pdf/suicide-datasheet-a.pdf.

GLOSSARY

acceptance: The final step before reconciliation of grief. To come to terms with the loss and accept that it has happened.

anniversary grief: A sudden rush of memories, intense emotions, and grief reactions triggered by the date of death, a birthday, holidays, or special occasions associated with a major loss.

anticipatory grief: Grieving begun in anticipation of a loss. The griever begins the process of grief before the actual death occurs.

bereavement: The "state" of grief.

comforting behaviors: Constructive behaviors that bring comfort to the griever.

complicated grief: An acute form of bereavement persisting for several years.

grief: The human response to loss. The emotions one experiences after the death of a loved one.

griever: A person experiencing grief.

internalization: The perception that the lost loved one is now *with* the griever in a new way.

message dream: A common dream among grievers in which the person who died is said to be sending a message to a person or persons still living. This is often reported by the dreamer as letting those left behind know that the deceased is at peace or doing well.

mourning: The behaviors and rituals of those in grief.

out of sync (synchronization): The feeling many people experience in the early stages of the grieving process when the world seems to have sped up or the griever has slowed down, creating the feeling of being out of synchronization with life.

practical secondary losses: Those practical concerns one must deal with after a loved one dies. As when a spouse dies and the widow or widower must now assume the responsibilities of that spouse as well as his or her own (e.g., mowing the grass, cleaning the house, or earning income lost to keep up mortgage payments).

rational suicide: The deliberate taking of one's own life as a reasonable choice by a terminally ill patient.

reconciliation of grief: Accepting that the death of a loved one cannot be changed and learning to incorporate the loss into one's life. A reconciliation chart is available in chapter 9.

re-grieving: Children re-grieve as they enter new developmental stages. For example, a girl who loses her mother at the age of five may re-grieve that loss when she reaches puberty. She reexperiences the loss of her mother throughout her childhood, almost as though it is happening all over again. Additional counseling may be required, geared toward her age and the issues that accompany it. Re-grieving can also occur in adults when a "trigger" places them back into symptoms of early grief.

secondary losses: When a loved one dies, the griever does not just suffer the loss of that individual; many other losses accompany the death, such as loss of self-esteem, status, or role.

"self" secondary losses: Those losses to self. These losses are less tangible and yet may be even more distressing than practical secondary losses. The self loses the relationship with that other person, which can produce lowered self-esteem and lack of confidence, among other ego losses.

story of the death: The words a griever uses to describe the loved one's death.

survivor's guilt: An overwhelming feeling of guilt over having survived when another or others have perished.

unresolved grief: A chronic reaction in which a person does not complete the reconciliation of a loss in a reasonable amount of time.

BIBLIOGRAPHY

BOOKS

Altschul, Sol, and George Pollock. *Childhood Bereavement and its Aftermath.* Madison, CT: International Universities Press, 1988.

Berg, Elisabeth. *Talk Before Sleep.* New York: Delta, 1997.

Bremner, D. *Does Stress Damage the Brain?* New York: W. W. Norton, 2002.

Brooks, Barbara, and Paula M. Siegel. *The Sacred Child: Helping Children Overcome Traumatic Events.* New York: Wiley, 1996.

Buck, Joy, PhD. "Policy and Re-Formation of Hospice: Lessons from the Past for the Future of Palliative Care." *Journal of Hospice & Palliative Nursing* 13, no. 6 (November–December 2011): S35–S43.

Collins, Judy. *Singing Lessons: A Memoir of Love, Loss, Hope and Healing.* New York: Pocket Books, 1998.

Corless, I., B. Germino, and M. Pittman. *Dying, Death, and Bereavement: Theoretical Perspectives and Other Ways of Knowing.* Boston: Jones and Bartlett, 1994.

Doka, Kenneth J., Ph.D. *Children Mourning, Mourning Children*. Washington, DC: Hospice Foundation of America, 1995.

Gitterman, Alex. *The Legacy of William Schwartz: Group Practice as Shared Interaction*. New York: Hawthorn Press, 1986.

Heath, Judy. *I Miss Matthew*. Charleston, SC: Book Surge, 2007.

Kennedy, Alexandra. *Losing a Parent: Passage to a New Way of Living*. San Francisco: HarperOne, 1991.

Kubler-Ross, Elisabeth, MD. *On Children and Death*. New York: Touchstone, 1983.

Kushner, Harold. *When Bad Things Happen to Good People*. New York: Avon Books, 1981.

Morgan, John D. *The Dying and the Bereaved Teenager*. Philadelphia: Charles Press, 1998.

Parkes, Colin, Pittu Laungani, and Bill Young. *Death and Bereavement Across Cultures*. London: Routledge, 1997.

Rando, Therese A. *How to Go on Living When Someone You Love Dies*. New York: Bantam Books, 1991.

Scaer, Robert. *The Body Bears the Burden: Trauma, Dissociation and Disease*. Binghamton, NY: Haworth Medical Press, 2001.

———. *The Trauma Spectrum: Hidden Wounds and Human Healing: Hidden Wounds and Human Resiliency*. New York: W. W. Norton, 2005.

Schaefer, Dan, and Christine Lyons. *How Do We Tell the Children?* New York: Newmarket Press, 1993.

Shapiro, Francine. *Eye Movement Desensitization and Reprocessing (EMDR): Basic Principles, Protocols, and Procedures*, 2nd ed. New York: Guilford Press, 2001.

Siegel, Bernie S., MD. *Love, Medicine & Miracles*. New York: Harper & Row, 1986.

Stroebe, Margaret S., Robert Hansson, Wolfgang Stroebe, and Henk Schut. *Handbook of Bereavement Research: Consequences, Coping, and Caring*. Washington, DC: American Psychological Association, 2001.

Winsch, Jane Loretta. *After the Funeral*. New York: Paulist Press, 1995.

Wolfelt, Alan D. *Healing the Bereaved Child*. Fort Collins, CO: Companion Press, 1996.

Wray, T. J., and Ann Back Price. *Grief Dreams*. San Francisco: Jossey-Bass, 2005.

WORLD WIDE WEB

Centers for Disease Control and Prevention. "Suicide and Self-Inflicted Injury." Official website, accessed October 8, 2014. www.cdc.gov /nchs/fastats/suicide.htm.

———. "Suicide: Facts at a Glance." Official website, accessed October 8, 2014. www.cdc.gov/violenceprevention/pdf/suicide-datasheet -a.pdf.

Fitzgerald, Helen. "The Bereaved Employee: Returning to Work." American Hospice Foundation official website, accessed October 8, 2014. http://americanhospice.org/the-bereaved-employee-returning -to-work/.

Garavaglia, Brian, PhD. "Avoiding the Tendency to Medicalize the Grieving Process: Reconciliation Rather than Resolution." *New Social Worker*, Summer 2006. www.socialworker.com/feature-articles /practice/Avoiding_the_Tendency_to_Medicalize_the_Grieving _Process%3A_Reconciliation_Rather_Than_Resolution/.

MedicineNet.com. "Loss, Grief, and Bereavement." Accessed October 8, 2014. www.medicinenet.com/loss_grief_and_bereavement/article .htm.

National Cancer Institute. "Types of Grief Reactions." Official website, accessed October 8, 2014. www.cancer.gov/cancertopics/pdq /supportivecare/bereavement/HealthProfessional/page3.

Sedona Method Course. "Grief Quotes: A Collection of Quotes About Loss and Death." Official website, accessed April 2007, www.sedona .com/html/grief-quotes.aspx.

Tyler, Kathryn. "Giving Time to Grieve: Compassionate Bereavement Leave Policies and Procedures Provide Support to Employees When

They Need It Most." Author's official website, accessed October 8, 2014. www.kathryntyler.com/giving_time_to_grieve.htm.

MAGAZINES, JOURNALS, NEWSPAPERS, AND BOOKLETS

Accord Aftercare Services. *Holiday Help: A Program for Hope and Healing*. Louisville: Accord Aftercare Services, 1996.

Aldwin, C. M., K. J. Sutton, G. Chiara, and A. Spiro III. "Age Differences in Stress Coping and Appraisal: Findings from the Normative Aging Study." *Journal of Gerontology: Psychological Sciences* 51, no. 4 (July 1996): 179–88.

Altschul, Sol, and George Pollock. *Childhood Bereavement and Its Aftermath*. Madison, CT: International Universities Press, 1988.

American Psychological Association. "Demand Continues for APA's 'Warning Signs.'" *Monitor on Psychology* 32, no. 1 (January 2001).

Bolten, Christopher, and Delpha J. Camp. "The Post-Funeral Ritual in Bereavement Counseling and Grief Work." *Journal of Gerontological Social Work* 13, no. 3/4 (1989): 49–59.

Carstensen, L., J. Gross, and H. Fung. "The Social Context of Emotional Experience." *Annual Review of Gerontology and Geriatrics* 17 (1997): 325–52.

Catlin, George."The Role of Culture in Grief." *Journal of Social Psychology* 133, no. 2 (April 1993): 173–78.

Cheever, Susan. "One Verse at a Time." *Newsday*, September 22, 1998.

Duff, Susanna. "Unresolved Grief Can Be Costly." *Employee Benefit News*, July 1999.

Erskine, John. *On Being Alone*. Commack, NY: Suffolk Community Center, 1996.

Forsyth, Sondra. "I'm in Agony & He Doesn't Care." *Mademoiselle*, September 1998, 173–74.

Freedman, Mitchell. "Camp Helps Kids Cope with Grief." *Newsday*, September 3, 1999.

Gelineau, Kristen. "For some, a Blue Christmas Is Enough." *Post and Courier*, December 21, 2006.

Grann, David. "Which Way Did He Run?" *New York Times Magazine*, January 13, 2002, 32–37.

Hannaford, Mary Joe. *Unchained Melodies: Families Growing Through Grief*. Atlanta: Active Parenting, 1992.

Krysinski, Patricia Rosenkranz. "Coping with Suicide: Beyond the Five-Day Bereavement Policy." *Death Studies* 17 (1993): 173–77.

Lordache, Loana, and Nancy C. Low. "The Over Diagnosis of Bipolar Disorder." *Journal of Psychiatry and Neuroscience* 35, no. 3 (May 2010): E3–4.

McCown, Darlene E., and Betty Davies. "Patterns of Grief in Young Children Following the Death of a Sibling." *Death Studies* 19 (1995): 41–53.

Millett, Nina. "Hospice: Challenging Society's Approach to Death." *Health and Social Work* 4, no. 1 (February 4, 1979): 131–50.

Moore, Julia, and Barbara Herlihy. "Grief Groups for Students Who Have Had a Parent Die." *School Counselor* 41 (1993): 54–60.

Norlander, Linda, and Kerstin McSteen. "The Kitchen Table Discussion: A Creative Way to Discuss End-of-Life Issues." *Home Healthcare Nurse* 18, no. 8 (September 2000): 532–39.

NYC Department of Health. *Strategies for SIDS Risk Reduction*. New York: NYC Department of Health, March 2004.

Parker-Pope, Tara. "For Some Bereaved, Pain Pills Without End." *New York Times: Health and Science*, October 10, 2007.

Pollock, George H. "Process and Affect: Mourning and Grief." *International Journal of Psychoanalysis* 59 (1978): 255–76.

Prigerson, Holly, and Paul Maciejewski. "An Empirical Examination of the Stage Theory of Grief." *Journal of the American Medical Association* 279 (February 21, 2007): 716–23.

Quindlen, Anna. "Grief Fades, Yet Loss Is Forever." *Ann Arbor News*, May 5, 1994.

———. "On Losing Your Mom." *Good Housekeeping*, February 1998, 86–87.

Rando, Therese A., PhD. "The Increasing Prevalence of Complicated Mourning: The Onslaught Is Just Beginning." *Omega: Journal of Death and Dying* 26, no. 1 (1993): 43–59.

———. "On Treating Those Bereaved by Sudden, Unanticipated Death." *Psychotherapy in Practice*, February 1996, 59–71.

Scherago, Marcia G. *Sibling Grief: How Parents Can Help the Child Whose Brother or Sister Has Died*. Redmond, WA: Medic Publishing, 1987.

Schwartz-Borden, Gwen. "Grief Work: Prevention and Intervention." *Social Casework: The Journal of Contemporary Social Work*, October 1986: 499–505.

Segal, Robert M. "Helping Children Express Grief Through Symbolic Communication." *Social Casework: The Journal of Contemporary Social Work*, December 1984.

Sheehan, George. "And Miles to Go Before I Sleep." The Best of Sheehan. *Runner's World,* March 1995, 111–12.

Sheehan, Pete. "Holidays Pose Special Problems for Those Who Are Grieving." *Long Island Catholic* 39, no. 33 (November 15, 2000).

Smith, Chris. "The Smoldering Fires of 9/11." *New York Magazine*, March 2002, 35–39.

Stone, Lois Greene. "Dealing with Death and Parents." *Humanist*, May/June 1996, 40–42.

Zisook, Sidney, and Lucy Lyons. "Bereavement and Unresolved Grief in Psychiatric Outpatients." *Omega: Journal of Death and Dying* 20, no. 4 (1990): 307–22.

INDEX